# Inside and Outside the Not So Big House

# Inside and Outside the Not So Big House

Sarah Susanka,
Julie Moir Messervy,
and Marc Vassallo

The Taunton Press

**The Taunton Press**
Inspiration for hands-on living®

The Taunton Press, Inc., 63 South Main Street, PO Box 5506, Newtown, CT 06470-5506
e-mail: tp@taunton.com

FRONT COVER PHOTOGRAPHERS: (clockwise from top left) Grey Crawford,
Ken Gutmaker, Ken Gutmaker, Grey Crawford; front flap: Ken Gutmaker
BACK COVER PHOTOGRAPHERS: (clockwise from top left) Grey Crawford,
Grey Crawford, Ken Gutmaker; back flap: Ken Gutmaker

LIBRARY OF CONGRESS CATALOGING-IN-PUBLICATION DATA

Susanka, Sarah.
  Inside and outside the not so big house / Sarah Susanka, Julie Moir Messervy, and
Marc Vassallo.
      p. cm.
  Combines two books: Inside the not so big house, published in 2005, and Outside
the not so big house, published in 2006.
  Includes bibliographical references and index.
  ISBN-13: 978-1-56158-930-2 (alk. paper)
  ISBN-10: 1-56158-930-6 (alk. paper)
  1.  Small houses. 2.  Architecture, Domestic. 3.  Interior decoration. 4.  Landscape
gardening.  I. Messervy, Julie Moir. II. Vassallo, Marc. III. Susanka, Sarah. Inside the
not so big house. IV. Susanka, Sarah. Outside the not so big house. V. Title.
  NA7125.S86 2006
  728'.37--dc22

                            2006011279

Printed in China
10 9 8 7 6 5 4 3 2 1

# Acknowledgments

## From Inside the Not So Big House

**from Sarah**   This book would not have been possible without the infectious enthusiasm and unusual combination of architectural and editorial skills brought to the table by my friend and colleague Marc Vassallo.

Putting a book together is no small undertaking, and with all the topics I want to cover to put answers into the hands of the homeowners who need them, I knew I could use some help with a number of the titles I have in mind.  Marc's background was perfect, and so was born the vision for a book I'd wanted to write for years, but simply hadn't had the time for. And even as we put the finishing touches on *Inside the Not So Big House*, our next one is on the drawing board—a book about small-scale remodelings.

I'll let Marc take it from here in extending our gratitude to all the other players who've made this book possible, but since he's unlikely to sing his own praises, I wanted to let you know that without Marc this book would not have been born for several more years.

**from Marc**   Everyone at The Taunton Press deserves our gratitude, especially Jim Childs, Maria Taylor, Paula Schlosser, Carol Singer, Maureen Graney, Wendi Mijal, Robyn Doyon Aitken, Katie Benoit, and most of all, Peter Chapman, our steadfast editor.

We'd like to thank our new friend, photographer Ken Gutmaker, and his wife, Linda, for criss-crossing the country to capture the wonderful photographs in this book. Thanks also to the architects whose designs appear here and to the homeowners who graciously shared their homes and a piece of their lives to make this book possible. We also want to acknowledge all the architects and designers who submitted work for our consideration.

At one point or another, virtually my entire family provided me with a place to work or a place to stay during visits to houses. A big thank-you goes to Lori and Barry Rochelle, Susan and Paul Morton, Paul and Jeremy Vassallo, Ted Vassallo, my second parents John and Sylvia Gatzy, and—not least—my mother, Josephine Vassallo. I'd also like to acknowledge my father, Domenic Vassallo, too long gone, who steered me toward architecture through his own love of design.

Thank you Phyllis Wender, my agent, for your good sense and perseverance.

Thanks of course to you, Sarah, my collaborator, for two very big things—your genius and your generosity.

Most of all I want to thank my wife, Linda, and my son, Nicky, for their boundless patience, good humor, and inspiration. Thanks for keeping the home fires burning. From me, this book is for you.

## From Outside the Not So Big House

*from Julie*   Writing a book is a lot like designing a garden: You seek to understand the elements involved, construct a frame in which to work, weave the parts together, and craft the details to get them right. Throughout, you need to return to the material time and again with fresh eyes.

Everyone who worked with me on this book has fresh eyes. Sarah is an articulate and tireless advocate for good design, using all her senses to express so eloquently what she sees and how to make it better. Seeing the world through Grey Crawford's camera lens as he photographed these properties was a privilege. Underneath his signature fedora is a pair of hawk eyes and fierce intellect that combine with a fine sense of humor and an easygoing working style. Executive Editor Maureen Graney helped me in the early stages to conceptualize the book and organize it properly. Editor Erica Sanders-Foege then took the editorial reins and guided me through its writing. With her incisive intelligence and dry humor, she sharpened and simplified my writing and helped teach me the Taunton way. Publisher Jim Childs and editor-in-chief Maria Taylor saw the possibilities in combining Sarah's and my visions. Art director Paula Schlosser's ability to graphically express the layout made it real for me from the start; design manager Carol Singer fine-tuned the design so that it flows.

Of course, many others played a part in making this book happen. I owe thanks to my literary agent, Christina Ward for her clear perspective and support; to my colleague, landscape architect Ed Hartranft, for his effervescent brilliance as a form-giver; and to landscape designer Amanda Sloan, who supports our design work with good humor, patience, and constant creativity. Virginia Small, who suggested my name to the Taunton book division, continues to shepherd me through the writing of my columns. I am grateful to all of these wonderful friends for their consistent support of my ideas.

And finally, I want to thank my family: my children, Max, Lindsey, and Charlotte, and my stepson, Luke; my parents, William and Alice Moir, and my sisters and brothers—you know who you are! I am lucky to be so loved. And with my soul mate, Steve Jonas at my side, I feel truly blessed.

# Contents

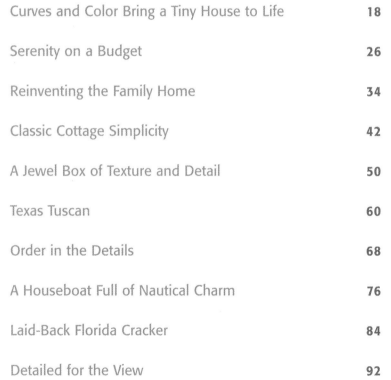

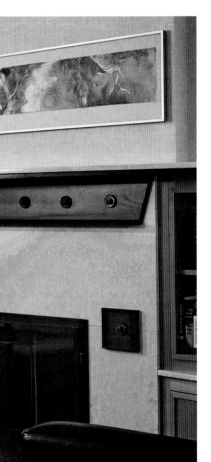

# Contents continued

# Preface

I started planning this book just a few months after my first book, *The Not So Big House,* was published in the fall of 1998. So many people had written to me asking how to make their own houses embody the spirit of building Not So Big. Many of them had noticed a level of detail that is absent in most newer homes today.

These readers wanted to know how to create for themselves some of the things they'd observed as they read and looked at the photos—things like the plate rail I'd included in my own St. Paul house, which I described in passing as a built-in detail that served many functions. This plate rail provided a place to exhibit some objects I loved; it housed a light cove; it provided a surface for the continuous maple trim band to wrap around kitchen and dining areas; and in the process of doing all these things, it created a sense of shelter for the activities taking place below. Or the ship's ladder allowing access to the tiny attic at the top of the same house. Several readers had written, wanting to know how to incorporate a similar detail into their own home. How steep was the stair, how wide, and how big were the cutouts for hands to grip properly?

I realized there were a lot of people looking for solutions to personalize their homes and make them more functional who, up until now, hadn't understood that this could be accomplished with features that are literally built in rather than brought to the house after construction (or remodeling) is complete.

The point of a book focusing on this more up-close view of house design was brought home even more clearly for me when one of The Taunton Press editorial staff told me she had completely misunderstood what I was aiming for. She had been mislead by the word "detail," which she explained to me means something akin to accessorizing—the art of decorating, if you will—to most non-architects. By contrast, what I wanted to describe were the special features of house design that are *permanently* attached to the interior and will remain there as the house passes to future owners. If you were able to turn your house upside down and shake it, these INSIDE details are the ones that wouldn't come off.

Through interactions with hundreds of interested homeowners, it has become a lot clearer to me how to explain this more "close up" level of home design. My goal is to help you make a house that, even before any of your belongings are brought in, still expresses something of your inner spirit and passion for life. As expressed by William Blake's famous aphorism, "All the world's in a grain of sand," a home that's designed well at every scale truly reflects its owners, whether you look at it from a distance or observe its smallest detail. The ideas you'll read about in the coming pages will help you build into your home some personal details that delight you daily and allow even the smallest elements to embody the character of the house as a whole.

# The Not So Big House Up Close

Attention to the small gives character to the whole.

## Shortly after I started my architectural training

I moved into a house with 15 other architecture students. I learned a lot from my fellow students, but what stands out most is the amazing education I got in how to look at my surroundings. I'd always been interested in architectural design, long before I knew what that was, drawing floor plans of imaginary houses as a child and building elaborate structures with blocks until well into my teens.

I loved visiting buildings of all types, checking out how they affected me spatially. But I'd always looked at the big picture when noting my experiences. I'd ask myself, how does this space make me feel? Does its shape and size please me? Would I want to spend more time here? What would I change? I had been blissfully unaware of the smaller features of the world around me.

The older architecture students helped me to tighten my focus— literally as you do when you zoom in with a camera lens. Instead of looking at a whole room, for example, I began to focus on the way two pieces of molding were brought

(Right) The smallest detail, like the way the flutes on the vertical window trim echo the horizontal lines of the top molding, reverberates at the level of the whole room.

together at the side (jamb) and top (head) of the door into the kitchen. I took note of the way each resident of our house had embellished his or her room, attaching intriguingly designed structures to the walls and floors, such as desk alcoves and drawing equipment containers, and even building up into the truss space above to create bed lofts and skylight shafts. Through it all, I got a crash course in what architects call "detailing." And like my fellow students I learned to zoom into this level of focus, no matter where I was.

For most non-architects, this level of reality is as invisible as it was to me before my initiation into the world of details. Although these small touches often go unnoticed, they have a huge effect on our experience of a place. One reason that so many older homes are venerated is because they have this zoomed-in attention to the little things, like the wall inset at the bottom of the stairway shown in the left photo on p. 9. Most people assume it's the building's age that gives it its charm, when in fact it's the attention to the smaller details that makes it feel so good. This example was in fact built only recently, yet it embodies the sensibility of the house it's a part of, adding to its integrity and character while expressing something that's more than skin deep about its owners in the process.

## Built-In Character

In my first book, *The Not So Big House*, I made the case that a house isn't really a home unless it is filled with the personality of its inhabitants. But how do you accomplish that? Most homeowners assume this means filling the space you have with things that have meaning to you, and certainly this is an important step in the right direction. But a

(Top) Even if you don't focus on the trim, it helps you make sense of the layers of space in this view from room to room. (Above and facing page) The window seat is treated as a little room. As you zoom in, the impact of details like trim, shelving, wide windowsills, and drawers adds up. The result is a space that's small in size but rich in character.

A wall niche with a small statue animates the entry area and serves as a focal point at the base of the stairs.

Attention to detail can give a room its charm, as in the way the wainscot wraps around the corner in this remodeled living room.

house that really sings has character that's built in, so that even if the house were completely emptied of furniture and objects collected over a lifetime, the house would still feel warm and inviting. It would still have a character all its own.

Sadly, all too many of the new houses and remodels built today would fail this test. To keep construction costs down, all the money available goes into square footage, leaving little or no money for the special details that can really make a house a beautiful place. The house in the photo on the facing page, on the other hand, would still be beautiful even without its occupants' belongings adorning its various surfaces.

In an effort to remedy this situation, I wrote *The Not So Big House* to help people looking for a more personal home understand what's missing in the average house. I suggested that the key to creating a home with intrinsic character is to keep the overall size down so that you can reapportion some dollars out of square footage and into the details that make the house a delight to live in. Although I've tried where possible in illustrating this book to find details that will not break the bank, they still do add to the cost of a home. A handy rule of thumb is that if you strive to reduce the square footage you were originally planning by about one third, and make available the dollars saved for personalizing your home, you'll have enough money to do the kind of detailing shown here.

In the short hallway shown at left, a lowered ceiling compresses space before releasing it into the taller master bedroom beyond, creating a satisfying sense of arrival.

This wall shelf was built with strips of basic pine lumber, but its elegant composition transcends the ordinariness of its materials.

## God Is in the Details

We've all heard the phrase, "God is in the details," made famous by architect Mies van der Rohe in 1959, but what does it really mean? What is a detail anyway? The details you'll see illustrated in this book are *not* what interior designers would call accessories—things like vases, wall hangings, and artwork. To use the analogy I used in the introduction, if you were to turn the house upside down and shake it, all these accessories would fall instantly from their various perches. The details we'll be discussing here are built right into the house, so they're attached permanently and won't fall off. They're designed in from the beginning, to help both personalize the house and make it function more efficiently.

To architects the word *detail* implies the marriage of materials to create design elements or combinations that are built in during the construction (or remodeling) process. The photo above is a classic example of what an architect means by the term. This medicine shelf, suspended above the toilet in a not so big bathroom, involves the interconnection of several wooden elements of different types. First, there is the 1x8 pine cap that stretches from one side of the alcove to the other, hugging the ceiling. Next there are the shelves themselves, made of 1x4 pine

We're drawn naturally to cozy spaces like this eating area, but for such spaces to feel comfortable and function well, all the parts—windowsill, seat back, tabletop—have to be sized just right.

boards. Then there are the pairs of vertical "suspenders," made of narrower pieces of the same wood species. And finally there are the wooden "pegs" between the vertical suspenders, which are made of cherry, to give a contrasting but complementary color.

In combination these four parts are brought together to create something that looks both beautiful and effortless. Yet like all good design, it took someone, in this case North Carolina architect Tina Govan, to conceive and develop the composition, include it as a drawing in the blueprints for the house, and to make sure it was executed in the way she intended by the craftsman who built it. The connection of one part to another is, strictly speaking, a detail, and when all these interconnection are considered together they become one larger detail. So the word itself implies multiple levels of design.

Let's look at a variety of these different levels of detail, so you get a sense for the kinds of information you'll find in the rest of the book.

## Details in Context

Most people think of details as a relatively small thing—a doorknob, a newel post, a shelf bracket—but the word *detail* can also refer to larger elements such as window seats and breakfast nooks, hearths and accent walls, built-in cabinets and kitchen islands. Take a look at the two photos on this page and the top left photo on p. 13 and you'll see

The quality and functionality of this narrow entry hall have been improved considerably with the addition of a small but thoughtfully outfitted and proportioned seating alcove.

details at this scale: a bench seat in a Minnesota mudroom flanked by cabinets on either side, and a triptych of windows above, that together create a practical but welcoming informal entryway for a family with young children; an informal eating area with benches and table proportioned just right for the body sizes of the homeowners, with a horizontal band that serves both as windowsill and apron for the window and as backsplash for the table; and a stairway with open risers, its treads spanning from side to side with no visible means of support. For the stairway to look so elegant, the architect or builder had to figure out how to support those treads and hide the fastening system from view. If I hadn't pointed out this particular detail to you, you probably wouldn't have wondered how it was done. Your eye simply accepts it. You may like the way it looks, but to duplicate it you need this information, or someone ingenious enough to create the same look.

The repetition of paint colors helps unite these rooms. Less obvious is the unifying effect of thin lines as a motif for everything from window trim to table legs, chair slats, and picture frames.

## Details in Combination

The word *detail* can also be used to describe materials and how they are used: concrete for countertops, hand-rubbed fir for ceiling beams, stainless steel for the stair rails. The top right photo shown on the facing page illustrates the marriage of two materials, wood and slate, interpenetrating to create an intriguing pattern at the same time

Each material in this entry area—slate, oak flooring, and embossed glass—expresses its unique nature in relation to the other materials. At the same time, the natural textures and colors of the materials work together to create a feeling of harmony.

Stair treads with no visible means of support seem to float, adding to the light, buoyant quality of the entire house.

Carrying the band of black tile around the window trim emphasizes the window and gives the small bathroom a unique look.

as they inventively solve the problem of where to stop one surface and start the next one. Obviously, if someone hadn't thought this detail through and drawn out what they were imagining, the chances of it being anything noteworthy would have been slim. But when designed and communicated to the craftspeople involved, the detail becomes an engaging aspect of the home.

*Details* can also refer to design elements that are not objects at all, but rather qualities that carry throughout the house, such as a palette of colors, a particular surface texture, or a character of glass that creates a particular quality of light. For example, the colors used in the remodeling shown in the photo on the facing page are carried throughout the house—sage green for trim, pale yellow for walls, and natural hardwood floors—which gives the whole a heightened sense of cohesiveness.

A type of detail that is familiar in older homes is the kind that defines the shape of something, such as the casing or trim that runs around all the doors and windows in a house, or the wainscot that wraps the bottom half of all the rooms on the main level of a home. The photo at left is an example of this type of detail. The black tile serves primarily as a baseboard and beltline, as these two lines define the perimeter of the room. But where the window interrupts the beltline, instead of stopping and starting the line, the black tile band carries

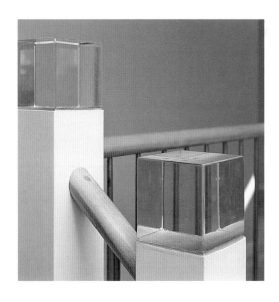

Green glass newel-post caps subtly connect these stairs to the ocean, unseen but just outside.

on around the window, giving the room a unique and attractive character in the process.

## Details in Focus

The details that can *sometimes* have the biggest impact are very small things indeed, like the wainscot cap we looked at earlier or the newel-post caps shown here. A reinterpretation of the traditional post cap, these are made of glass, and add a delightfully contemporary flair to a simple cottage.

My favorite detail in this category is the horizontal cherry lattice that I've used in a number of houses I've designed over the last few years. I use it both to create a segment of lowered ceiling to separate one space from another, as well as to add some geometrical patterning and visual weight. The effect is engaging, especially at night when the light from recessed cans above filters through the lattice to create fascinating patterns on the floor below. I first saw a detail similar to this one in the old section of Kyoto when I traveled to Japan a few years ago. I was so intrigued by the detail that I started using it in my own work as soon as I returned. My St. Paul house was the first experiment, and ever since then I've been refining both the proportions and the method of construction. Horizontal lattice is a relatively simple detail to build, but one that can have a significant effect on the pleasure you derive from your house.

Details that resolve the meeting of materials are the ones that are almost completely invisible to someone who doesn't know what to look for, and yet they can be the most elegant. The photo shown at right on the facing page will give you an idea of how to train your eye to notice

them. In this tiny master bathroom it was desirable to use every trick in the book to make the room look larger. So the architect brought the mirror all the way to the countertop as well as to the adjacent door jamb. There's not even a C-channel at the edge of the mirror (the little border you find on most mirrors that actually cups its ends so you don't see the edges), so your eye is led to believe that there's no wall there at all. It looks as though there are two sinks directly facing each other, though of course this is an optical illusion. It's the detailing of how the mirror meets the countertop that creates the effect.

Another such detail is the marriage of materials around the window boxes on an interior porch shown in the bottom left photo on p. 16. The vertical wood brackets, made to look like fins, secure perforated steel flower boxes that serve in place of railings. As these same fins extend below the opening, they terminate a few inches short of the flat casing on either side, and a square-head stainless-steel bolt holds the entire assembly in place. This is the kind of detail that, as soon as I see it, I know for certain that an architect has been involved. To make it look this crafted, the architect had to carefully draw all the interrelationships between the various parts, and track down a source for both the square-head bolts and the perforated metal.

Small detail, big impact: a mirror that meets the countertop creates the illusion of more space.

This charming bed alcove is detailed at every level to emphasize human scale. The entire alcove is a detail within the larger room; the beadboard paneling and curved trim are details of the alcove; and the trim itself is detailed with a rosette and glass marble.

No accidents here. This detail is a labor of love, and though it may seem obsessive for many homeowners it clearly indicates the refinement that's possible when you pay attention to the little details that make a house personal.

## What It All Adds Up To

Appreciating details is really just a process of learning to zoom in and focus on what's important at this smaller scale of consideration. Some details are so simple they're hardly noticeable, and they blend in perfectly. Other details intentionally draw attention to themselves as they perform their task. Best of all, in design there is no single right answer. There are literally millions of solutions to every challenge. All you have to do is let go into the process and allow the creative juices to roll.

My hope is that all the creative details in this book will inspire you to turn your home into your own creative playground. A house that's simply lived in can provide shelter, but it doesn't do much in the way

of inspiration. A house filled with the kinds of details you'll see here can be a highly personal expression of all that has meaning to you. It will be, in a very real way, a reflection of who you really are. And there will be no doubt in anyone's mind that this is HOME in the best sense of the word.

(Left) While performing the role of safety railings, the tapered wood fins and perforated steel planters add depth, texture, and personality.

(Facing page) A large window, oriented to the view, gains visual power through contrast with a small window that offers a mere glimpse.

A single gentle curve impacts the dynamics of a whole space.

<< The smallest trim piece contributes to the overall effect.

Furnishings can be an opportunity to add flashes of color.

Wide openings allow adjacent rooms to appear larger because they visually borrow space from one another.

# Curves and Color Bring a Tiny House to Life

**When David and Sukie bought** a 1,280-sq.-ft. fixer-upper in Brookline, Massachusetts, back in 1988, they assumed it was a starter home. But Sukie, an avid gardener, fell in love with the soaring paper birch in the backyard, and David, an architect, recognized that the house had great natural light and kept imagining possibilities. Today, their children have gone off to college, but the family remains happily at home in what is still a small house. Remodeling in phases, they updated, opened up the downstairs, and added a garden study with master bedroom above. What makes this modest house so special is the way David and Sukie handled color, light, and scale to unify the house; used curves and small details to add interest; and framed interior views to create a sense of spaciousness.

It might have been tempting to tear down the walls between rooms completely, but David and Sukie had a different idea, one more in keeping with the traditional spirit of the 1920s-era house. They opted to keep the rooms small but to expand the openings between them to 5 ft. or 6 ft.,

**outside the house**

## A Clever Trick for Round Corner Trim

The living room fireplace is a zero-clearance insert; it's housed in a drywall hearth that could be added to nearly any house. Its simple embellishments include a raised granite hearthstone, a gently curved mantel, and round trim made from ordinary wood closet rods, notched to fit the hearth corner as shown in the drawing below. The same closet rod detail is used on the outside corners of the wainscoting.

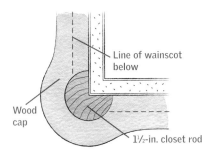

Line of wainscot below

Wood cap

1½-in. closet rod

**Living room** The focus of the living room is a hearth that's been added into the space, much as the writing alcove was added to the reading nook (see the left photo on p. 24). Pushing the hearth into the room brings the fireplace closer to the sitting area in the center of the room and creates a pocket of space at either side, perfect for a small table or chair. It's counterintuitive to take away floor space in a small room, but sometimes doing so increases both the distinctiveness and the usefulness of the space.

roughly twice the width of a typical doorway. With four walls intact, each room retains a sense of itself, but the wide openings allow adjacent rooms to appear larger because they visually borrow space from one another.

Take the kitchen and dining room, for example. Sukie and David kept the kitchen as an efficient galley and left the dining room the size it was: big enough for a dining table but no bigger. But where the two rooms used to connect through a doorway, there is now a cooking peninsula under a double arch (see the photo on p. 18). The archway defines a transition area below it and frames the view in either direction. The thickness of the arch also creates a sense of spatial depth. Standing in the kitchen looking through the double arches, you experience the dining room as a place beyond.

the way it's done

## A Rectangular Bay Window

A bay window doesn't have to be three windows at an angle to one another. The bay window at the far end of the dining room is a 1-ft. bump-out with a pair of double-hung windows but solid sides that feel like the sides of a really thick wall. The integrity of the bay is enhanced by painting everything within it—window, trim, and walls—the same color. The extra inches expand the space of the dining room and provides enough depth for a narrow window seat, widened here with the barest of curves. It's actually a two-story bay; upstairs, it provides space for book-shelves in a child's bedroom.

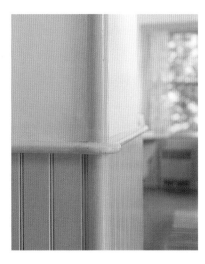

**Harmony through repetition of color and form**  The pale green color used for all painted wood trim and surfaces throughout the house helps tie together otherwise disparate elements. Less immediately obvious are the lines that embellish the woodwork: for instance, the gouged lines known as "flutes" on the door jambs (see the photo above right) and the newel post (above left), or the grooves—or "beads"—in the bead-board wainscoting. Even the ribbed glass fronts of the kitchen cabinets pick up on the lines.

**Simple details add up**  The cooking peninsula is one of the most attention-getting elements in the house, and yet it's a surprisingly simple construction. The countertop is plastic laminate, softened and spruced up on its edges with wood trim. A similar trim approach has been taken with the tile on the backsplash. The real impact comes from the brackets holding up the counter and forming sides for a display shelf. Each bracket is simply a 1-in.-thick piece of plywood, but the power is in how thoughtfully the plywood has been shaped, and in the concentrated repetition of the curves.

**Reading nook** The alcove in the reading nook was created by adding bookshelves within a room just big enough for an overstuffed chair and ottoman. The impression is of a desk set into the extra space within a thick wall, giving the illusion of more space even though there is less floor area than before.

**Garden room** A painted wood floor, wainscoting, and ample light from two pairs of windows contribute to the airy, back-porch feel of the garden room. The curved desktop and wavy bracket add some whimsy, while subtle touches like the wide frame around the bead board on the ceiling keep the look crisp.

THE IMPORTANCE OF A CURVE  The double arches between the dining room and kitchen add visual interest and frame an interior view. They also define a narrow space in between, an effect enhanced by the bead-board ceiling. If you take away the arches and the bead board, the two rooms bleed into each other, and the transitional space is lost. Remove the curved brackets from the cooking peninsula, and the impact of their refrain is lost as well.

**Entry**  Even a small room like this entry is an opportunity to work with the colors, materials, and details established in the main spaces. The painted floor and ceiling make this a less formal indoor-outdoor space, akin to the garden room, but here the wainscoting is higher, allowing the top trim band to function as a coat rail.

Framed openings aren't the only detail that bring the rooms together. Sukie and David chose a serene palette of colors—cream, sage green, pale spring green, and soft brown—that they maintained from room to room, helping to harmonize the whole house. They also introduced graceful curves throughout the house to break up the somewhat boxy lines of the little rooms. The curves occur at many levels of scale. They can be generous, like the double arches between the kitchen and dining room; whimsical, like the squiggled brackets supporting the garden-room desk or the cooking peninsula countertop; subtle, like the slight sweep of the window seat in the dining room, the fireplace mantel, or the slim writing desk in the reading nook; or unassuming, like the corner trim on the hearth, the molding capping the wainscoting, or the gently rounded trim surrounding the tiled backsplash.

Whether choosing colors, selecting materials, or shaping trim and other details, David and Sukie have been mindful to work with, not against, the diminutive scale of their house. Even the furnishings are in keeping with the scale of house. Most of the furniture pieces are low, making the ceilings feel higher, and the chairs and sofas have legs so that space flows under them. Some might consider this degree of attention fussy, but it's precisely David and Sukie's unwavering approach to detail that makes their tiny house so enduringly livable.

A small, framed interior view hints at space beyond without giving it all away. ∨∨

Think of a freestanding >> cabinet as a pod of space, both object and container.

In a simple composition of basic materials, beauty lies in honesty of expression.

A modest house can be beautiful in its simplicity.

# Serenity
# on a Budget

A Not So Big House is not necessarily an inexpensive house. But if you keep the size of the house small and stick with common materials, basic construction methods, and simple details, you can indeed build or remodel on a very limited budget. It helps to pare down your notion of home to its essence and to embrace simplicity—in your house and in your life. But you will not have to give up beauty and delight, nor do without a few special features and spaces that will satisfy your soul.

The retirement house Philip and Nancy built in a passive-solar cohousing community in Durham, North Carolina, offers proof that you can create a tranquil home on a budget that won't raise your blood pressure. When the couple approached architect Tina Govan about designing a simple home, they had read *The Not So Big House* and wanted to incorporate many Not So Big ideas into their home. Tina was equally familiar with Not So Big principles, and she shared the couple's vision of building modestly and efficiently. There was another connection: Tina had worked in Japan; Philip and

**outside the house**

**Hanging shelves, wall shelves**  Open shelves are not only efficient and inexpensive but also an elegant expression of the very nature of simplicity. Nothing is present except what is absolutely necessary.

Nancy had lived there for a time; and Japanese architectural elements and principles run through *The Not So Big House*. So it was no stretch for Tina to give the house a Japanese leaning, as Philip and Nancy requested.

The house Tina designed, with lots of collaboration from Philip and Nancy, was built within a slim budget yet it provides Philip and Nancy with everything they wanted. Although the house is deliberately spare, the life lived in it is not spartan. Nancy and Philip each have a private space for creative endeavors, and the small second floor is a quiet (and very Japanese) away room with tatami mats for yoga and meditation.

## The palette of interior materials is truly minimal: concrete

(sealed but left its natural color) for the main-level floor; drywall (painted white) for all walls, ceilings, and soffits; clear-stained Southern yellow pine for shelving, stairs, and all trim; natural birch plywood for built-ins; standard hollow-core doors; laminate countertops; and basic white appliances. Add *shoji* screens and tatami mats for the away room upstairs, and that's about it.

## An Expressive Hanging Shelf

Even in a minimalist interior, it's possible to create variations on a theme. This wall shelf in the bathroom is simple and inexpensive to build; it's just pine boards and a few lag bolts and screws. It's also visually in tune with similar shelves in the kitchen and, more subtly, with the pattern of thin wood slats on the shoji screen in the living room.

**In the kitchen** The kitchen isn't a room with four walls but an area separated from the living area by a dropped soffit and a partial wall, and from the dining area by a work island. It could not be more simply appointed: concrete floor, narrow pine storage shelves, and laminate countertops edged with a thin strip of pine.

**Dining room** The dining area is defined on three sides by a dropped soffit. The soffit is narrow above the doors to the terrace (left) and to the screened porch (right) and wide where it defines the entry area and separates the dining area from the living area. The built-in cabinet provides a further separation between the dining area and the entry area.

## A Grid of Under-Stair Storage

The shelves beneath the stairs make the most of what is often unused space. By lining up with the grid of square rails and spindles, the shelves help accentuate the essential stepped nature of the staircase. The staggered ends of the horizontal rails further the stair-step effect. The rails and spindles continue to become the face frames of the shelves. (Even a simple detail like this requires a thoughtful eye for design.)

The way these materials are used, however, is maximal rather than minimal, because the result is the maximum amount of usable space for the least amount of money. Swinging doors and cabinet doors are eliminated wherever possible in favor of pocket doors and open cabinets. Thickened walls contain shelves. Space under the stairs is used for clothing storage on one side and media storage on the other. Aligning the pocket doors eliminates the need for hallways, and the open floor plan reduces the number of interior walls. In several places, the walls between adjacent areas are partial walls; elsewhere, freestanding cabinetry doubles as a wall between two spaces. There are a few items that add cost, namely the shoji screens and the dropped soffit that helps define discrete spaces in the absence of interior walls. But overall, the basic materials and space-saving tactics keep costs well within the limited budget.

**Laundry hall** The short hall from the kitchen to the bath saves space by doubling as a laundry area. The bath occupies two rooms, one with a sink and commode, the other—seen here beyond the pocket door—with a sink and shower.

## The spaces within this unassuming house invariably

add up to more than the sum of their off-the-shelf parts. The entry area—just 4 ft. by about 6 ft. 4 in.—is a wonderful example of a space that is small and inexpensive but also hardworking and beautiful. This little entry has a seat with some shoe storage below it, a coat closet, storage cabinets, and two elegant spots for displaying flowers and favorite objects: illuminated glass shelves and a deep, recessed shelf, called a *tokonoma* in Japan. All this, but no expensive materials and no labor-intensive details. The cabinet door pulls are blocks of pine with a curve cut out of them for your hand. Like the rest of the house—the materials, the details, and the spaces themselves—the door pulls are beautiful in their simplicity.

**A flexible boundary** As the Japanese have known for centuries, a shoji (like other translucent screens) is perfect for creating a flexible degree of openness. Because light passes through it, a shoji screen suggests the space on the other side even when it's closed. This shoji slips neatly into the middle of a two-sided bookcase. Though it's attached to one wall, the bookcase feels like a free-standing object because there's space between it and the ceiling.

**Long views and cross-ventilation** When the shoji screen is open, the bookcase frames a view from the home office through the living room to the window in the entry area. The entry window lines up with one in the office to generate cross-ventilation as well as long views. The wood tracks on which the shoji slides remain in place to reinforce the framed view.

**Minimalist trim for a partial wall** The half-walls in the living room are surfaced in drywall with finished corners. A 1x4 strip of wood is screwed to the narrow piece of drywall on the top of the wall, and a 5½-in.-wide strip of finished wood is attached to the wood strip, creating a slight reveal. The effect is richer than the simplicity of the materials and construction would suggest.

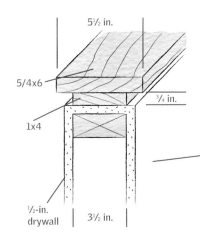

5½ in.

5/4x6

¾ in.

1x4

½-in. drywall

3½ in.

**An entry pod** The freestanding entry cabinet is a pure expression of a "pod of space," an element that is both an object *in* space and a container *of* space. This pod is both a solid and a void, with storage space concealed behind doors and an open display shelf that in a Japanese house would be called a *tokonoma*. You could place a similar pod beyond a door that opens directly into a living room and, with this move alone, create a defined entry area and add storage.

Simplicity is a state of mind as much as an absence of unnecessary detail.

It's okay to mix >> several kinds of wood in one space as long as they go together.

^
^
Positioned just right, even a tiny alcove can take in the whole outdoors.

Although the house has nearly doubled in size, the spaces are still small.

# Reinventing the Family Home

Of all types of buildings—museums, libraries, schools, and so on—none is reinvented as often as the house. There's a unique idea of home for every person, couple, family, or group, and for each there's a house to suit. If you and your household can't find what you're looking for in a house that's already built, and if you aren't in a position to build new, you can always find an existing house and reinvent it.

Sabrina and Douglas and their young children have the good fortune to live in Los Angeles, where people and houses reinvent themselves all the time. Douglas, an architect, was able to take a quiet, single-story 1920s Spanish-style house and transform it into a dynamic and contemporary two-story house that fits his growing family as well as the innovative, forward-thinking spirit of the city.

Douglas has a refreshingly open attitude toward how spaces can function in a house. Realizing that the small existing living room would always feel partly like a foyer and acknowledging that his informal family didn't want a

**outside the house**

**A slice of indoor-outdoor space** A floor-to-ceiling framed panel of glass cuts diagonally from the end of the family room back toward the kitchen, stealing just enough indoor space from the outdoor terrace for a child's play table. By angling inward, the glass panel avoids blocking the existing windows over the kitchen sink (visible to the left beyond the glass). It also creates a fun triangular space that feels like an adjunct alcove beside the home office alcove (see the floor plan on p. 41).

**Enter into art**  Turning the original living room into an open gallery creates a serene welcome space as well as a place for art. A subtle visual trick has been employed on the far wall of the gallery, which has been painted the same color as the others, but three shades darker. This slightly darker wall appears to recede, making the room feel larger.

traditional living room, anyway, Douglas fashioned the living room into an open gallery/foyer for displaying his painting and sculpture and the work of other artists. The family has fewer choices of where to sit, but the open gallery welcomes guests with artwork and provides breathing space for the adjacent dining room and even for the kitchen beyond. Douglas took the same approach with the detached garage in the backyard, which he turned into a full-sized playhouse for his three boys. The garage-turned-playhouse is in full view of the kitchen and just a hop, skip, and jump from the family room. The family room, in turn, occupies space at the back of the house that had been a bedroom and one of two first-floor baths, rendered unnecessary by the second-floor addition.

## Upstairs, Douglas's playful approach continues in the

tall, angled spaces. In the master bedroom (see the photo on p. 38), the vaulted ceiling allows for a large 5-ft. by 5-ft. skylight over the bed; in one of the two children's bedrooms, the tall ceiling space is open now but will one day accommodate a sleeping loft, enabling the entire floor to be used for deskwork and play. There's already a ladder concealed in a hall closet that climbs to a secret hideaway above the other children's bedroom.

**Translucent wall panel** There's more than one way to separate two adjacent spaces. In a traditional house, a half-wall with columns might be one option. In this contemporary house, a translucent glass panel screens the powder-room door but allows light to filter through.

**Built-in window seat** Here's a great example of a window seat that's been created by building into a room rather than by bumping out, though the effect is similar to a cantilevered bay window. The angularity of the room is softened by the gentle curve in the seat.

## A Simple Vanity Mirror

The master bath deftly mixes three sizes of square tiles and three types of green slate, including Kirkstone for the vanity top and the elegant little shelf above the back-splash. The vanity mirror, designed and built by the architect, achieves maximum bang for the buck. It's a simple framed mirror hung on blocking so it floats 1 in. away from the wall. Before it was installed, a standard light track was mounted on the back, facing up, and gooseneck lights were snapped in.

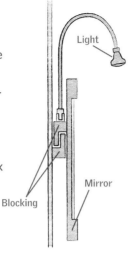

Light

Blocking

Mirror

A number of large and small details contribute to the open and expansive character of the refashioned family room (see the photos on pp. 40–41). Typical of the honest approach this house takes, there's been no attempt to hide the TV. In fact, it's the focal point of a full wall of cabinets. The maple cabinets allow for the depth of the TV at the center, but then they angle back toward the corners of the room. The light-hued maple, the smoothness of the flat-panel doors, and the receding lines keep the cabinetry from overpowering the space. Like the cabinets, the large sliding doors between the family room and the backyard have minimal visual weight.

Clean lines continue in the kitchen, which opens to the family room and dining room. An angled wall of glass creates space for a kid-size play table in the family room without blocking the windows above the kitchen sink. The kitchen proper is no bigger than a stand-up galley, but the countertop steps up to become an eat-in bar for four stools that occupy a narrow space between the dining room and family room. Having the kitchen open to nearly the entire first floor makes it command central for family life. For all its contemporary flair, the house has at its heart the most ancient of communal spaces: a single common area for cooking and eating and living together.

**Stairway windows** A vertical stack of translucent windows adds light to the stairway while providing privacy at the side of the house.

**Concealing a door frame** A sliding door unit includes the doors themselves as well as a larger frame that houses tracks on which the doors slide. Typically, the side pieces of the unit frame abut the sides of the opening, so when the door is closed, you see both door frame and unit frame. But here the fir columns to either side of the door units have a channel cut into them so that the 1-in. unit frame fits within the column. Now when the doors are closed, you see only one frame, not both. It's a subtle bit of streamlining, but it makes a difference.

**Calm port in a storm** The home office alcove centered on the wall between the family room and the backyard enables parents to contemplate the garden and keep an eye on the children's playhouse in the converted garage out back. The large window helps the alcove feel like part of the garden and maintains the open feel of the long family-room wall.

**Everything in its place** A wall of cabinetry makes the most of the relatively small family room. The TV is in line with the room, as it must be for viewing from the sitting area, but the cabinets and shelves angle back toward the corners of the room. This carefully balanced composition of solid and void, centered on the TV and the floor-to-ceiling stack of cabinets to its right, is far more interesting than uniform cabinets all set to the depth of the TV.

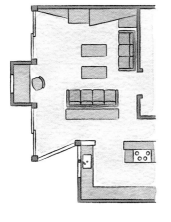

**Kitchen-family room connection.** Although the kitchen itself is quite small, it interlocks spatially with the family room. The two rooms, in effect, borrow space from one another. But this kitchen-family room combo is not one large, undifferentiated great room. The low walls and alcoves define distinct areas for sitting, deskwork, play, and cooking, allowing for both expansiveness and intimacy.

Subtle shifts in color make a difference, especially in a simple house.

You don't need expensive materials to make a space more interesting.

When there >> are very few details, each one gains in importance.

The constant play of light is almost the only detail you need.

# Classic Cottage Simplicity

This small cottage on Block Island, off the coast of Rhode Island, is the epitome of simplicity. The homeowners came to architect James Estes with a collection of photos of Block Island houses that exhibited traditional cottage elements: weathered gray shingles, porches with low-pitched roofs, and steeply pitched dormers that extend from the face of the house, known, fittingly, as Block Island dormers. What attracted the owners to Block Island was the crisp light and rugged landscape, right out of an Andrew Wyeth painting, as well as the pared-down, no-frills aesthetic of the island's early buildings. They wanted a bare-bones place for themselves and for visits from their grown children and guests.

James designed a house true to classic Block Island cottage form, but he threw in a twist. The roof of the attached front porch continues through the house—where it is the vaulted ceiling of the living room—and comes out the other side as the roof of the back-entry porch. The main

**outside the house**

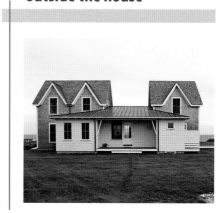

**Big kitchen window** This large double-hung window is a good illustration of leaving well enough alone. Because it is simply trimmed and painted, and because there is nothing around it to distract you, it has a greatly heightened presence, as does the view beyond.

mass of the house has, in effect, been cut in two, and so has two sets of stairs, each leading to dormer bedrooms on one side or the other.

## Inside, the bright, open spaces reflect the simplicity

and purity of the exterior forms. There's a subtle order, a quietness to the details, and an overarching restraint that is Shaker-like, though the interior is not in the Shaker style. The interior is not without details, of course, but, to a considerable degree, the stripped-down spaces serve as a stage for the ocean, which is the real focus, as it should be at the seaside.

Perhaps the easiest way to understand how the simplicity of the exterior impacts the quality of the interior is to look at the double-hung windows. These windows are really big; on the first floor, they're 3 ft. 10 in. by 6 ft. 9 in., the maximum stock size available from the manufacturer. By scaling the windows larger than our eye imagines they might be, James has made the house appear smaller than it actually is, as well as simpler, more pure in form. Each window sash is divided vertically by just a single muntin, so each window unit becomes a block of four tall panes. These are windows a

**Living room** The 8-ft.-tall doors and 2-ft.-tall transom windows lend a graceful proportion to the whole living room; you enjoy the spaciousness and the big view but don't feel overwhelmed by the room's height. A crisp order is established when the sliding doors are closed and the vertical door sashes line up precisely with the sashes on the transom windows.

## It Takes a Good Plumber

For this cottage, the impact of the large double-hung windows on the exterior was paramount; a smaller window set over the sink would have broken the spell cast by the tall windows and called attention to itself: "Oh, that must be where the sink is!" Leaving the window tall has a playful, stunning impact inside. The sink appears to float, and a plane of light reaches the floor where you'd least expect it. Notice how the window trim, rather than carrying below the countertop, instead turns and becomes the backsplash and then the base trim of the cabinets.

**Screened porch** The screened porch is a platonic square, stripped of all but its most essential structural elements. Its screen panels, divided by a slim rail, have a graphic visual impact similar to that of the double-hung windows. The strict order of the screen walls, the lack of embellishment, and the pure floor shape make the porch a quiet point from which to sit and watch the ocean.

**Bedroom** The window perfectly centered on this bedroom dormer reflects the perfection of form seen on the exterior of the house. If the window were off center even a touch, your eye would notice it; you'd feel vaguely unsettled. The simple bed, almost a caricature of itself, further emphasizes purity of form; its vibrant color suits a room this plain.

child would draw. On its sweeping hillside, the simple house shape with its simple windows produces an arresting, agreeable effect.

Inside, the effect is much the same. On the ocean side of the kitchen, a single, oversized double-hung window rests on the baseboard and tops out just shy of the ceiling (see the photo on p. 44). The window's crisp white trim and four oversized panes frame the ocean in a strikingly straightforward manner. Surrounding the window is an unadorned pale gray wall. The ocean captured in the window provides the only true color. The effect is calming, even sublime. Imagine how different the quality of the space (and the view) would be if the wall was paneled in mahogany and the window was divided into 12 panes over 12; you'd perhaps feel you were in a Georgian manor, a very different place from a Block Island cottage.

The living room is, in essence, somewhere between an indoor room and an outdoor room, and the way it is detailed follows suit (see the photo on p. 48). Instead of the smooth drywall ceiling found in the other interior spaces, it has exposed rafters with a tongue-and-groove wood ceiling, all

KITCHEN CABINET NICHE Sometimes, the absence of something is more powerful than its presence. That's the case with the in-fill cabinets between the upper cabinets and the countertop in the kitchen. A display niche has been created by leaving one cabinet unit out; the missing cabinet also allows for more counter space beside the sink. Add a cabinet, and the breathing room and striking niche disappear.

**Bath vanity** The unexpected but welcome shelf above the master bathroom vanity is a simple, elegant, and highly useful detail, the result of creative design rather than of money spent.

painted white. This ceiling is literally a continuation of the porch ceilings on either side. Although an interior ceiling of exposed rafters looks simple, it raises a challenging question: where to put the insulation? The answer, in this case, is a sheet of rigid foam insulation topped with a sheet of plywood; the two-layer panel is known as a "nail-base" insulation panel because the roofing material can be nailed right onto the plywood layer. The panels are about 4 in. thick, and they sit right on top of the tongue-and-groove ceiling.

## Not surprisingly, the living room has the qualities of a porch. Exposed rafters are only part of the reason why. The side walls of the living room are also the sides of the two house pieces split apart by the room; these side walls have been treated as smooth plaster planes to emphasize the form of the house pieces they're part of. In keeping with the sense of the living room as negative space, the entire wall facing the ocean consists of doors and transom windows. In a modern house, such a wall might literally have been all glass, perhaps without any visible frames. Here the doors and transom windows are framed, but the intent is the same: to make this wall disappear so space flows continuously between the living room and the porch, and light pours in.

**The right height for a porch rail** Porch rails (as well as porch windowsills) are typically set 36 in. above the floor or higher, for safety or to meet code requirements. Unfortunately, high porch rails block the view when you're sitting and greatly diminish the open feeling that draws people out to porches in the first place. The horizontal rails dividing these screen panels are set 30 in. above the floor, about even with the surface of the tabletop.

**Defining a dining area** It doesn't take a lot to define discrete areas within an open plan. The dining area is divided from the living room by a simply detailed built-in bookshelf and two columns. The second-story wall above the columns is a little lower than the dining-area ceiling, so from within it reads like a beam, further distinguishing the more intimate dining area from the tall living room.

**More than meets the eye** The twin stairs could hardly be more straightforward, yet each is refined by a surprising number of subtle details. The most obvious refinement is the gracefully tapered newel post. Less immediately obvious are the bottom tread that wraps around the stair wall; the bead-board wall itself, painted a pale gray to emphasize the brighter alternating pattern of white risers and wood treads; the riser and tread pattern; and the railing, which is wood, in contrast to the white spindles.

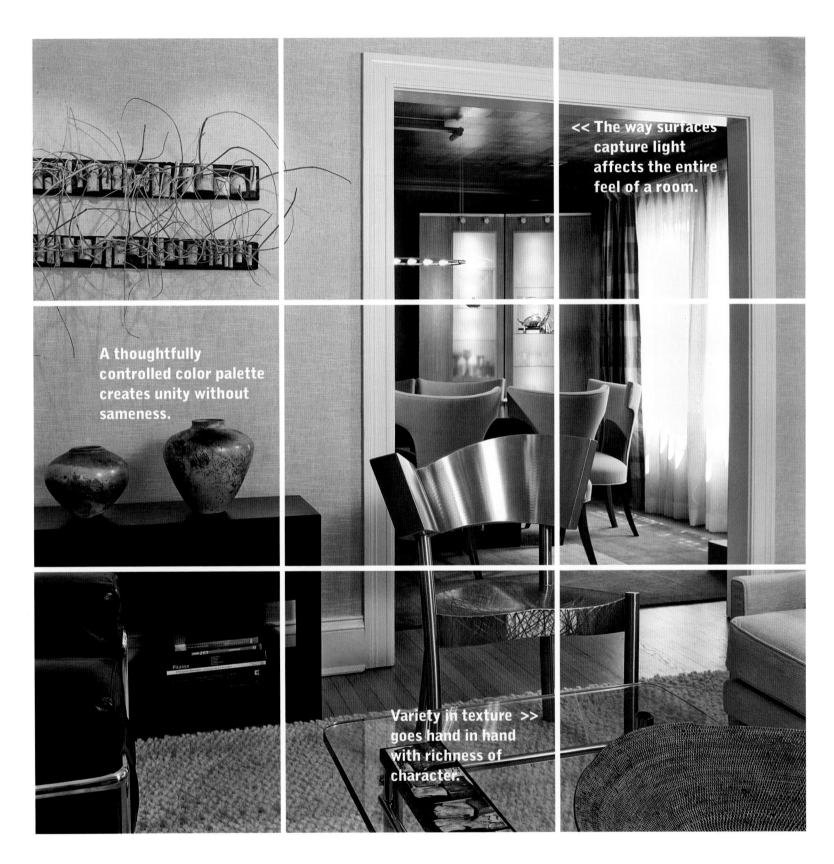

<< The way surfaces capture light affects the entire feel of a room.

A thoughtfully controlled color palette creates unity without sameness.

Variety in texture >> goes hand in hand with richness of character.

This in-town remodel achieves coherence through imaginative variations on a theme.

# A Jewel Box of Texture and Detail

The empty-nester couple who own this house could have bought or built a large house in the suburbs beyond West Hartford, Connecticut, but they chose instead to buy a small house in an older neighborhood, within walking distance of shops, restaurants, and a farmer's market. The couple initially hired architect Jamie Wolf to reconsider the living room, because they didn't like the traditional fireplace or the colonial cabinetry. What began as a consultation about color became a larger conversation about design, then a living-room remodel, and ultimately a transformation of the entire house. Jamie designed an "indoor back porch" that mitigates the elevation change between the kitchen and the cozy backyard; otherwise, the rooms stayed where they were. But the owners encouraged Jamie, and interior designer Peter Robbins, to think boldly (but respectfully) about the opportunities each space presented. The resulting remodel exemplifies richness of detail, imaginative use of space, thoughtfulness in design at every scale, and a balanced use of materials, all executed with an extraordinary degree of craft.

**outside the house**

**Variations on a theme** The transformation of the entire house interior began with a remodel of the living room. Ideas, colors, materials, and details established in this room are maintained or reinterpreted in every other room of the house, creating a harmonious whole. Here are just a few examples.

**Steel bolts and wire mesh** In the living room, black bolts with washers attach the steel mantel to the chimney face. The bolts and washers reappear, polished this time, to attach the railing brackets between the kitchen and the indoor back porch. Wire mesh door panels conceal the existing radiators in the living room; between the kitchen and indoor back porch, wire mesh is fashioned into planter boxes that serve in place of railings.

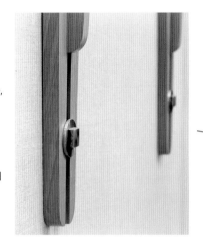

**Details that lean** In the living room, the lower cabinets angle, or slant, from the wide speaker cabinets in the corners to the narrow chimney face. This notion inspired tilted or leaning window trim, which energizes a number of windows, such as this one over the kitchen sink.

**Groups of squares** In the living room, the lower cabinets are divided into squares. In the indoor back porch, a group of three square awning windows is introduced. And in the upstairs study shown at left, the three square windows reappear in slightly different form; the bookcase is a grid that's four squares by four squares, trimmed similarly to the living-room cabinets.

**Sunroom**  The sunroom is detailed to take advantage of its diminutive scale. A room this tiny doesn't handle furniture very well; prop yourself on a chair, and you'd feel like you were on display for passersby. So instead, a futon has been set on a plinth below a wide window-sill. Glass plant shelves span the windows, bringing the room down to the futon level.

## Bedroom Wall as Theater

It's amazing how much is happening on this side wall of the master bedroom. Instead of a ho-hum flat wall and a standard door to the dressing room, there's a layered wall with a shoji-like translucent screen that slides on wood tracks to hide behind fabric panels, which seem to float a few inches from the smooth drywall. A soffit above the layered wall brings down the scale of the room (whose high ceiling soars into

what had been attic space) and provides a place for recessed lights. Although this setup is somewhat complex and requires considerable craftsmanship to con-struct, it is plainly detailed and quite restful, especially at night, when the fabric panels are backlit.

The house isn't lavish—it has no golden chandeliers or marble staircases—but the remodel was not inexpensive. The owners were willing to invest in quality materials and expert craftsmanship as well as in design time for the many things designed expressly for the house. They also invested their own time to collaborate with Wolf and Robbins. What they have for their investment is a home that's tailored to their needs and tuned precisely to their sense of style and expression. At just over 2,000 sq. ft., the house is a finely wrought jewel box, which makes perfect sense when you learn that one of the owners is a jewelry artist.

## In redefining the character of the living room

and the tiny sunroom adjacent to it, Jamie arrived at a palette of colors and materials and an approach to details that includes anigre (a light, warmly colored wood) cabinets, pale limestone countertops, wire-mesh door panels, bold but simple steel elements, and glass shelving. These choices were

**Kitchen** The kitchen features a harmonious mix of materials, textures, and colors. The cabinets are made from two different varieties of wood, not just one. The upper cabinet door panels are a combination of wire mesh and textured glass. Part of the peninsula is stained; part of it is painted. The mix is far more interesting than a whole kitchen of uniform cabinetry bought by the linear foot.

**Powder room** Small and simple, a powder room is a perfect place to pull out all the stops. In this tiny, playful room, nearly every design idea in the house is given fresh, even whimsical expression. The idea of three square windows, for instance, reappears as three square display niches.

**Master bath** If the house is a jewel box, the master bath is a gem. The deeper-than-usual tub works for a bath or a shower and is flooded with light cascading from a skylight. The impact of the light is amplified by the contrast between the larger, brighter tiles above the tub and the smaller, darker tiles in the rest of the room.

influenced by practical requirements, of course, but also by Jamie's artistic sense of what feels right. The skewed angle of the low cabinets on either side of the hearth (see the photo on p. 53) can be explained as making up the difference in depth between the deep speaker cabinet in the corner and the narrow chimney face, but the truth is also that the angled cabinet feels right. Same with the curved track for the spotlights above; it just looks good. True, the curve of the track echoes the gentle arc of the limestone mantel, but the track could just as easily be straight.

## Design is an exploration of possibilities. As the remodel

continued from room to room, Jamie arrived at fresh interpretations of the ideas introduced in the living room and sunroom. For instance, the black steel bolts that fasten the mantel brackets above the living-room fireplace reappear in polished form to pin wood railings to the half-wall between the

**Indoor back porch**

Generous sliding doors to the backyard garden keep the 9-ft.-wide indoor back porch from feeling too narrow. The groupings of three awning windows, the tilted window trim above the sliding doors, and the mesh planters and angled wood brackets work together to animate the space and visually relieve its tallness.

## picture this

THE SUBTLE REFINEMENT OF A GRID OF SQUARES  The stairs represent one of the last vestiges of the original neocolonial house. But the wallpaper, made up of squares of slightly varied neutral hues, ties the stair hall to the new look of the house, where squares and neutral tones predominate. As you come to appreciate when it's taken away, the wallpaper grid also adds a quiet energy and a measure of refinement.

indoor back porch and the kitchen. Jamie also introduced entirely new ideas. Several details that are repeated upstairs first took shape in the indoor porch addition, including the grouping of three square awning windows. Similar windows appear in the stairwell and in the upstairs study. The wallpaper and floating lattice ceiling in the upstairs hallway feature squares meant to echo the awning windows in spirit.

Another detail that first appeared in the indoor porch is a window with trim that leans into the room. Tilting the side trim inward is a simple thing to do, but it generates a subtle energy. In the indoor porch, the tilted trim also emphasizes the thickness of the wall into which the windows are set. But then the lean of the window trim in the vertical is really a variation of the lean of the living-room cabinets in the horizontal, so the lean is not something that first appeared in the porch after all. When a high degree of care and attention has been given to unifying materials, colors, textures, and details, there's almost no end to the connections you can find. It's through unity of effect—which does not mean sameness—that this house achieves coherence.

Archetypal forms >>
like arches and squares
resonate with us
at a deep level.

One of the surest >>
ways to create unity
is through the
repetition of form.

Especially in a
bright and airy house,
dark floors add
solidity and substance.

Finding peace and tranquility is easy in a light-filled home.

# Texas Tuscan

You might think that regional styles, by definition, would not be transportable from one region to another. But when the two regions have a similar climate, no matter how far apart they are, the vernacular architecture of one place can befit the other. So it is with Tuscany and Texas—at least those parts of Texas that are both hot and dry. In the arid, hardscrabble land around Austin, Texas, for instance, the villa architecture that evolved in the Tuscan hills makes perfect sense.

All of this came home to architect Steve Zagorski as he traveled in Tuscany, where he was captivated by the small villas dotting the hillsides, which he saw as "basically boxes, with or without ornament." The opportunity to explore Texas Tuscan architecture (as Steve calls it) came when clients Philip and Anne asked him to design a house in Austin that would be small and real rather than large and fake.

The house Steve designed for Philip and Anne is a nearly perfect square (not counting the garage) of roughly 40 ft. by 40 ft. It has a tiled roof, wood pergolas, a narrow portal

**outside the house**

**Punched opening** The thick wall between the dining room and the kitchen provides more separation than connection, allowing each space to express itself as an individual room. Even though it's quite wide, the opening between the rooms feels like it's been punched through the wall. The considerable thickness of the wall helps define the countertop, which occupies a kind of transitional space within the wall.

**Under-stair storage** These inset cabinets and shelves help to express the sculptural quality of the staircase. The archetypal zigzag of the stairs is amplified by the dark stair treads set against the white plaster.

WHAT A LITTLE DEPTH WILL DO
The niche in the wall under the stairs allows even small art objects to have the impact of a much larger art piece because your eye takes in the entire composition: the archetypal form of the arch; the sides of the niche, bathed in light from above; and the grouping of three objects. The niche at the far end of the stair hall has the same effect. As you can see, two paintings hung on flat walls would not have the impact of the two niches.

between the house and the garage, an arched loggia above the front door, and walls of creamy Austin limestone. The interior spaces are, by intention, tall boxes arranged one beside the other; even the stairwell is a box, albeit two stories high. This approach to building is not only true to Texas Tuscan form but also economical; all else being equal, constructing a series of boxlike volumes is less expensive than building complex spaces with lots of ins and outs.

Within the boxy volumes, it's relatively easy and inexpensive to add a few steps of floor height or to alter the ceiling, as Steve does in the dining room with a raised floor and a doubled ceiling vault known by architects as a "groin vault" (see the photo on p. 60). The groin vault transforms the walls as well as the ceiling, giving them an arched shape that mimics the windows and doors.

Above all, it's the shape of the rooms, the thickness of the walls, and the pure form of the arched openings that connect this house with the villas Steve saw in Tuscany. The connection is especially powerful because classical Tuscan architecture relies on archetypal forms that require no translation. We respond at a deep level to squares and arches, just as we respond instinctively to the light that's so important in Philip and Anne's house.

## The largest and most important space in the house,

the living room, is also the purest expression of Texas Tuscan architecture. The room is essentially an unadorned 10-ft.-tall space, yet it has tremendous presence (see the photo on pp. 66–67). In many of the houses we've

**Up to the den** The steps through the opening between the living room and the den are another feature that emphasizes wall thickness. Placing the den three steps above the living room helps define it as a distinct space.

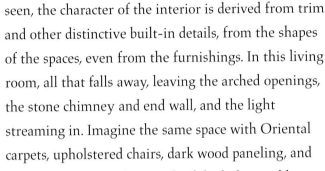

**Stair central** The ethereal character of the interior reaches its apogee in the soaring two-story stair hall. Placing the stairs in the middle of the vertical space gives them a floating, processional quality. The thoughtful placement of religious icons in the twin wall niches lends a contemplative air.

seen, the character of the interior is derived from trim and other distinctive built-in details, from the shapes of the spaces, even from the furnishings. In this living room, all that falls away, leaving the arched openings, the stone chimney and end wall, and the light streaming in. Imagine the same space with Oriental carpets, upholstered chairs, dark wood paneling, and thick trim. It might be a beautiful room, but much of the light would be absorbed by the rich materials. With so much else to consider, we might not focus as readily on the light.

For many of us in this country, our sense of home derives from the northern climates of England, Germany, and Scandinavia. We equate comfort with sitting in a cozy inglenook by the fire, safe from the howling winds. In the temperate zones, a tall stone and plaster box like Philip and Anne's living room probably wouldn't conjure up the feelings of warmth we associate with home. But the situation in a hot, dry place like Austin is very nearly the opposite of what it is in the vast temperate regions of our continent. A tall space where the hottest air stays above us feels welcoming indeed. Just looking at the stone and plaster, we sense the absence of the heat they are absorbing.

The radiant and transporting quality of sunlight may have very definite connotations in an Italian church; in a house, the effect of light is equally profound if less numinous. Quite apart from whatever spiritual beliefs we may hold, we all respond to light and can find great peace and tranquility in a light-filled home.

**Second-floor loggia**   In many center-hall houses, a bath or closet occupies the space above the front door and foyer. Here a small, covered terrace (or *loggia*) offers a quiet, shaded place between the master bedroom and study. The loggia is just 9 ft. 4 in. by 10 ft 4 in., but it makes all the difference.

## Forced Perspective

The tub alcove in the master bathroom plays with Renaissance notions of symmetry and perspective. Although the alcove looks grand, it's simply a standard tub built into a 6-ft.-wide alcove between the water closet and shower. The tub is set a little high, allowing for a gracefully curved step. Plain, tumbled limestone tiles are embellished with decorative ceramic tiles (a great way to get maximum impact from just a few expensive tiles). The deep arch over the tub is angled to create a forced perspective, a trick of the eye favored by Italian painters and sculptors. The point isn't to fool anyone but to have some fun and punch up the visual appeal of the bath.

**Making a little stone go a long way** Stone on an interior wall is expensive because it has to be laid to the inside of a wood-framed, insulated wall; stonework thus takes the place of much less expensive trowel-finished drywall. By featuring stone on the most prominent wall in the house, the whole interior of the main floor benefits. The impact of the stone is heightened by doors to either side of the hearth that let you experience the doubled stone wall by passing through it.

**Surfaces as a stage for light** What you experience in the living room is not just light itself but the play of light on the reflective surfaces of the thick plaster window openings and the glossy wood floor.

**Form and light in combination** The archetypal form of the arch figures prominently in the living room and is repeated throughout the interior, as in the dining-room window. The character of this window vignette is derived primarily from the interplay of the thick arched opening and natural light in the absence of distractions from heavy details or furnishings.

**Repetition of form** The niche at the foot of the stairs mirrors the arched windows in form, and, like the windows, it helps express the thickness of the walls. The recessed light illuminates the small painting, but it also accentuates the sides of the niche, just as sunlight accentuates the sides of the arched window openings.

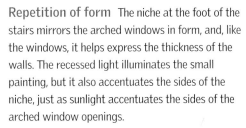

<< A twist of 45 degrees may be all it takes to make the old appear new again.

<< Size the roof overhangs right, and you won't need curtains to block the sun.

An underlying ordering system lends coherence to every detail in the house.

Logic and order are immediately apparent in this "pinwheel" house.

# Order in the Details

Most architects would agree that design constraints—modest budgets, odd-shaped sites, height restrictions—are a virtue because they channel creativity along certain lines. Paradoxically, the challenges imposed by limits can be more compelling than the unfettered freedom of a blank slate. So architect Frederick Noyes had a good thing when a retired couple asked him to design a one-story cottage for their visiting children and grandchildren (and for themselves should they no longer be able to negotiate stairs). The hitch? The cottage could be no bigger than 800 sq. ft., the maximum allowable size for a second house on their property on Martha's Vineyard, Massachusetts.

To make the most of so little space, Fred actually imposed further constraints by establishing two underlying ordering systems. One ordering system is the pinwheel form of the house: a tall main space in the center with four smaller spaces overlapping like spokes around it. The other ordering system is a 6-ft. module that regulates everything

**outside the house**

**Entry**  The overlap of space between the main living/dining room and the smaller spaces surrounding it is subtle but effective. The wood-paneled wall and the brick floor define the entry area proper, but the floating beam extends the entry experience ever so slightly into the tall volume of the main space. It also defines a transition area between the main space and the lattice porch.

from the arrangement of the interior spaces to the placement of walls and windows to the nature of details.

The two ordering systems unify the house. Even though you may not see the 6-ft. module, you experience it. The interior spaces feel crisp and composed, yet there isn't a quality of stiffness or rigidity about the house. This is because the pinwheel form generates layered volumes that share space in a dynamic way, one borrowing from the next. Space flows easily between the smaller spaces (bedrooms and kitchen) and the main space (living and dining area), and between the main space and the outdoor spaces (lattice porch, screened porch, and open deck).

Natural light also enlivens the spaces. Because the glass gable ends of the tall main space face east and west, they transmit even light across the vaulted white ceiling for most of the day. Stronger, more direct light hits the screened porch, the lattice porch, and the small kitchen window; thus, the brightest light dances around the edges of the main space, animating it without overwhelming (or overheating) it. The drama of natural light combined with the overlapping of space makes the house seem much larger than its square footage.

## Built-In Bedroom Utility

The master bedroom with vaulted ceiling is, in essence, a smaller version of the main living/dining space. A horizontal band of fir, not unlike the floating beam in the larger main space, defines a dresser niche and a desk niche on either side of a closet. The horizontal band makes more sense in this open interior than a solid-walled soffit would. People worry needlessly about matching wood; here, the fir trim nicely sets off the birch closet doors and dresser.

**Living-room hearth** The rectangular panel of the chimney brick and the solid wall panel above the mantel help emphasize the pure geometry of the wood framework. In a similar manner, extending the glass gable windows to the ceiling plane emphasizes the pure form of the vaulted ceiling, which almost seems to float free of the end wall.

**An implied soffit**  A floating beam defines the portion of the main living/dining space shared by the kitchen. The beam functions like an implied soffit above the kitchen island, creating a more intimate sitting area. At the same time, it brings down the apparent height of the living/dining space, keeping it from feeling too tall. And the beams attached laterally to the main beam provide an anchor for light fixtures and open shelves.

**Honest shelves**  The shelving unit is simply an open box (birch plywood faced with strips of solid birch) clipped to the floating beams with steel brackets. Everything is on display, not just the glasses and dishes but the brackets and the shelves themselves. Open shelves provide a degree of separation between the kitchen and the living/dining room while allowing space to flow freely.

**The result of order, not expense**  The appliances, countertops, cabinetry, and wood shelves in this kitchen could hardly be more ordinary. Their crisp, tidy look is not the result of money spent but of time taken to establish a loose symmetry about the window at the center, to line up beams with cabinets, and to work with the 6-ft. module that underlies the organization of the entire house. The clean composition gives simple elements like stock cabinets and a plain wood backsplash a dignity they wouldn't have if they'd been put together haphazardly.

**Lattice porch** In a house that doesn't draw hard lines between inside and out, the lattice porch feels like a room even though it is clearly an outdoor space. The roomlike nature of this minimally enclosed porch is partly the result of having the same dimensions and volume as the screened porch and each of the bedrooms.

**picture this**

DEGREES OF ENCLOSURE The west gable end of the main living/dining space is divided into panels by fir framing members. Fixed glass fills each of the panels except the hearth panel, creating a strong connection between inside and outside and enabling the wide roof overhang and the angled brick chimney to be experienced from the main space. The overall effect of the wall would be very different if more of the panels were solid wall.

The way the interior is detailed reinforces both the quality of light and the feeling of overlapping space. In detail after detail, openness is emphasized. Where there could have been a solid wall above the hearth, instead there are smartly framed clerestory windows. Over the kitchen, where you might expect a solid soffit, there is an open frame of floating beams. In place of a kitchen cabinet with doors is an open grid of shelves. What could have been a solid beam spanning the center of the main living/dining space becomes a doubled beam with a slim gap of space between the planks.

The main space is a perfect square in plan, which you might think would make it a static place. But the two free-floating beams that stretch between the gable ends and the double beam that crosses the center of the space divide the square into implied rectangles. The floating beam on the south side of the main space helps define the kitchen area, which occupies a portion of the main space as well as its own

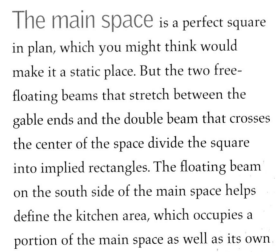

**In the corner** Glass doors and panels of fixed glass break down the corner of the living/dining room so that space seems to continue into the screened porch. Being able to see into adjacent spaces makes the house feel larger than it actually is.

**Two-door bathroom**
Bathrooms with two doors can make guests uncomfortable, but in this tiny house, where everything has to do double duty, two doors enable the bath to serve both the children's bedroom and the entry area, which shares a hardworking brick floor with the bath.

**Double-duty bathroom** A pleated window shade is cleverly used to conceal the stacked washer/dryer from the rest of the master bath. A closet door would have gotten in the way of the door to the room.

smaller space. Likewise, the floating beam on the north side of the main space creates a subtle transition zone just beyond the tiny entry area. These beams are set exactly 3 ft. (half of a 6-ft. module) into the main space, and because everything conforms to the same modular system, the beams line up precisely in the center of a 6-ft. window-and-door module to either side of the hearth, which, no surprise, is itself 6 ft. wide (see the photo on p. 71).

If you're quick with math, you'll have figured out that the main space is 18 ft. by 18 ft., three modules by three modules. But the point of a modular system is not mathematical rigor; it is clarity of expression, beauty, and beyond that, delight. It is a house whose logic and order are immediately apparent. The materials and details are simple and straightforward. To the degree that they draw attention to themselves, they also accentuate the qualities of light, order, and spaciousness inherent in the overall design. It would be hard to say which you like better in a house as tightly conceived as this, the parts or the whole.

There's an elusive
yet undeniable charm
in the simple fairness
of a curve.

A very small house
can achieve the snugness
and refinement of
a tailored suit.

Particleboard is
a perfectly decent
material when it's
treated with integrity.
v
v

Economy reigns in a floating home where every inch counts.

# A Houseboat
# Full of Nautical Charm

A wooden boat is the essence of the maxim "a place for everything and everything in its place." In the necessarily compact cabin of a sailboat, every square inch must be used, and in a well-crafted wooden boat, every square inch is also lovely to look at. All Not So Big Houses embrace a kind of graceful economy, but perhaps none more so than a small floating house, occupying as it does a middle point between a house and a boat.

Having scouted fishing boats for 20 years with vague domestic notions in the back of their minds, recent empty-nesters Barry and Val pared down their possessions, sold their 3,000-sq.-ft. house in Idaho, and moved into a dilapidated 700-sq.-ft. single-story houseboat on Lake Union in Seattle, Washington. They kept the floating log "footprint" of the 1920s houseboat, but little else remains beyond one porthole and the charm of the original, reinterpreted in two stories and an aesthetic that combines 1920s Craftsman-style bungalow and 1960s cabin cruiser. Barry and Val are part of a diminutive floating community of kayaks and ducks and creative

**outside the house**

**Window seat** The bright window seat at the top of the stairs is a made-to-order reading spot for a book picked from the stairway bookshelves. The seat lifts up to reveal storage underneath.

neighbors, with sweeping views of the Space Needle and the Seattle skyline crisscrossed by the comings and goings of seaplanes. But it's inside, where the artfulness of boatbuilding meets the art of home building, that this little house comes into its own as a comfortable nest for empty-nesters.

## Storage is a theme running through the house. As

often as not, a seemingly mundane storage problem gives rise not only to a functional solution but also to an unexpected flourish. For example, what appear to be column bases at either side of the fireplace turn out to be pull-out shelves for videos and CDs (see the top left and bottom right photos on p. 81). Similar pull-out shelves are fitted into even the slimmest sections of the kitchen and entry area. The one TV in the house swivels around in its cabinet to face either the living room or the bedroom. The stairway doubles as a library, with shelves on three sides marching upward with the steps. The

---

**the way it's done**

## Window Seat With Rollaway Bed

This window seat in a cozy corner of the second-floor workspace turns into a bed with a few elegant moves that call to mind the compact economy of a VW™ camper perhaps more than a boat cabin. The drawer (which is a useful storage bin) rolls out to become, along with the seat top, a base for a double bed. A hinged plywood panel folds down to the opened drawer. One of two pads (previously stacked together as a seat cushion) is simply pulled forward over the drawer to complete the bed.

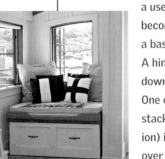

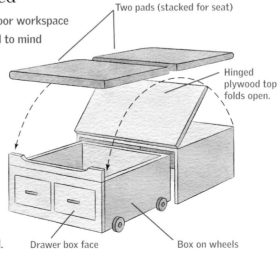

Two pads (stacked for seat)

Hinged plywood top folds open.

Drawer box face

Box on wheels

**Library stairs**   The stairway as library is one of the most pleasing and useful elements you can incorporate into a new house or a remodel. With the addition of just 10 in. on all sides, the stairway becomes a room full of books. You might think books would overwhelm a small space, but their visual richness is, if anything, more enchanting in this tight stairway, with its lighthouse-shaped newel posts and arched ceiling.

**Ceiling in three dimensions** Because it's built up from many individual pieces, the coffered ceiling in the living room has a richly textured, three-dimensional quality that helps relieve the low (several inches less than the standard 8 ft.) ceiling height. The contrast of the hand-rubbed fir beams against the white bead board adds visual interest and keeps the ceiling from feeling too dark and heavy.

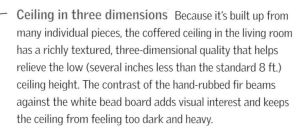

**A nautical echo** Subtle thematic connections invariably enhance the character of a house. The round vintage photograph in its circular frame feels just right above the mantel, though it's hard to say exactly why—until you see the ship's porthole around the corner.

**Furniture-quality cabinetry and a boatbuilder's approach to storage** Fine craftsmanship is especially appropriate in a very small house, where it can't help but be seen from up close; craftsmanship is also more affordable in a small house, where there isn't too much to detail. These cherry cabinets have slim, shiplike proportions and trim lines, with flat panels set off by what's known to furniture makers as a parting bead. The panels under the columns cleverly slide out to reveal storage shelves, just as they might in a boat.

**The perfect spot for a TV** Half-hiding the television behind leaded-glass doors to one side of the fireplace maintains the classic look of the hearth and its surrounding cabinetry. In a house where everything does double duty, the TV is no exception: It swivels within its cabinet so it can be viewed from the bed in the master bedroom.

## Windows to Bathe By

This nearly open-air tub is the
bathing equivalent of a corner window seat. The clear glass of the
adjacent shower, the glossy white
walls and trim, and the tall casement windows contribute to the airy
quality of the bath. White curtains
hung gingerly from thin metal cables
provide privacy without diminishing
the open feel; the cables are like the
guy lines of a sailboat, in keeping
with the nautical character of the
house. But it's the way the windows
meet the lip of the tub that has the
greatest impact on the bathing
experience. Bringing windows right
down to tub level is really the only
way to ensure a view for a bather
lying back in a tub.

**Kitchen**  Among the many smart appointments in this efficient kitchen
are two ideas that make sense in a kitchen of any size. One is to continue
the countertop material up to the windowsill to create a simple and
elegant backsplash, as has been done here with soapstone. The other is to
build separate cooktop and oven units into the lower cabinetry, avoiding
the awkward, vaguely out-of-place look of some single-unit ranges.

**French doors**  French doors extend the living-room space onto the waterside deck, establishing a beguiling contrast between the tidiness of the paneled interior and the jumbled neighborhood of floating decks, boats, and houses.

space under the stairs (accessible from outside) holds bicycles, snowboards, fishing gear, and anything else you might imagine in an attic or garage.

## Yet the houseboat never feels cramped, whether

you're upstairs under the bowed ceiling or downstairs in the kitchen, living room, bedroom, and bath. Barry and Val have a modest amount of stuff and lead tidy, disciplined lives, but that only explains the lack of clutter, not the overall feeling of tranquility. The calm character of the interior stems as much from the beauty of its proportions as from the thoughtfulness of its parts.

The living room is a pleasing 16 ft. by 16 ft. square, richly appointed with dark fir wainscoting, beams, and trim. With just a single seating area in front of its substantial hearth and a small dining table off to one side, it feels satisfyingly snug and cozy.

The living room feels calm, not cramped (and this could apply to any space in the house), because Barry has shown admirable restraint. There's a ton of storage tucked into the house, but, strictly speaking, there's room for a ton more. Barry has the good sense to provide enough storage but not so much that shelves and drawers and cabinet doors overwhelm the spaces. There's lots of wood paneling, cabinetry, and trim, but in every case the dark wood is balanced by white space, whether it's painted bead board or swatches of drywall. The spaces themselves are simply not crammed too full of furniture and artwork and other stuff, so even in this tiny cocoon, there's ample room to breathe and grow.

<< A coherent design can bring polished mahogany together with whitewashed pine.

In the effort to >> get everything right, don't forget to have fun.

The one rule of eclecticism is this: If it fits, it fits.

Vintage materials and a playful attitude lend an informal air to this modest beach house.

# Laid-Back Florida Cracker

Architects are sometimes criticized for liking their work too much ever to allow curtains or drapes to hide any of it. In this architect's own house, curtains were part of the design from the beginning. Evoking a time gone by, the cottage has no formal closets; in place of closet doors, simple curtains hang from galvanized rods. In a similar vein, operable shutters filter light from the front porch; the baths are outfitted with free-standing porcelain tubs; and the doorknobs are old rim-locks from the late 1800s.

Architect Jim Strickland designed this remarkable beach retreat in WaterColor, Florida, for himself and his wife, Linda, and their extended family. Although it's a new house, it's meant to look and feel like a laid-back fish camp that's been passed down from generation to generation. Authenticity is paramount in the design, along with informality and durability. Harkening back to cottages he remembered as a child, Jim created an inspired meld of simple spaces, vintage materials and fixtures, and well-worn

**outside the house**

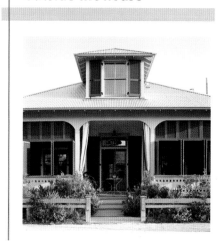

furnishings that manages to feel honest and inviting without ever seeming too precious. In just more than 2,000 sq. ft., Jim has also slipped in a modern heating and cooling system, contemporary appliances, and four bathrooms. The cottage may look and feel like a Florida cracker, as such a house is called in the regional vernacular, but it's as comfortable and convenient as any new home.

## Jim's architectural firm, Historical

Concepts, designs new buildings that have the patina of age, so it's no surprise he employed a trick or two in his own cottage for creating a vintage look. His approach is widely applicable, even in a house that doesn't aim for a strict historical effect, because it relies on using inexpensive building materials in imaginative ways and celebrating the imperfections of old fixtures, worn furnishings, and family hand-me-downs, many of which can be had for a song. It might seem easier to be playful and informal in a second home, but there's no good reason not to adopt the same attitude with a primary residence. If you're on a limited budget, then using reclaimed or inexpensive materials will save you money and may allow you to pick and choose a few key materials or elements on which to splurge.

**Barn door** The barn door between the master bedroom and bath makes sense because there isn't enough room for a door swing. A sliding-panel door feels at home in a house where opened shutters and curtains (like the one at right in the photo) remain visible. A pocket door would work but is less in keeping.

**Stair hall and master bath**  The trim on the wall in the stair hall illustrates the idea of a simple pattern overlay. The grid pattern of the trim breaks up the large wall surface into smaller panels, adding visual interest and creating an order that helps position the family photos. In the master bath, the grid of trim lends order to the photos, the mirrors, the towel hook, and the antique gas lights (rewired for electricity).

**Framed opening** A framed door opening with transom window above separates the stair hall from the living room in a way that makes the stair hall appear almost as outdoor space, maintaining the easy indoor-outdoor quality that begins on the front porch.

**Front porch** Operable shutters give the porch a vintage feel, but they're not just for looks. Like operable shutters of old, these provide cooling shade, privacy from a street that's only steps away, and shelter from inclement weather.

**Utilitarian kitchen furniture** Because the cabinets stop at various distances from the ceiling and they're topped with strong crown moldings, they feel more like old-fashioned kitchen furniture pieces than contemporary built-in cabinetry. In place of rows of matching cabinets, there's a mix of open shelves, small, breadboard-like countertops, and cabinet units with the loose feel of stacked Shaker boxes.

**Functional appeal** Placing a dish rack across the kitchen window is a brilliant way to provide both light and privacy at the side of the house, where the neighbors are so close you could ask them to pass the salt. A dish rack has the straightforward appeal of utility. Similarly, the contemporary stainless-steel range makes sense in this kitchen because, like the dish rack, its beauty lies in its pure expression of functionality.

**No need to match** Many contemporary kitchens feel monolithic, the result of too much cabinetry made from a single wood, with floors, walls, and trim of the same or a very similar hue. This kitchen features a variety of wood species and other materials, held together not by literal sameness but by a shared sensibility. Mahogany French doors, whitewashed pine walls, painted wood trim and cabinetry, and stained heart pine countertop: Each, in its fashion, is a simple and honest expression of its purpose.

# A Child's Bed with a Pedigree

This child's bed is set within a dormer off the open bunk space of the second floor. The bed could have been placed farther into the dormer, but it's much more interesting—and more fun to play on—with curtains on two sides and a little space between the mattress and the window (practical, too, because its base hides ductwork behind the drawers). The idea for the bed-as-alcove came from Thomas Jefferson's bed at Monticello, a reminder that you can borrow ideas from another period or style and recast them in your own.

**Children's bath** Two old vanities, relieved of rust and painted yellow, were expertly replumbed and fitted into the children's bath. Placing the two vanities together, along with the twin medicine cabinets, more than doubles the impact.

Many of the materials used to finish the interior of the cottage do double or triple duty: providing a durable and functional surface, contributing to the casual ambience, and often costing little to buy and install. The walls, for instance, are #2 Southern yellow pine—the cheapest lumber in the home center—given a light whitewash that utterly transforms them. The wide boards are simply nailed to the studs, one beside the other, with no tongues and grooves or other joinery to complicate things.

Cracks between the boards, which naturally develop as the wood shrinks and expands with the weather, only add character. The floors are treated in a similar fashion. Some are #2 Southern yellow pine, like the walls; these floorboards are painted once, then a second time with a slightly different color, so the color of the first coat will start to show through as the top coat wears. The effect is of an older generation's color choice reasserting itself over time.

Other floors, particularly those in the main living spaces and central stair hall, are reclaimed antique heart pine. Admittedly, they're more expensive than the new yellow pine, but the old planks have been left just as they are, some slightly thicker than others and some with beetle damage, though the worst spots have been patched with new wood. The rough-edged planks were butted together without joinery, painted with a wash, then sanded by hand, buffed, sealed, and waxed. The stair treads have been sanded down in the middle to suggest years of use. It's all very convincing; even the new patches look old.

**Upstairs hall**  The Dutch door (only the top opens) adds a playful touch to the second-floor stair hall. The white curtains swivel to the sides of the window on pivoting rods. Recalling the operable shutters on the porch, swiveling curtains don't block the window when swung open.

With exposed ceiling joists, the structure is the decoration.

<< Even a detail as simple as a stair tread can be made highly expressive.

Plain, polished materials provide an ideal surface for the play of light.

What the mostly white interior gives up in color
it gains back in intensity.

# Detailed
# for the View

**This Rhode Island house sits** on a waterfront property on
the East Passage of Narragansett Bay. The site is very long, front to back,
with an unusually narrow waterfront; the most expansive ocean views are
not straight ahead but beyond the southeast corner of the property, a tricky
site on which to build. The owners hired architect Peter Twombly, whose
partner James Estes designed the cottage we looked at on pp. 42–49. Each of
these architects has his own approach to design, though they share a broad
aesthetic. With this house and the cottage on nearby Block
Island, we have an opportunity to see two distinct yet
related ways to detail an honest, straight-ahead house.

**outside the house**

Peter oriented the house lengthwise on the site, with
a narrow gable end directly facing the water. The rooms are
arranged lineally, each with ocean views to its south side.
On the waterfront end, the living room and the master
bedroom above also open to the view through corner windows. The placement of the house and its organization are
large design moves and not in themselves details. But at

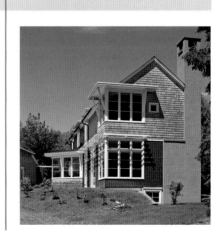

## Getting Shelves to Float

The four long, white shelves in the living room (see the bottom left photo on p. 114) were attached to the wall studs with metal brackets before the drywall was installed. The brackets are sandwiched within each shelf, which is constructed like a long box. This is one of several ways to attach shelves to a wall without visible means of support so they appear to float; it looks seamless and highly convincing, but it requires construction ahead of drywall installation (in a remodel, the old drywall would have to be removed first).

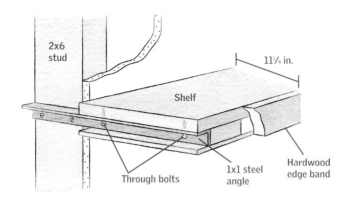

2x6 stud

11¼ in.

Shelf

Through bolts

1x1 steel angle

Hardwood edge band

every opportunity, Peter has detailed the interior with the linear orientation of the house and its oblique ocean views firmly in mind.

## Let's look at the corner windows in the living room.

Especially in this calm space, the corner grouping of two triple windows with transom windows above (the most glass in one place anywhere in the house) all but screams: "The view is over here!" The same is true of the corner windows upstairs in the master bedroom. On the other hand, the little square window in the master bedroom addresses the view in exactly the opposite way, by providing a contained glimpse. Think of it as a square porthole on the bow of a ship.

The linearity of the house is emphasized in the grooved wall below the stairs and, strikingly, in the long floating shelves that guide you into the living room from the entry hall. You probably don't stop to think about the grooves or the shelves, but as you experience the house over time, moving along its length or taking in a long view, these linear elements reinforce the

A WINDOW LIKE A MINIATURE PAINTING The small, square window in the master bedroom acknowledges the center of the house on the exterior, under the oceanside gable, and inside, where it marks the center of the room. The window also lines up with the middle of the corner windows, lending balance and order to the wall opposite the bed. Most of all, the small window offers a framed glimpse in counterpoint to the expansive view offered by the corner windows. Take away the window, and the room becomes much less interesting.

**Degrees of separation** The half-wall with columns and the steps to either side provide just the right amount of separation between the living room/dining area and the kitchen. The columns mark the width of the kitchen at the center of the house, while space slips easily past them, creating long views and allowing for circulation around—not through—the dining area.

## A Staircase Detailed on a Budget

The staircase is the first thing you notice when you step inside; its beguiling geometry animates the entry hall and makes moving through the house a pleasure. Yet this signature element is the result of good design, not great expense.

The curved lower treads embrace the hall the way falling water spreads out after hitting a flat stone. The stair wall has a classic cottage look, though it's surfaced in inexpensive medium-density fiberboard (MDF) scored to look like true tongue-and-groove paneling.

The inexpensive metal spindles were going to be painted white, but they looked better with a clear seal instead. The simple glass blocks capping the newel posts refract light like the old deck lights on a wooden boat; befitting a cottage, they have the quality of sea glass.

**Stock cabinet with custom end**   To keep costs down, the kitchen cabinets are stock units, but they're spruced up with 2-in.-thick end panels made from maple plywood. The end panels keep you from seeing the toekick reveal in profile, which never looks right. A little of the money saved went toward honed slate countertops, which match the simple elegance of the light maple cabinets.

**Study bookshelf** The bookshelves in the study are a playful, vertical variation of the floating shelves in the living room. The square window creates a brightly lit display shelf.

**A subtle detail** The top shelf is set cleanly into the window trim, and the shelf and the trim are the exact same width. This is just the sort of detail we generally don't see and therefore don't request of a builder. And so it gets done wrong. The more you look for such details in well-designed houses, the more you'll see them, and you'll be in a position to ask for them in your own home.

horizontal nature of the house and the site whether you acknowledge them or not.

If linearity and ocean views are two of the larger design issues, another was staying within a reasonable budget. The living room (the owners call it the "not so great room") manages to be the important room in the house without undue expense. It gains additional height not by occupying the roof but by stepping down a foot. It's expensive to build a room with a soaring roof because then you can't build what amounts to relatively cheaper rooms above it. By setting the living-room ceiling at the same height as the ceilings in the rest of the first floor, Peter has enabled the second floor to be occupied over the living room. Exposing the second-floor joists also adds visual weight and character to the living room. The solid fir joists were not cheap, but they double as structure and decoration. Finally, the expense of the stone fireplace surround was balanced by surfacing the exterior of the chimney in stucco rather than in more stone.

Let's take another look at the Block Island cottage (see pp. 42–49). Where this house comes closest to the cottage is not in any particular material or detail. The real connection lies in the similar way both architects, Peter Twombly and James Estes, approach materials and details, and in their mutual concern for the proportioning of parts, the massing of forms, and the placement of elements. These are big architectural ideas, but in the house shown here, as in the Block Island cottage, big ideas have been brought down to domestic scale. The result, in both cases, is simply a home that makes sense.

**Light from below**  A halogen uplight is a wonderful light fixture for illuminating a ceiling and bouncing reflected light all over a space. With a dimmer switch, you can create a variety of effects, from the ceiling appearing as a bright plane to the ceiling casting the barest warm glow.

**Turning a problem into an opportunity**  Building a house rarely goes without a hitch. In this case, the firebox ended up off center—6 in. farther from the wall than from the built-in media cabinet. The error was reconciled with a few judiciously placed slabs of the same bluestone used for the hearth and mantel. There's more space on the right side of the firebox than on the left, but now the overall stonework composition feels balanced and more interesting. The bluestone rectangle above the mantel is the same size as the rectangular opening at the top of the cabinet, a bit of visual play that brings a smile to your face should you notice it.

**A detail in tune with the orientation of the whole**  Shelves that attach to the wall without brackets or other visible means of vertical support are well suited to a long house on a long site with a long view because we see only their horizontal dimension. Below the floating shelves, a built-up maple plinth carries the line of the bottom stair tread from the hallway.

A trim band set >> roughly at door height keeps tall ceilings from seeming too tall.

^
^
When trim is well crafted, even straight lines become highly expressive.

Few materials warm a space as well as orangey woods like fir and cherry.

Craftsman-style details and built-ins add richness to small spaces.

# Craftsman Character on a Narrow Lot

Standing up, the human body occupies a spot on the floor roughly 2 ft. by 2 ft., or 4 sq. ft. This mathematical fact doesn't seem to have entered the calculations of people who build houses of 5,000 sq. ft. and 6,000 sq. ft. Just hearing about homes this large skews our sense of scale to the point where we have trouble realizing how little space is required for comfortable living. Forget about these megahouses with their 26-ft. by 46-ft. great rooms and think instead of that virtual 4 sq. ft. surrounding you, because it's the key to realizing how much home you can have in a modest amount of space.

This house in Seattle, Washington, was built in 1905 with 750 sq. ft. on the main floor and 550 sq. ft. upstairs, and even at that size, it's stuffed onto a narrow lot of just 4,000 sq. ft. The owners bought the house as a starter home but became so connected to the neighborhood they decided to stay. Zoning laws prohibited tearing down and rebuilding on the undersized lot; instead, the couple hired architect Gail Wong to add to the house. They wanted more space for

**outside the house**

**Kitchen cabinets** These custom-built cherry cabinets have a three-dimensional quality that's hard to achieve with stock cabinetry. If you're in the market for higher-end stock cabinetry, do a little homework; you'll often find that custom-built cabinetry costs the same.

themselves and their young son, but they didn't want to sacrifice too much of their small backyard.

Gail extended the house a mere 14 ft. at the back and reconfigured the roof to create more usable space upstairs. The house now has 2,150 sq. ft. of living space within its narrow confines, and it still doesn't have any large spaces. On the contrary, the new spaces offer testament to the pleasures and functionality of modest dimensions; the primary new space, the family room, is just 10 ft. wide. The addition may be small, but the payoff is big. By choosing to stay in their narrow home on its narrow lot, and by accepting the constraints imposed by a modest addition of space, the owners were able to put their money toward materials, trim, cabinetry, and built-ins that give the formerly nondescript house the warmth and character of a Craftsman-style bungalow.

## The Craftsman style is apt for this remodel because

this style, which evolved in the early 20th century, celebrates not only craftsmanship and handwork but also the domestic scale and the comforts of home. For instance, take a look at how the new family room and rejuvenated first floor embody both these aspects of the Craftsman style (see the photos on pp. 106–107). The family room is 23 ft. long, 9 ft. high, and, as already mentioned, just 10 ft. wide. To keep the room from feeling

Cherry built-ins The height of the divider between a kitchen and an adjacent space has a huge impact. There's no right or wrong height, just differing degrees of openness and separation. This built-in strikes a nice balance: The upper counter conceals the sink from the family room but allows someone standing to look through.

picture this

THE IMPACT OF A CURVE The curve in this desk embraces the corner as part of the worksurface, and it relieves the linearity of the desk and the space, so this narrow room (you're seeing 90 percent of it) doesn't feel like a mere slot. With the curve removed, you lose its pleasing roundness, and the corner of the desk becomes less usable.

**Half-wall with columns** In this second-floor bedroom, a half-wall with columns provides the perfect degree of separation between the bed area and the study area. Beyond the bed, casement windows with large, unobstructed openings satisfy code requirements for emergency egress more easily than a double-hung window would, yet the muntins dividing the sash give the casement the traditional look of a double-hung.

uncomfortably tall and narrow, Gail divided it into two areas: a nearly square sitting area that's in line with the original dining room and living room, and a slightly larger rectangular area for an all-purpose table between the kitchen and the back deck. Taking advantage of the tall ceiling, Gail defined each area by a lowered soffit that creates a kind of tray ceiling centered above it. The lowered soffit between these areas houses speakers and ductwork.

Each part of the family room features built-ins that enhance the comfort, human scale, and functionality of the entire room. The area with the table features a stunning wall of cherry cabinets (see the left photo on p. 102) that provides a ton of storage and offers views into the kitchen yet maintains a suitable degree of separation. The orange tone of the cherry, the thin muntins dividing the glass cabinet doors, and the many facets of the paneled construction add visual richness to the family room and soften the feel of the space. The sitting area features a simple hearth surrounding a gas fireplace and a deep window seat that's so thoughtfully proportioned and finely detailed it draws you to it from across the house.

**Master-bath tile** A band of decorative tiles (thoughtfully in line with the window frame) breaks up the tiled wall surface. Cutting tiles above and below the band requires a little extra work, but it maintains the centering of the square tiles on the window. Art glass in the lower frame of the window adds visual interest and maintains privacy.

**Master-bedroom window seat** The window seat in the master bedroom is the right size for sitting or reclining because it isn't too tall at the edges. Within the triangular form of the dormer, stepped windows provide wall surface for two sconces, which do a better job of providing light for reading than overhead lights.

## Sizing Up an Informal Eating Booth

This eating booth is sized right for the homeowners who use it every day, but it might not be right for everyone. If you plan to build an eating booth, it's a good idea to try out a few restaurant booths first to discover what feels right. Just bring along a tape measure.

A couple of points to keep in mind: The padded back should have a slight tilt; a ledge or sill behind the top of the seat back, even if it's just a couple of inches wide, gives the booth a more spacious feel; the edge of the seat should overhang the base of the bench, so people can place their feet a little behind their knee; it's usually best if the tabletop overlaps the seat by 4 in. or 5 in. (though the table shown here does not have this overlap); and a table with a center leg makes it easier to get in and out of the booth. If you have extra inches, resist the temptation to make the table or seats too wide—add inches to the sills behind the seats instead.

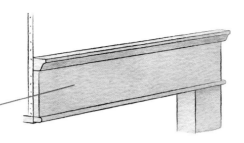

**Classic Craftsman-style trim**  The trim around the window seat is straightforward, honest, and expressive. It has just two pieces that are not absolutely necessary: the crown molding across the top and the narrow spline just above the opening. The crown molding and the spline combine with the wide top trim piece (like a bare-bones Greek frieze) to give the whole framed composition greater weight at the top, an arrangement that has felt right for more than 2,000 years.

**The ultimate window seat**  This window seat is the whole nine yards: wide enough (and cushioned enough) to be a daybed, built of rich cherry, with drawers below and four well-proportioned windows above. But what really sets it apart are a couple of thoughtful details. The wide sill that wraps around the seat provides a place to rest a book or a cup of coffee and keeps your head from bumping against the wall; the bookcases on either side don't hold a lot of books but add immeasurably to the cozy feel; and the gently sloped trim at the front offers a bit of extra containment, lending the window seat the snugness of a boat.

**A simple but dignified hearth**  There's nothing complicated or ornate about this fireplace surround. Its two materials, cherry wood and green limestone, are unadorned save for the angled Shaker-style crown molding across the top. The pleasure is in the thoughtful proportions and in the materials themselves, the warm grain of the cherry and the mottled patina of the limestone.

A shelf of books compels the curiosity seeker in us to walk toward it. ⌄

A roof overhang carries >> the ceiling plane outside, extending interior space.

⌃⌃
The best way to experience a really thick wall is to pass along its full depth.

Light and space, encouraged by thoughtful details, connect inside to outside.

# Rooms Afloat above a Garden

An active gardener in Manchester, Massachusetts, Olga asked architects Gitta Robinson and Richard Grisaru for a home that responded to her passion in two ways: She wanted large expanses of glass and ample doorways that would allow her to enjoy the garden, and she needed a place to keep her growing collection of houseplants, as well as potted plants that have to be brought indoors during the winter.

The steep site suggested tucking a garage, mudroom, and office under the main level, and this lower walkout basement level establishes the main floor a little above grade. From the upper garden side, the house appears to never quite touch the ground. Outside, Richard and Gitta accentuated the house's light touch on the land with wide roof overhangs and a long wooden deck that extends over a garden pool. Inside, he established a floating, almost weightless, quality with ample openings between adjacent rooms, a layout that lets in lots of bright daylight, and a series of details that cantilever and in some cases appear to hover above the floor.

**outside the house**

**A sign of lightness to come** One of the first things you see upon entering the house is the gap in the corner between two translucent panels that serve as stair rails. You may not consciously notice the open corner, but your mind likely registers the idea of openness it signals, subtly setting you up to experience the lightness and airiness of the entire house.

## Purple Sliders

The purple doors that slide out from either side of the hearth aren't pulled open often, but when they are, they make a real statement. The doors also enable the library (which has its own full bath) to be used as a guest bedroom or, in the future, as a main-floor master bedroom. The firebox has been painted with heat-resistant black paint, which looks much less new and stark than white firebrick.

A perfect example of a detail that floats is the hearthstone, a polished concrete slab that extends from the chimney mass like a thick shelf, 15 in. above the floor. You feel the full weight of the hearthstone, visibly spanning as it does the length and breadth of the chimney into which it is pinned, and yet it hovers. Space flows under the hearthstone just as it flows under the wooden deck outside.

In a slightly less literal way, the entire chimney is an object floating in the middle of a long space, dividing the living-room side from the library side. It's an artful composition in its own right and an illustration of the Not So Big concept of useful beauty. The chimney mass is not simply a sculptural object. It's a wall that divides two spaces, a sound buffer, a fireplace, a media center, an impromptu seat, a display area, a surface that reflects natural and artificial light into the rooms, and a place to conceal two large pocket doors; it's even a place for storing firewood.

Take a close look at the chimney in the photo at left. All of its parts have been considered and arranged with great care, yet in a way that ends up looking effortless. A firebox is typically placed slap-bang in the middle of the chimney, but it doesn't have to be. By placing the firebox to one side, Richard and Gitta have allowed the white wall (plaster over concrete block, in this case) to become a blank canvas

**Entry and landing** The second step from the entry to the stair hall extends along the side wall, combining with the picture frame to make the artwork on the wall seem more important.

for whatever is displayed in front of it. Placing the firebox to one side also leaves space behind the blank wall for the firewood niche. Richard and Gitta take a similar approach with the cherry media cabinet that is set into its own niche within the chimney mass to the left of the firebox. The hearthstone would be a logical place for the bottom of the cabinet, but instead the cabinet hovers above it, again reinforcing the floating theme and also creating a display area on the hearthstone.

Along with the media cabinet, most of the wood elements throughout the house, whether of cherry or oak, satisfy the definition of useful beauty,

**Conservatory** The fixed-glass window in the stone-tiled plant conservatory (at the far end of the stair hall) takes up the entire wall and is minimally detailed to feel almost as if it isn't there. Glass panels in the floor allow light to reach the mudroom on the lower level and appear with the plants as little reflecting pools, blurring the distinction between the conservatory and the garden.

## the way it's done

### Floating Stair Treads

Many people love the buoyant, weightless look of open stairs, which have solid treads but no risers. It's more difficult to build open stairs now that the maximum allowable gap in any part of a stairway has been reduced to 4 in. One trick I've employed is to add a strip of wood underneath each tread, recessed from the edge to decrease the gap between the treads without overly increasing their apparent thickness. But how to attach the "floating" treads to the walls? On this stair, metal clips are recessed into each end of these treads, one of the least obtrusive of several options.

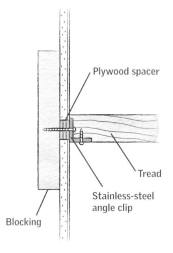

Plywood spacer

Tread

Stainless-steel angle clip

Blocking

**Library ladder** A simple but elegant handcrafted oak ladder is all it takes to make what is otherwise a room with a long bookshelf feel more like a proper library. The ladder rungs and the handholds lend a tactile quality to the room, as do the books, of course.

providing storage or some other function while also adding warmth and texture. In an interior as white and brightly lit as this one, wood is an ideal accent material. Given the linear nature of wood, it's no surprise that many of the floating details—the stair treads, for instance, or the breakfast-nook seats—are made of wood; these, too, embody useful beauty. And it would be hard to imagine a more straightforward expression of useful beauty than the handcrafted oak ladder in the library.

**Breakfast nook** The breakfast nook feels like a place of its own because it's defined by the corner windows. Even with a deck just beyond the windows, this corner spot feels perched above the garden outside. The near seat is cantilevered, another variation on the theme of lightness and floating.

**Low shelves** Low bookshelves run the length of the west wall beneath windows to the garden. The long shelves slip past the hearth to connect the library to the living room. Light from the glass door at the far end of the library draws you toward the garden just outside.

The house contains many details and elements that subtly appear to defy gravity, but the sense of buoyancy one feels in this interior is arguably affected most by the quality of light. The house has been oriented so that the kitchen and dining room face south, which makes these two heavily used spaces very bright on sunny days. The windows in the living room and library face east and west, so the light there shifts across the hours of the day. The stair hall, with its tall wall of glass, serves as a kind of light bridge connecting the living room/library and the dining room/kitchen.

But the form and orientation of the house are not the only reasons the interior feels so airy. The spaces also feel open because they're made up of elements that allow light to pass through them. Of course, the windows and glass doors let light in from outside. But once inside, the light continues to flow, through the openings between the stair treads, through the translucent stair panels, through the glass doors of the cabinet between the kitchen and dining room, and through glass panels set into the conservatory floor. Light and space are rather similar in the way they flow, and in this house, it's both light and space, encouraged by thoughtful details, that connect inside to outside even as the house floats above the garden.

**A not-quite-see-through cabinet** The display cabinet suspended between the kitchen and the dining room dances on the line between openness and containment. Its thin glass shelves, lit from within, and the slim reveal that ever-so-slightly separates the door frames from the ceiling give the cabinet a floating quality. Clear glass on the kitchen side lets you see the glassware displayed within; translucent glass on the dining-room side dampens the impact of the glassware, creating a slightly more formal, less cluttered feel.

**Sizing a sink window** The way the window behind the sink comes to rest flush with the countertop is an elegant detail, but it's one that requires some forethought. Assuming you want the tops of all the windows to line up, you need a window that fits exactly between the head of the rough opening and the countertop. Few stock windows do. Rather than spend money on a custom window, I often use a stock window behind the sink to set the head height of all the windows in the house.

**Cut-out cabinet corner** Stopping the lower cabinets short of the end of the countertop softens the look of the corner and lets the countertop overhang just enough to read as though it's floating, a theme repeated throughout the interior.

<< A lowered ceiling plane adds intimacy to the area below it.

Space appears >> to flow more freely when it has an object to move around.

<< Distinctive materials distinguish special elements from their surroundings.

Opening up the house makes an ordinary ranch more livable . . .
and more beautiful.

# A Modest Ranch Opens Up

### Steve and Courtney's ongoing ranch remodel

in Atlanta has been a labor of love since the couple bought the house in
1998. Built in the 1960s, the understated 2,100-sq.-ft. ranch had good lines
and enough space for the family of four; it simply needed updating. From
the beginning, Steve and Courtney knew they wanted "better not bigger
space." By adding just 80 sq. ft. to the kitchen, and through a combination
of small moves inside, Steve, an architect, created a surprisingly sophisticated
ensemble of interior spaces. The room functions remain where they had
been in the original, but now the spaces themselves overlap each other. Opening up the house involved judiciously
removing some of the long wall at the center, varying the
height of the ceilings, and adding furniturelike components,
such as a breakfast booth, a tall display cabinet, a round
worktable, and media cabinets. These built-in details
(mostly of cherry, though the round table is beech) combine with carefully controlled natural and artificial light

**outside the house**

**detail in focus**

## A Cabinet That Does Double Duty

This cherry cabinet provides storage and a display area while also serving as the back of the breakfast nook. Its Masonite panel doors are just right for kid art. There are square piers on either side of the cabinet; one stops below the floating ceiling, an expression of support, but the other continues past the ceiling, stopping just slightly above it, a playful way to emphasize the sculptural qualities of both the ceiling and the cabinet.

and custom-sized rugs to define distinct functional areas while letting space flow.

In the original ranch, the interior was divided right down the middle by a structural wall that supported the ceiling joists at their centers. With just two doors through it, the wall effectively cut off views and the flow of space from one side of the house to the other. To bring the rooms together, Steve opened the wall between the family room and living room and widened the opening between the kitchen and dining room. The fairly long central wall that remains now reads as a distinct object within the interior. It's a thick plane with space flowing around it, no longer a wall with doorways piercing through it. The central white wall adds reflected light to the rooms on both sides and serves, with the other white walls, as backdrop for the worktable, media cabinets, and other wood elements.

## Along with the central wall, the ceilings have been redefined

to create spatial zones rather than distinct rooms. It's the variation in ceiling height, more than the walls, that tells you you're in a particular area of the interior. In the kitchen addition, the ceiling vaults upward in the opposite direction to the original roof, creating a brightly lit clerestory area above the whole expanded kitchen. To take advantage of the additional light and to tie the kitchen and family room closely together, the family-room ceiling has been opened up to the original roofline, vaulting up to the central wall. Light from the clerestory windows now illuminates the family room as well as the kitchen. On the other side of the central wall, the flat ceiling has been maintained at its original height. The change in the ceiling from vaulted to flat helps to differentiate the family room from the living room.

**Media cabinet detail**
There's nothing fussy about the built-in media cabinet. Because of its recessed base and the lack of a solid corner, the cabinet appears to hover just above the floor, reinforcing your sense that space is flowing freely within the interior.

## The drama of a lowered ceiling plane

Though it's a relatively simple detail, the lowered ceiling plane achieves many things at once. By spanning the entire width of the house, it stitches together the spaces on either side of the central wall; it allows you to experience the wood accent wall and the wood display cabinet as bookends, further linking the two sides; and it helps define the dining area, the breakfast booth, and a sink work area. Finally, the floating section frames views between the family room and kitchen and from the kitchen into the family room.

**Objects in space** The wall that divides the living room and family room feels like a plane in space because of its apparent thickness and because it meets the ceiling without any trim. There's no framed doorway between the two rooms, just free-flowing space. The hub of the house is the round, built-in table that continues as a media cabinet along the central wall. The table, like the wall, appears as a sculptural object, but it's differentiated from the wall as well as from space around it by its warm color and rounded shape.

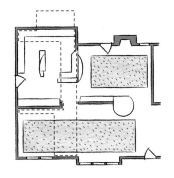

**Delineating activity areas underfoot** A long rug, designed and made for the house, defines a sitting area in both the living room and the dining area; on the other side of the wall, a more compact custom rug defines a family-room sitting area. The rugs run perpendicular to the floating ceiling plane, creating a kind of plaid effect, a stitching together of space similarly explored by Frank Lloyd Wright. The rugs have bold stripes and squares that relate from one rug to the other, a subtle way to unify the rooms.

**A soffit lends the hearth intimacy** The soffit extends beyond the chimney and across the window, tying the chimney and window together in a balanced composition. It's the perfect surface on which to locate two spotlights for illuminating artwork on the mantel.

**A well-defined kitchen** The kitchen reads as a smaller, contained space within the large, open space of the overall interior, rather than as a discrete room. The floating ceiling and the degree of openness contribute to this effect, as does the wood half-wall and cabinetry, which together define the kitchen as a distinct entity.

The most striking ceiling innovation is a lowered horizontal plane that begins outside as a trellis extending beyond the kitchen addition and then carries through the kitchen as a free-floating plane, defining an intimate breakfast booth below it. The plane rests on a display cabinet, then slips through the central wall and becomes a lowered (though no longer floating) ceiling defining the dining area from the slightly taller living room to one side and the slightly taller family music area to the other.

This horizontal ceiling plane is a great example of a detail that does double duty, defining distinct areas of space below it and animating the whole interior. Take a look at the photo on p. 123, and you can almost feel the ceiling plane thrust through the central spine of the house. It's the physical embodiment of spatial flow.

**Window treatments**

Although they're closely connected, the living room and the dining room each have their own character because of the way their windows have been treated. Set high, the dining-room windows provide light and also containment, so dining doesn't become a public display. The casual living room is defined by its bay of floor-to-ceiling windows.

**Kitchen island** Though it is quite functional, the kitchen island is the most purely sculptural of the wood built-ins within the interior. The top is for working on, but because it's transparent glass, your eye rests on the curve of the thick cherry shelf, a mirror of the curved countertop between the kitchen and family room.

Local materials, by their nature, help connect a house to its surroundings.

A corner window >> makes you believe the room ends outside, in the distance.

<< Diagonal views stretch space across the longest dimension of a room.

This split-level ranch remodel feels at one with its forest setting.

# The Nature of Materials

It's wonderful when a house is so thoroughly rooted in the land that it becomes an integral part of its surroundings. Sadly, too few houses are built with this kind of sensitivity, and a remodel isn't likely to create a connection to the land that didn't exist in the first place. But you might be surprised by how many older houses have a latent sense of place, buried under years of outmoded styling and bad decisions, just waiting for someone to come along and make it manifest.

If you had seen the 1960s rambler Andy and Rose bought in Bellevue, Washington, before its transformation, you'd never have guessed it had the bones of a forest house. It looked like a split-level ranch that could be in any suburb anywhere, not like a house set deep in the woods. Inside, the house was dark and dreary, divided down the middle by a white stone fireplace and indoor barbeque, with cavelike rooms further divided by the awkward split-level design. Outside, the house was a long, white box that sliced through the treed landscape in an unsettled way.

**outside the house**

**A box within a box**  If the open, pavilionlike interior can be seen as a box defined by a broad roof, then the three-sided partition between the kitchen and the dining room is like a box within that box. As an object, the partition helps you read the open space around it; as a "pod of space," it contains kitchen cabinetry and a countertop work area within. The razor-thin gap between the top of the partition and the central beam creates a subtle tension that emphasizes the heft of the beam and the form of the partition more than a wide gap would.

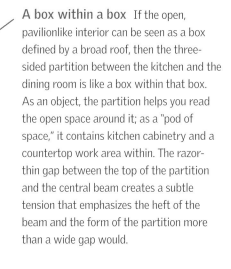

**Materials that express themselves naturally**  The interior is unified by natural materials that echo the earthy tones of the surrounding forest. Although the materials are clearly related by the colors and hues of nature, each also expresses the unique qualities of its own nature: Glass is glass, wood is wood, and stone is stone. This might seem a given, but often we treat materials in ways that contradict their true nature, and when we do that, even local, natural materials can lose their sense of place.

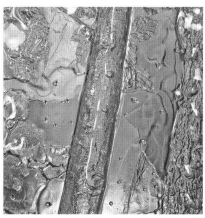

**Stairs to office** The open corner of the upper-level home office and the stair railings resolve the split of the split-level floor plan, visually connecting the office to the main level. The office feels a bit like a loft; it's possible to focus on work there and yet not feel removed from the family life below.

Andy and Rose first approached architect and design-builder Julie Campbell for a new roof and windows, but Julie quickly convinced them that with a thorough remodeling the house had the potential to be a bright, open pavilion in the woods. Julie extended the roof overhangs, created porches and decks, and replaced the roofing, windows, and siding with materials whose textures, colors, and forms befit the landscape. Sliding glass doors, skylights, and corner windows were added; a glass-covered canopy was built above the entry; and the dining-room wall was repositioned farther under the roof, creating a narrow veranda that feels like a Japanese *engawa*. The house now appears as a contemporary cross between a Japanese house and the traditional longhouse of the indigenous Northwest Coast peoples.

## The original house had a huge fir beam at the center of

the main level, with smaller but still substantial beams resting on it and in turn supporting a ceiling of fir boards, but all of this had been painted white or was concealed by interior walls. The first order of business was to strip off the paint so that the roof overhead would recover its Northwest character. To open up the main level and further emphasize the sheltering roof, the central chimney and all the walls were removed. A stone chimney was built on an exterior wall of the living room, and the interior walls were replaced with partitions that stop short of the ceiling, so you experience the full sweep of the roof.

LESS IS MORE One of the discoveries made during remodeling was that the central fir beam ended at the entry area. An obvious response would have been to continue the beam by butting another beam to it. But by accentuating the end of the beam on top of the tree-trunk column, the heft of the beam becomes stunningly apparent, and the openness of the ceiling above it is maintained. Extending the beam is not a bad idea, as you can see, but it's far less dramatic than exposing its end grain.

**A unified interior**  There's considerable textural variety and spatial complexity in the open interior, and yet there is also a cohesive quality to the whole. The dominant roof unifies the space underneath it, and complementary colors, mostly of a warm, orangey hue, pull together materials of varying texture. The repetition of black details—brackets, tiles, countertop, fireplace surround, light fixtures—further unifies the look of the interior.

The kitchen is defined by a translucent glass panel that's clipped to the ceiling and by a boxlike partition that functions as a "pod of space" (see the photo on pp. 128–129). This pod contains cabinetry on the kitchen side and provides a wall surface on the dining-room side for a large painting. The coat closet is also a pod of space, providing storage at the entry area and defining one corner of the living room. All of the materials—from the kitchen wall tiles to the fireplace stonework to the fir cabinetry—have an earthy feel that ties them to the outdoors. Even the glass panel has an outdoor connection in its patterned imprint of trees and plants found on the property.

To speak separately of changes outside and changes inside is to misrepresent the house, because the real change has been in the blurring of indoors and out. Especially in the entry sequence, Julie has taken a very

detail in focus

## The Interplay of Stone and Wood

One of the best ways to express the nature of one material is to place it in contrast with a second material. Interspersing square slate tiles and lengths of oak floorboards heightens our appreciation of the qualities of each material. This particular effect requires the careful work of an expert flooring installer, but the interplay of stone and wood gently grabs our attention even as it eases the transition from the slate terrace outside to the wood entry area inside.

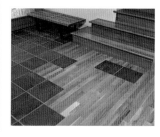

**Home office** A clerestory window above the stairs throws light into the office and hallway. In a typical split-level, you feel you might hit your head on the ceiling each time you start down from the top of the stairs. Here, the stairs begin well away from the wall, and the clerestory eliminates the feeling that you're walking right at something solid.

**Entry sequence**  The melding of indoors and out is marvelously expressed in the entry sequence, which begins under a glass-covered canopy supported by two colossal tree-trunk columns. The slate pavers of the terrace continue into the house, passing through the doorway without the interruption of a threshold—a subtle but powerful detail. The sequence ends with another colossal fir column.

Japanese approach to easing the indoor-outdoor transition. The most prominent element of the interior is the thick trunk of a Douglas fir, stripped of its bark, that supports the central beam and defines the far inside corner of the entry. This natural fir column mirrors two similar tree-trunk columns holding up the glass-covered canopy above the entry terrace outside.

And all three fir columns mimic the tall firs growing on the property. The indoor-outdoor transition is also softened at the floor level. The grid pattern of slate pavers covering the outdoor entry terrace moves seamlessly inside but then breaks down one tile at a time to mesh with the wood flooring.

In the original house, there was almost no connection between the main level and either the lower or upper levels. Now when Andy or Rose or their young daughter stands at the top of the upper-level stairs, they see down through rails into the open main level and out through a clerestory window to the stone chimney and the trees beyond. From the very spot where the house had been the darkest and most disconnected, it's now possible to experience a broad sense of unity.

<< Tracing a line of trim allows us to experience the three-dimensionality of space.

Thin window muntins >> add human scale without diminishing openness.

A hall made wide and filled with light becomes a room to spend time in.

> Trim creates contrast as well as continuity.

# Simple Trim, Substantial Impact

Sharon and Brett's house in Asheville, North Carolina, was built new, but it presents a perfect opportunity to talk about traditional home details and why people like them. Architect Jim Samsel honored the couple's request for a house with the character of their previous home, a Craftsman-style bungalow they'd restored in Atlanta. As Jim took cues from the land, the new house evolved from a bungalow into a mountain cottage, still with Craftsman-style trim and details inside, but now with a cruciform plan that neatly fits both the site and Sharon and Brett's requirements. You get a sense of the cruciform shape when approaching the projecting front of the house, but the real impact is felt when you step inside. A cruciform is admirably suited to a Not So Big House because it enables small rooms projecting from the center each to have windows on two or three sides, creating spaciousness without undue square footage.

Upon entering, the first thing you notice is the pleasant contrast established by the dark trim against the white walls.

**outside the house**

**A fine balance**  You don't have to divide an entire window to get the impact of divided panes. With thin muntins dividing just the top quarter of each sash, these casement windows strike a balance between the openness of contemporary undivided windows and the sheltering quality of traditional divided windows. The muntins also keep these windows from feeling too tall.

The trim is stained Southern yellow pine, but it looks like rich oak. The impact of the trim is amplified by its width—7¼ in. for the baseboards and 5½ in. for the crown molding and the head trim above the windows—and also by the consistent way the trim has been applied from room to room. Trim of a contrasting color to the walls adds visual punch and, more significantly, differentiates the various parts of the interior—floors, windows, doors, walls—from each other, thereby creating visual complexity.

## At the same time the trim creates contrast, it also creates continuity. The constancy of the trim ties the spaces together. The color and material of the trim stitch together the floor, cabinets, windows, and doors (all are of similar hue if not always of the same wood). The lines of the trim pull together the furnishings, especially the Craftsman-style and Mission-style chairs, sofas, and tables, in whose own lines and colors the trim is echoed. The trim in this house is doing a lot of work, even though it's not ornate or

**detail in focus**

### Rhythm of the Rails

Stair rails are too often spaced the minimum 4 in. apart, which doesn't always look good. Here a simple rhythm has been established: three rails really close together, then a gap, then three rails, and so on. Although the rails themselves are nothing fancy—just 2x2 pine—their thoughtful placement adds character to the stair hall (as does the graceful wall niche).

**Stone hearth**  Tennessee fieldstone gives the hearth visual weight and makes it stand out as a special element. With stone on only its bottom half, the hearth does not overpower the small room, and there's a plain wall on which to hang artwork.

### Display cabinets add useful beauty

Small cabinets with glass doors add display space for items used only on occasion. The storage cabinets would have looked too tall if they had run uninterrupted to the ceiling, and the top shelves would have been difficult to reach. In this interior, where the full ceiling height has been maintained throughout, soffits would have looked out of place.

### Harmony on a small scale

Although the sink area is composed of a number of different materials—wood, tile, and solid-surface countertop—the overall effect is harmonious. The sink and countertop are a single unit, with no seams to keep clean, and yet the white sink set within the green stonelike counter surface feels like an old-fashioned farmhouse sink.

### Slender French doors

There's a delightful slimness to the trim and other interior elements that's in tune with the 10-ft. height of the rooms. The exterior doorway in the dining area (to the right of the photo on the facing page) is a narrow 4 ft. wide and a tall 8 ft. high. Each of the French doors, therefore, is unusually narrow, with panes divided by slim horizontal muntins to emphasize the vertical. Thinness and linearity are further accentuated by a slim groove cut into the face of the wood door frame, visible in the photo at far right.

### Dividing a wall with a chair rail

Chair rails were originally meant to keep chair backs from damaging the plaster, but a rail makes sense simply to bring down the apparent height of a wall and add character to a room. This rail is a nicely stained but otherwise unadorned 1x2 strip of pine, set 36 in. from the floor, even with the countertop, which continues the line into the kitchen.

complicated. Not surprisingly, the blandness of today's stock houses is often partly the result of a lack of trim.

Why is it that even simple trim evokes such strong feelings of domesticity? We respond first to the visual effect of trim. Trim relates to our hands, and our hands in turn to our sense of scale. Looking at trim, you can imagine your hand running along it, you can figure the size of the things trimmed. And in this house, where the trim material is a richly stained oak, you respond further to the natural warmth of wood. You might not think consciously about any of this, but you feel it all the same.

**Interior window**  A small interior window adds interest to the stairwell as well as to the desk alcove in the home office on the other side.

**The chair rail continues**  For scale and consistency, the chair rail that figures prominently in the dining area continues in the kitchen area, even where there's just a few inches of wall. Maintaining the chair rail helps you read the kitchen area and the dining area as one larger space.

**A CONTINUOUS BAND OF TILE** This master bath presents a contemporary take on the old-fashioned look of white tile. In a more traditional bath, the black trim tile would have stopped at the wood window trim. Here, the tile band continues around the window (and then around the double windows over the tub), strengthening the impact of the window. Stop the trim at the window, and the whole room becomes less interesting. Centering the towel bar (and the floor register) on the window heightens the impact.

**Details in the trim** Though the trim in this house is exceedingly simple, it's not without subtle embellishment. The head trim above the doors and windows is a touch wider and thicker than the side trim, and it protrudes beyond the side trim, weighting the top ever so slightly. The trim at the base of the doorjambs and posts is just a little thicker than the baseboard, creating a reveal.

## While the trim and wood details lend Sharon and

Brett's home a traditional air, the floor plan gives it a modern quality of openness and flow. The kitchen and dining areas are essentially one room, though subtle cues define one area from the other: for instance, the positioning of the sink counter in a bay that protrudes beyond the dining room. The most pronounced sense of openness, surprisingly, is at the very center of the cruciform plan, which typically feels hemmed in by the rooms springing from it. In Sharon and Brett's house, what begins as a stone-floored front hall expands into a wide gallery for displaying artwork.

The gallery, not the trim, may be the real secret to the domestic quality of the house. In the end, the trim works so well because the spaces themselves work so well, which is why merely adding trim to an ill-conceived house rarely creates the kind of place you see here.

**Substantial trim can make an ordinary wall feel more consequential.**

**<< In a very small house, a little layering of space goes a long way.**

**An opening in a >> thick wall is a great place to tuck in a little storage.**

The details are what make this tiny apartment a joy to live in.

# Grace, Elegance, and Storage—in 650 sq. ft.

**This one-bedroom apartment** in a 1908 Beaux Arts building in Washington, D.C., first belonged to Gail, an architect, whose plans for her modest 650-sq.-ft. home were fully realized only after she met and later married Tom, a builder. Ten years after Gail bought a most ordinary apartment, it's now an extraordinary—and extraordinarily compact—example of carefully established interior views, double-duty elements, well-proportioned spaces, and clever storage, all of it detailed with imaginative colors and richly built-up trim that takes advantage of the apartment's thick walls and high ceilings. The classical trim ties the apartment to the elegant, heavily corniced exterior of the building and to the historic neighborhood. But more than that, the details are what make the apartment a joy to live in.

Design is a process that frequently begins as a conversation, a discussion of possibilities around the table, maybe even a polite argument or two. This is how it was for Gail and Tom. Confronted with a bath, bedroom, living room,

**outside the house**

143

and kitchen, lined up just like that, they considered removing the wall between the living room and kitchen entirely, making at least one big, open space. But where to put the washer and dryer? The design Gail and Tom arrived at— think of it as a single, grand detail—solved the washer and dryer problem *and* supplied a feeling of spaciousness. It also made the kitchen work much better and created a new space of sorts, a virtual dining room.

What had been a wall with a door between the living room and kitchen has become a paneled opening that is 10 ft. wide and 34 in. deep, exactly the width of the dining table that rests against one side of the opening. The table acts as a room divider, defining the edge of the living room on one side and the edge of the kitchen on the other. The top panels of the opening, which are several inches lower than the ceiling in the rooms to either side, define a transitional space that, in effect, is a dining room, albeit a very narrow one. At night, with lights dimmed in the kitchen and living room, the two lights hanging above the table reinforce the sense that you're sitting in a distinct dining space.

The dining table, it turns out, is not what determined the width of the paneled opening. Rather, the width was set by the closetlike pantries on either side of the opening. Gail and Tom decided to put the dryer inside the inner pantry and the washer in the pantry next to the exterior wall, where it had to be for plumbing reasons. The space above the opening houses the dryer vent on its run to the exterior wall. There's a slight inconvenience to

## Taking Cues from What's Already There

The original transom window above the door to the bathroom provided a cue to detailing the rest of the space. To keep the tiny room from feeling too tall, wainscoting was added to the height of the door, its trim line giving your eye a place to rest below the full ceiling height, thus making the space seem lower. A second transom window was added over the tub, creating an enclosed bathing nook. The thick wall of the bath was used to store and hang towels, but for visual continuity, the trim line above the wainscoting was maintained across the towel niche.

**Galley kitchen** In this foreshortened view, you can see how the dining table, set into the wide opening to the living room, maintains the former edge of the galley kitchen without making the kitchen feel narrow and cramped, as it did when there was a wall in place of the opening.

having the dryer separate from the washer, rather than stacked, but now there's twice the usable countertop surface, one countertop above each appliance.

## Storage is tucked everywhere in this little apartment:

under the window in the kitchen, within the thick wall of the bath, in the hall leading to the bedroom. The living room felt too long, so Gail and Tom shortened it by building in a bookshelf at one end and cabinets under the windows at the other end, thus adding storage and improving the proportions of the room without affecting its functionality.

As is often the case, storage goes hand in hand with trim, simply because cabinets, closet doors, and shelving create lots of edges and openings to be trimmed, making the plain walls of the original apartment more useful and visually interesting. Throughout the apartment, raised panels and

### picture this

THE IMPORTANCE OF BEING PANELED
The paneling in this apartment bedroom adds visual interest while reflecting light from the two windows. Remove the paneling, and the bay window effect is less pronounced; the wall and the room become more ordinary (though a painting on the bare wall would help).

## What to Do with a Flat-Screen TV

You can hang a flat-screen TV on a wall, of course, but here's an option for setting one into a bookshelf. The TV screen is mounted on a fabric-covered sheet of Homasote®, a paper-based fiberboard. The sheet, with holes cut in it for speakers, is set halfway into the shelf, leaving space behind it for the speakers themselves and wiring (and, in this case, a TV tuner, since the screen is just a monitor).

paneled cabinet doors are used to break up the surface of the walls. In the wide doorway from foyer to living room, the panels are cabinet doors, opened by touch latches rather than door pulls. Here the trim *is* the storage (or at least the access to it).

In an old house, nothing lines up, floors dip, walls are out of plumb. Trim is a great way to add impact and at the same time deal with the imperfections of construction, time, or both. In a modern house with little or no trim, on the other hand, materials have to come together perfectly; everything has to fit just right; lines have to be straight and edges crisp. In this traditional space, trim cleans up the mess and becomes a key characteristic of the apartment's personality.

**Pantries on either side** There are two pantries in the kitchen, one on either side of the big opening. The left pantry has a washing machine below a usable countertop, plus space for a food processor and mixer. The dryer is in the right pantry, along with a second countertop and space for a microwave, toaster oven, and coffee maker.

**Storage, storage everywhere** This is a good example of getting more by giving up just a little floor space. Cabinets under the windows add storage and a display area while shortening the otherwise long room, improving its proportions. The wall has been made to appear like a large bay window by angling the corners. The built-out corners hide heating pipes and provide room for built-in stereo speakers.

**Hidden storage** A deep closet in the dressing area down the hall has been treated like a pantry, with hinged shelves that swing out to reveal more storage behind.

**Opening up—but not all the way** In place of a wall between the living room and kitchen, a wide opening defines a narrow zone of space for the dining table and for pantries to either side of the opening. The dining table divides the living room from the kitchen while allowing a strong visual connection between the spaces. Getting rid of the wall entirely would have created one large room but no distinct place for the dining table and no pantries.

A little metal, by way of >> contrast, brings out the warmth of wood.

Four-foot-six is >> a nice width for an opening, neither too big nor too small.

^^
A movable interior element literally puts people in touch with a home.

A few key details tie the rooms together and create a unity of effect.

# Rooms Defined but Not Confined

## What began as a nondescript 1960s house,

something of a sore thumb on a boulevard of elegant 1920s homes, has been transformed into a house that befits its well-established Minneapolis neighborhood. From the start, homeowners Beth and Rick opted for high-quality materials rather than an overabundance of space, a Not So Big approach gladly embraced by architect Jean Rehkamp Larson.

Remodeling meant gutting the entire interior of the house and then adding space at the back for a kitchen, family room, and mudroom. Jean cleverly placed the front hall, mudroom, stairs, and powder room all on one side, creating privacy there and freeing up the main spaces front to back so they could more easily connect to each other. Where a smidgen of extra space was needed on the sides, Jean bumped out rooms or alcoves just a foot or two beyond the original walls. Within the house, she allowed the spaces to open to one another without losing their identity as individual rooms. As Jean puts it, the rooms are "defined but not confined."

**outside the house**

**A kitchen window mini-bay** You don't need thick walls to enjoy wide windowsills. As you can see from inside and outside, these corner windows are part of a slim bay that juts beyond the wall 6 in., just enough to allow for a wide sill above the sink and countertop.

**Degrees of separation** You have choices about how much or little the wall divides two spaces. A partial wall can feel like a true wall with holes punched in it, like columns, or like built-in furniture. To divide this kitchen and family room, the architect considered cabinetry alone—which would have made the two spaces feel more like one big kitchen—but settled on a combination of wall-like piers and a counter-height wood cabinet, with a thick shelf above. The shelf's metal support rods echo those above the dining-room interior windows.

**The delight of an unexpected detail** The main countertop of the kitchen island is in line with the countertops and the partial wall. The small lower countertop, supported by brackets but otherwise suspended from the island, offers a bit of a twist. It has its own logic, being just the right height for pulling up a chair instead of a stool.

## Throwing in a Curve

You don't have to have tall ceilings to vary their height. The curved ceiling that's been added within this short, 8-ft.-high hallway takes away a few inches of headroom yet heightens the sense of transition between the front entry and the mudroom (the interior window throws a little light into the stairs to the basement). The dark cherry paneling accentuates the shape of the curve and distinguishes it from the regular flat ceilings.

**Mudroom alcove**   The alcove added to this existing mudroom contributes to its usefulness and its character. The bench offers an opportunity for some color and a place to sit; the cherry cabinets augment an existing closet and warm up the look of the room; and the windows bring in natural light. Like the window seat upstairs, the alcove is cantilevered from the existing house structure and does not require a foundation.

**Front hall** Throughout the house, metal is used as an accent to the more dominant wood trim and paneling. The stainless-steel rails liven up the look of the stairs yet complement the blond maple and red cherry wood. You won't find metalwork like this at a home center, but a good architect can design it for you and have it made to order by a local fabricator.

Keeping the rooms small and discrete means there are no huge spaces in the house. On the other hand, it's by encountering a series of spaces that you get to enjoy the expansive effects of layering. *Layering* may sound like an obscure architectural notion, but it's simply a word used to describe the very tangible experience of being in one space while seeing into and through other spaces. And it's the details as much as the rooms themselves that sustain the illusion of more space than is actually there. The sliding windows between the dining room and the eating area of the kitchen are a perfect example of a detail that creates a layering effect. Look at the left photo on p. 156. The family room, seen through a wide, unframed opening, seems really close, almost part of the dining room. But looking past or through the window frames, you have a restricted view of the eating area and a mere glimpse of the kitchen; you feel there is more space beyond the windows to explore, perhaps to arrive at later. In this way, layering creates interest—even intrigue—as well as spaciousness.

At the same time, a few key details tie the rooms together and create a unity of effect, a sense that no matter which room you're in, you're still in the same house. The most prominent continuous details

the way it's done

## Clipping on a Little Extra Space

A great way to increase elbow room without undue expense is to cantilever a small bay or alcove from the existing structure of the house, thereby adding a pocket of space to a room without having to build a new foundation. A wall is opened up, as if for a new window or door, but instead of adding a flat window or door frame, a framed box is "clipped" on, usually by tying its floor joists to the existing floor joists. In the photos below, you can see how a window seat was cantilevered from what had been the end of an upstairs hallway.

**Separate but connected** The yellow wall between the dining room and eating area and the pale green and white wall between the family room and kitchen are variations on a theme. Both walls partially divide two rooms, limiting views and access but maintaining a spatial connection.

are the crown molding running along the top of the walls—a two-piece affair consisting of blond maple and dark cherry—and the baseboard, a thick band of cherry with a beveled cherry cap that juts out a touch, giving ample weight to the bottom of the walls.

With respect to defining versus confining, the openings are a bit ambiguous, in an entirely successful way. The primary openings between the main rooms are around 4 ft. 6 in. wide, an ideal width for creating a strong connection between adjacent rooms while maintaining each room's integrity as a separate space.

Ultimately, each room has its own identity. The most distinctive room is the dining room, which gains a suitable degree of formality not by being the most elaborate room but by being the most differentiated. Its position, sandwiched between the living room, eating area, and family room with just one exterior wall, could have condemned it to feel like leftover space. Instead, it's arguably the most visually arresting room in the house. Where the other main rooms are painted a pale green, the dining room is a rich yellow. The other rooms retain the original flat ceilings, but in the dining room the ceiling has been arched and paneled in cherry. The dining-room ceiling, like all the ceilings in this house, is a standard 8 ft. high, but there's still room for a curve, slight enough to ensure sufficient headroom, deep enough to make an impact.

## A Simple Rail for Plates or Pictures

People ask me all the time how to make a plate rail like the one I have in my house. The photo at left shows one that's equally straightforward. The typical soffit built above the upper cabinets becomes a wood rail that the pictures or plates rest on. The rail is simply a piece of plywood faced with trim to create a lip. The continuation of the soffit and trim above both the cabinets and the display area keeps the look crisp, as does maintaining the same width for both the plate rail and bottom rail of the cabinet face.

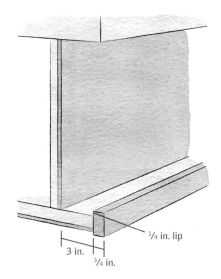

¼ in. lip

3 in.

¾ in.

**Eating area**   In the eating area off the kitchen, details for display (the picture rail and the wall for children's art), for storage (the cabinets and shelves), and for privacy (the sliding interior windows) come together to create a cozy feel and an intimate scale, perfect for a kids' meal or perhaps a board game with the whole family.

A single running >> line of trim elegantly emphasizes the horizontal.

The interplay of color, texture, and light generates a quiet energy.

^^
A wall longer than the room itself appears to extend space outward.

This suburban ranch was remodeled to emphasize light, color, texture, and openness.

# The Illusion of More Space

Looking at this house in Bethesda, Maryland, you'd never guess it was once a typical suburban ranch house from the 1950s, contemporary in its approach to one-story living but otherwise low-slung, dimly lit, and unremarkable. When the owners sat down to work with architect Mark McInturff, they expressed a modest goal: Honor the original intent of the house but open it up and strengthen the connection between the interior and the patio, which the couple and their two children already used as an outdoor room.

What is striking about the house now is the play of natural light, the radiance and texture of brightly lit stucco, the crispness of the wall and trim colors, and especially the flow of space. The original house, in spite of its many windows and glass doors, seemed to trap space and hold it tight; it felt dark and cramped. The remodeled house feels considerably larger and more open, even though only a small family room was added. The changes Mark introduced have allowed space to move more easily from room

**outside the house**

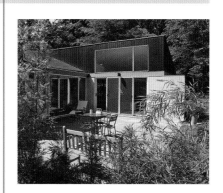

**Floating corner**  You read the yellow stucco wall in the family room as a plane around which space flows, not as a wall that defines the corner of the room. The low retaining wall outside feels more like the edge of the room than do the windows; in effect, space continues from inside to outside, and the room expands beyond its walls.

to room and from inside to outside, creating the illusion that the house contains more space.

Lighter surfaces help the house feel more open, as does daylight streaming in from skylights and clerestory windows above the rooms. But the really big change is in the way certain key walls have been treated. Let's look first at the most important wall in the house: the yellow stucco wall (see the photo on p. 158). This central spine divides the more public dining room and living room from the more private kitchen, breakfast area, and family room. The yellow wall begins at the front, carries through the original width of the house, and continues past the family-room addition, ending outside at the far corner of the backyard patio. With this wall, Mark has introduced a detail that's larger—and more dramatic—than any room in the house. Wherever you are in the main living spaces, as your eye follows the yellow wall along its considerable length, you experience a feeling of expansiveness.

## The impact of the wall is only partly the result of its length.
The wall has also been given visual importance by the way it's been detailed: by its distinctive shape, material, color, texture, and trim. The regular walls of the house, whether new or old, are 2x4 studs clad in drywall, painted white. The central spine is 12 in. thick, made from plywood over

## Line and Color

The crisp look of the dining room is achieved not with lavish detail but with attention to line and color. The copper trim line above the stucco wall and the thin metal window mullions are highlighted with bold colors. The rear wall of the room— just plain drywall—is accented by being painted dark gray, a suitable backdrop for bringing out the lines of the furniture. The stucco was colored before it was applied; integrally colored stucco dries with subtle changes in value not achievable by painting the stucco after it's been applied.

**Details that repeat**  A subtle repetition of rectangular planes lends the kitchen a sense of balance and order. The refrigerator door echoes the window, the tabletop echoes the window seat, and the skylight echoes the stainless-steel backsplash behind the stove. The forms reinforce each other but never overwhelm; their unity creates a feeling of calm.

WHERE A WALL MEETS THE CEILING One of the most important details in this house is the green copper trim line that carries around the top of each stucco wall. The bright line emphasizes the overall horizontality of the house and the importance of crisp lines to the sleek feel of the interior. The color of the line and its slight indentation from the wall surface also differentiate the stucco walls from the ceiling. Working in tandem with the colored stucco, the green line makes the thick walls much more expressive than they would be if they were white.

2x10 studs, finished with stucco and painted pale yellow. The yellow stucco wall has no base trim, just a slim gap—what architects call a "reveal"—between itself and the floor, which allows you to feel the weight of the wall rather than the weight of the trim. Gaps in the wall further emphasize its thickness and heft. The top of the wall is recessed slightly and trimmed in bright-green copper. The indentation and the copper line separate the wall from the ceiling, allowing you to read the wall as a distinct and separate object.

Because it continues outside, the yellow stucco wall had to be made from materials that can withstand weather. Stone or brick would have worked, but stucco was versatile and within budget and looked just right. The copper trim is also an outdoor material. Having a wall on the inside that's made from exterior wall materials further strengthens the indoor-outdoor connection and the illusion that space continues beyond the strict boundaries of the house.

Other thickened stucco walls work in concert with the yellow wall. A light gray wall defines the front entry and one side of the dining room, and, outside, a charcoal gray stucco retaining wall defines the patio and slips past the family room, suggesting that the room really ends at this low wall, beyond the floor-to-ceiling windows. The stucco walls unify the look of the

## Breakfast area

Sometimes restraint and a can of paint are all that's required. In the breakfast area, the original ceiling, paneled in cheap-looking dark wood, has been painted a bright apple green. The cheery color and the low height of the ceiling define the area as a small, intimate space apart from the taller family room and the more functional kitchen.

house and create a larger three-dimensional effect that complements the sculptural qualities of each individual wall.

## The delicately colored, textured walls are also perfectly suited to capturing and reflecting light from above. In the family room, northern light enters through a tall clerestory window in the vaulted ceiling, illuminating the yellow wall on either side of the sliding glass doors below the clerestory. In the dining room, a skylight spills light onto the gray wall and the yellow wall that bookend the space, washing them with even light or hitting them with a dazzling beam, depending on the time of day and season. The endless play of light, even on cloudy days, generates a quiet kind of energy within the walls of this simple home that more than makes up for relatively low ceilings and modest square footage.

### the way it's done

## Window Minimalism

One hallmark of modernism is the window that isn't there, or at least that tries not to be. When the expression of a window is minimal, you look past the window. Instead of focusing on window trim and the view it frames, you experience the immediacy of the outdoors. The illustration at left shows how the window sill has been hidden by drywall.

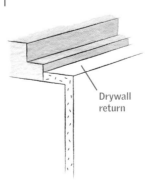

Drywall
return

**A composition of thoughtful details**  The original entry area has been given a crisp look with a few simple design moves. Sandblasting the glass door but leaving its wide sidelight clear provides some visual privacy and two distinctly contrasting qualities of light. A niche cut into the gray stucco wall reinforces the thick feel of the wall. The wall's thickness is further emphasized by a narrow gap, which also gives visitors an anticipatory glimpse into the dining room.

**Signaling the entry**  The green ceiling juts into the living room, signaling the importance of the entry and tying the ceiling to the rest of the interior. The ceiling feels almost like one of the thick stucco walls turned on its side.

**Amplifying the impact of light**  Two very deliberate details transform the way natural light enters and illuminates the dining room. One detail is the hole cut into the horizontal ceiling plane, which partially diffuses light from the skylight in the sloped roof above. The second detail is a window that's flush with the surface of the stucco wall. As you can see, this allows direct sunlight to enter through the south-facing window and strike the textured wall, filling the room with soft light.

**Achieving balance**  Although the kitchen is not strictly symmetrical, it feels balanced. This is largely the result of balancing the apparent weight of things on either side of the room. For instance, the yellow stucco wall and the group of three windows have roughly the same visual weight. The room also feels balanced because the powerful combination of the built-in refrigerator and the skylight keeps pulling your eye back to the center of the space.

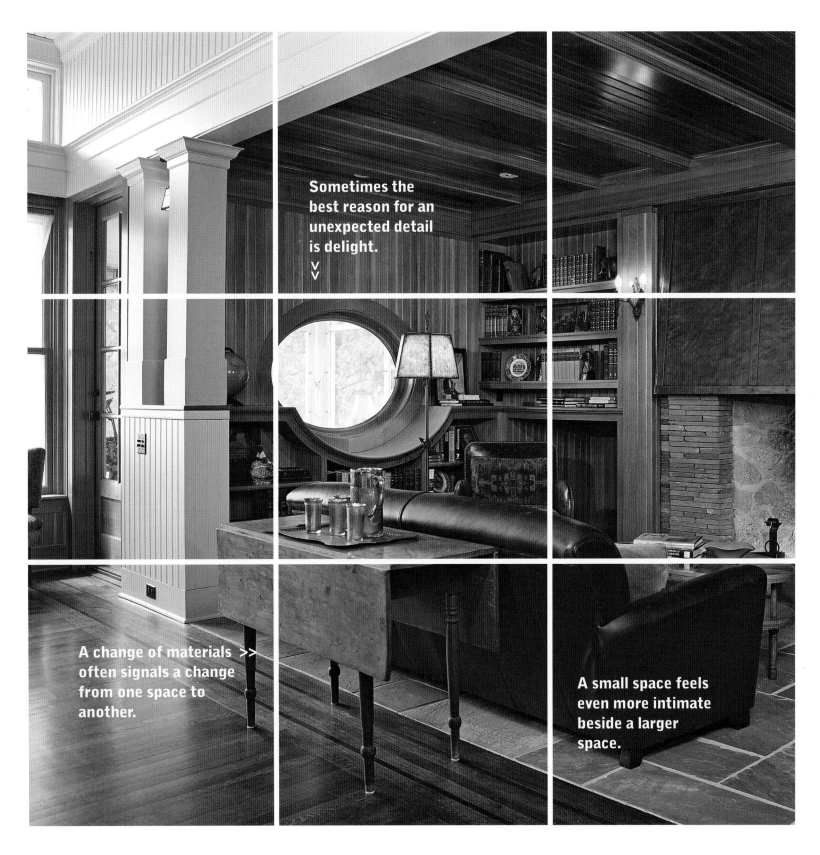

Sometimes the
best reason for an
unexpected detail
is delight.
V
V

A change of materials >>
often signals a change
from one space to
another.

A small space feels
even more intimate
beside a larger
space.

This house has a quality that's hard to define but easy to recognize: charm.

# Creating Coziness in a Large Cottage

When the owners built their year-round house on White Bear Lake, within the St. Paul, Minnesota, city limits, they wanted it to feel like one of the easygoing lake cottages that Minnesotans have repaired to for summers and on weekends for generations. Still, with three children, they needed a fair amount of space. Architect Tom Ellison designed a cottage home that gave the family the space it required as well as warmth and coziness. At over 4,000 sq. ft., the house is a not-so-small Not So Big House, but it masterfully achieves the casual qualities and domestic scale of a much smaller cottage or cabin.

The informality apparent on the inside of the house begins with three design ideas that initially seem to have more to do with the exterior than the interior. In fact, these big moves set up the interior details for success. First, in keeping with the lake cottage tradition, Tom designed the house to appear as a one-story dwelling; the bedrooms upstairs are within the volume of the roof. This gives the

**outside the house**

WINDOW MUNTINS HELP US JUDGE SCALE  This snug sitting area is actually a stair landing. Besides minimal floor area, many details contribute to its diminutive scale, some built in, like the wainscoting, some not, like the books. The muntins that divide the upper window sash into panes mark increments that relate to our hands. Take away the muntins (and the curtains), and the space loses scale and intimacy to the big outdoors.

house a cottage look outside, but it also gives the bedrooms a sheltered quality, enhanced by dormers, alcoves, and nooks under the eaves of the sweeping roof. Second, Tom did not attempt to give each room a grand view; this allows for a variety of spaces within the house, some with expansive views of the lake, some with intimate views into adjacent spaces. Finally, Tom gave the house a casual "massing," bringing together smaller house forms and roofs so it looks as though there may have been additions to the house over time.

## The human scale of the individual details makes

this house feel like a home, but the details wouldn't be nearly as effective without the attention Tom paid to the scale of the house overall. Without overarching design moves like the ones Tom used, the sheer size of a larger

**Entry** A lowered ceiling and wood trim create a welcoming and intimately scaled entryway into a house that soon opens up to a big view. Within the entry, you have a chance to pause upon arriving before taking in the whole house.

**Master bedroom alcove** The framed opening and the dark wood set this alcove apart from the rest of the master bedroom, while the small square windows lend it intimacy. The tall double-hung windows in the main space of the room soak in the view. In contrast, the low window in the alcove offers a private glimpse available only to someone sitting in the leather chairs.

**Quality without formality**
Where its traditional styling makes sense, bead board, sometimes called matchstick paneling, has qualities of scale and detail perfectly suited to a Not So Big House. The fir bead board in this hallway adds warmth and texture while maintaining a relaxed, cottage-like feel.

## An Understanding of Craft Comes First

The charm of this child's bed alcove comes from its compact size and also from the way it's been shaped and constructed, almost as though it were a piece of furniture. To get this level of detail, you need an architect who understands materials, tools, and how things fit together, and who can communicate with the craftspeople who execute the design. Or you need a craftsperson who understands design. Although there's room for spur-of-the-moment ideas, like embedding a purple marble into the trimwork, quality craftsmanship doesn't just happen—it has to be planned.

house often works against attempts to add small details; the rooms end up as big, decorated boxes, not visually complex yet humanly scaled rooms.

Tom employs another concept—what he calls "counterpoint"—at many levels of detail. The light and airy living room has as its counterpoint an inglenook with lower ceilings and a much warmer, cozier feel (see the photo on p. 166). Within the inglenook, an oval window is a bright counterpoint to the stone floor, wood walls, and copper fireplace hood. The same oval window, because of its unique shape and singular position, serves as a counterpoint to the row of double-hung windows in the living room. In turn, the double-hung windows and surrounding trim are a warm, natural fir color, with fir wainscoting below, in counterpoint to the transom windows above, which are painted white, as is the wide trim band and the ceiling.

## Counterpoint creates variety, complexity, richness of detail.

You understand one material or color not by itself but in relation to another. Rooms and elements within rooms are not duplicates of each other but rather variations on a theme. The idea that everything doesn't have to be identical is very liberating, and it works so long as the materials, colors, and details are broadly related. The eclectic attitude of the house itself enables the owners to take a mix-and-match approach to furnishing, which, in concert with the relaxed materials and details built into the house itself, contributes to the cottage feel.

**Living room**  The open but comfortable feel of the living room—and the details that create it—has been carefully thought through by the architect. Painting the upper third of the room white and leaving the lower two-thirds natural wood brings down the apparent height of the space and emphasizes the view through the lower windows.

**Variations on a theme** The coffered ceilings in the kitchen (right) and in the living room (left) are clearly related, yet the built-up moldings that thicken and embellish the beams are different in each room. In the more formal living room, the molding has a deep, graceful curve to it; in the less formal kitchen, the molding has a narrow, more ordinary cove.

**Wide sill above a sink** The materials in the sink bay—slate countertop, crisply painted wood cabinets, bead-board backsplash, natural fir windows—have a sense of quality and craftsmanship but not of formality. The sill is simply an 11½-in.-wide piece of fir, supported by curved brackets, the sort of detail that could be worked into almost any kitchen to give the look of a bay window and the usefulness of a shelf.

**A seemingly accidental alcove** In keeping with the informality of the kitchen, the cooking alcove feels as though it could be space borrowed from a former closet or a bump-out added later. The trim framing the opening sets the alcove apart from the main space of the kitchen and accentuates the thickness of the opening, as though to build the alcove an exterior wall had to be breached. The effect is enhanced by the stained-glass windows and the spice rack, which disappear above the framed opening, creating a pleasant catch-as-catch-can appearance.

The straight grain
of natural fir, the patina
of stained concrete:
Who needs gold?

When everything else
in a space is dialed
back, light comes
to the fore. >>

There's ample room
inside a simple
house for what's
inside you to be felt.

Japanese elements create a home that's as beautiful as it is serene.

# Zen Warmth

At the heart of Zen Buddhism is the idea of emptiness. Properly understood, the Zen notion of emptiness, far from being chilly, is in fact radiant. It's a concept that suggests that an interior space can be plain and still be warm. In the *Tao te Ching*, the ancient Chinese sage Lao Tzu extols emptiness in a seemingly less metaphysical, more pragmatic way:

*We pierce doors and windows to make a house;*
*And it is on these spaces where there is nothing that the*
*usefulness of the house depends.*
*Therefore just as we take advantage of what is, we should*
*recognize the usefulness of what is not.*

But you don't have to embrace Eastern philosophy to appreciate the qualities of extreme simplicity in the 1,160-sq.-ft., one-story house architect Fiona O'Neill designed for herself on a coastal hillside in the Sea Ranch in northern California.

**outside the house**

175

**Flush media cabinet** The flush built-in media cabinet maintains visual calm by hiding clutter and also through its crisp lines. In this house, lines themselves take the place of trim, as does the thin gap between the cabinet doors or the equally thin gap between the drywall and the wood ceiling band, a slim gap the architect fondly calls a "spider crack."

**Fiona's small house is an elegant blend** of no-non-sense Western barn on the outside and pared-down Japanese house on the inside. Like the traditional Japanese house, Fiona's house is essentially one room, divided from time to time into smaller areas by the movable *shojis*. The house is also Japanese at an even deeper level: Its small, plain space exemplifies the Japanese notion of *wabi*, or "calm simplicity."

Fiona admires Japanese architecture and design for its elegance, serene quality, and deep respect for materials. All three are evident in even the smallest aspects of the house. Consider the materials them-selves: clear-stained, vertical-grained Douglas fir; poured concrete with a trowel finish and an acid wash; drywall painted a buttery hue; bronze

**Bedroom closet** Closets to either side of the bed (along with a lowered ceiling) form a cozy alcove. Similarly, twin closets create a thickened opening between the master bedroom and bath. *Shoji* panels slide to conceal the closets or close off the bath. Each closet or *shoji* is a single element that does many things, the essence of simplicity.

## Shoji for the 21st Century

These *shoji* screens, which were built by a local cabinetmaker, have a traditional look as well as a few con-temporary touches.

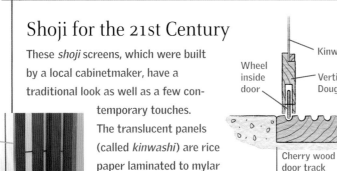

The translucent panels (called *kinwashi*) are rice paper laminated to mylar for strength and water resistance.

The fir frames have wheels inside the bottom rail. The wheels travel in grooves cut into a cherry plank set within the concrete floor.

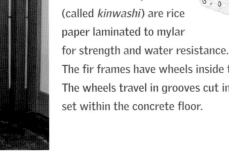

Kinwashi panel

Wheel inside door

Vertical-grain Douglas fir door

Cherry wood door track

Concrete floor

**Kitchen** This carefully composed kitchen emphasizes the line where one material meets another: Wood meets drywall; slate tile meets wood; stainless steel meets slate tile. A skylight placed flush with the wall enables the wall to become a reflector, setting up yet another line, where raking light strikes the cabinets and countertop.

## Making the Most of Wall Thickness

Here's a detail you can adapt to almost any existing wall. The narrow wood shelves and the rich red accent color behind them have turned the slim space within this otherwise ordinary wall into storage and display area. The barn door between the living room and master bedroom plays a dual role, closing off the doorway or concealing the shelves.

anodized aluminum windows. None of these is extravagant, though each is handled with great care.

Look closely at the framed window in the solid wall at the center of the main space (seen obliquely in the photo on p. 174 and straight on in the photo at right). The wall is set a couple of feet into the space, emphasizing its solidity in contrast to the triple sliding glass doors at either side. The undivided and unadorned window captures a framed view of the trees beyond. Architects call such a glimpsed view a "Zen view," for the story of a Buddhist monk whose only view of the distant ocean was through a narrow slit in the stone wall of the courtyard beyond his house. Of course, in Fiona's house, there's more of the view through the glass doors, but the Zen view still has impact, especially because it's in line with the entry door at the opposite side of the main space. Rather than stepping into the house and confronting a long, uninterrupted wall of glass, you first take in the solid wall, the calming arrangement of egg-shaped stones, and the alluring Zen view.

**Kitchen counter detail** This tidy combination of modest materials—straight-grained fir, copper-flecked slate tiles, laminate countertop—shows that the effect of the whole can be more than the sum of its parts, and that a few distinctive materials (wood and tile) can elevate an ordinary one (the laminate).

## Besides Japanese aesthetics, there was another consideration Fiona had to take into account: cost. Quite simply, she had a very limited budget. Many people mistakenly think the more you spend on materials, the more beauty you will have. Often, the opposite is true. In fact, if you design and build with integrity and respect, you can achieve beauty whether your materials cost $2 or $50 per sq. ft.

**The flexible use of limited space** Shoji screens or similar sliding translucent panels make perfect sense in a Not So Big House, where space is limited and often must be used in more ways than one. In this house, the four shoji panels between the living room and the adjacent study greatly affect one's perception of space depending on how they are positioned. The shoji screens, handsome in their own right, also serve as the dominant decorative element of the interior.

**Four panels fully closed** With the panels closed, the spaces to either side each become smaller and more intimate. Light flows through the panels, yet even with the shoji closed, there is very little acoustical privacy.

**Two panels slightly open** The slim opening provides a sense of space beyond while maintaining a clear separation between the rooms, much like a narrow doorway.

**One panel at the center** With a single panel at the center of the two spaces, you perceive the study area to the left of the panel as an area distinct from the open area to the right, and you get only a hint of the bay window. In turn, the privacy of the window seat is preserved.

**Four panels to one side** With the panels staggered on the right side, space flows freely, but you still sense there are two rooms. The more private area leading into the guest bathroom is blocked by panels; your eye gravitates naturally toward the desk to the left.

A line of trim helps >> anchor art and other items placed on the wall.

A stairway can be a stage for displaying things, not just a bunch of steps.

Even in a mostly >> horizontal house, certain details should be vertical.

A variety of ceiling effects combine to define and differentiate space.

# Ceilings Shine in Rooms without Walls

**Ed and Maureen raised their children** in an urbane, exquisitely crafted Prairie School home designed by architect William Purcell in Minneapolis in 1911. When they hired Susanka Studios to design their retirement home in Stowe, Vermont, they wanted the same open feeling of their old house but in a more straightforward design suited to their simpler lives and the Vermont countryside. As empty-nesters, they required a much less formal floor plan, with only spaces they would use every day—they didn't even need a formal dining room. Ed and Maureen wanted lots of natural light, views to the surrounding farmland and mountains, and places here and there made expressly for displaying their favorite antiques and artwork. Above all, though, they wanted a feeling of openness.

Even in a house with a high degree of openness, it's important to give each activity area some spatial definition. In an open house, there are few walls to accomplish this task, so I turn to the ceiling plane. Because it's relatively easy for a builder to lower sections of ceiling from the

**outside the house**

**Kitchen cabinet close-up** Placing the kitchen window flush with the cabinetry allows natural light to wash across the glass cabinet doors, making this side of the kitchen brighter.

structural joists above, I start with an 8-ft. or 9-ft. ceiling, then drop soffits, ceiling sections, or lattice to define the spaces.

In this house, I used three strategies— dropped soffits, floating lattice panels, and lowered ceilings—to modulate the actual or apparent height of the spaces. Although you aren't consciously aware of how the ceiling details affect your sense of space, they have significant impact at a subliminal level. Your eye notices changes in height and subtly recognizes the distinction between one space and another. For instance, in the short hall connecting the living room and master bedroom, I lowered the entire ceiling (see the photo on p. 186). Stepping under the low ceiling of this relatively narrow space creates a feeling of compression after the full height of the living room, as though you're moving through a tunnel. There's a subtle sense of release when you again reach full ceiling height in the master bedroom.

The key to keeping the various ceiling details from seeming like a hodgepodge is to have something tangible to which their height is keyed. In this house, the key is a continuous horizontal trim line—simply a 1x3 piece of maple, or occasionally cherry—that runs throughout the house just above the top trim of the windows. (I set the continuous trim line to the tallest item to be trimmed, the built-in refrigerator; the windows followed from there, suitably high for Ed, who is tall.) Wherever there's a soffit,

**Kitchen** In the kitchen, the cherry window trim becomes the top trim of the upper cabinets, neatly filling the gap between the cabinets and the dropped soffit. The soffit is set to the main trim line, which you can see continuing into the dining room in the foreground.

detail in focus

## Shelter around an Activity

A soffit dropped below the main trim line helps define and shelter the sink, countertop, and cooking range work areas. A dropped soffit is also an ideal place to locate task lighting. The floating cherry lattice is aligned with the maple trim but serves a different purpose from the soffit, in this case defining the kitchen space and separating it slightly from the dining area.

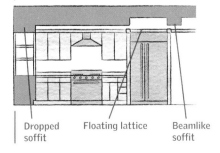

Dropped soffit    Floating lattice    Beamlike soffit

whether over a window seat, a kitchen counter, or a display shelf, it's set to the height of the trim line. The lattice panels are similarly set to the trim line.

## The architectural details built into the house are important, of course, but so are the things we own. Fittingly, elements like soffits, nooks, deep shelves, and even staircases can provide a place for our favorite belongings at the same time as they embellish the spaces we live in. A handful of Ed and Maureen's favorite antiques are gathered together in the "away room," my term for a small, quiet space set apart from the more open and lively rest of the house. The away room (in this house it's essentially a sitting parlor) is tucked behind the hearth, which it shares with the living room; in the photo on pp. 190–191, you can see the away room peeking through the display shelves and the two-sided fireplace.

Other places for the display of cherished antiques, collectibles, and art objects include shelves by the hearth and a deep nook in the short hall between the entry and living room; the nook provides a place for an artful floor chest and shelves of Maureen's mother's china. By spreading out the lower stairs and dropping a soffit

**Hall to master bedroom**   The entire ceiling in the hall to the master bedroom has been lowered to the height of the continuous trim line, so you feel a sense of compression between the full height of the living room and the full height of the bedroom. A glass door to a covered terrace and light from the window seat in the bedroom keep the hall from feeling cramped.

**Master bedroom** A snug window seat in the master bedroom looks out to a small, private meadow. As with other window seats and nooks in the house, the ceiling above has been lowered to just above the window trim, increasing the cozy feel.

**Laundry room** In the laundry room, a soffit is dropped below the horizontal trim line that runs through the house, providing a sense of shelter above the countertops. Without the soffit and trim, the space would feel like a narrow slot instead of a room.

## A Simple Floating Lattice

I'm often asked how to make the floating lattices I've used in several houses I've designed. The lattice in this house is made from slats of 1x3-in. solid cherry, spaced 2 in. apart. A narrow ledger strip has been added to the bottom of the long 1x3 rails, making them a little deeper than the slats. The slats are attached to the rails with screws; the ledge is there more to create clean-looking joints than to support the slats. The entire lattice is attached with metal anchor rods. Light from ceiling fixtures above the lattice is able to filter through; there are no lights in the lattice itself.

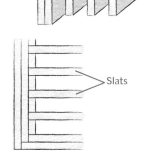

Rails

Slats

**A window seat at the entry** When framing a window within a window seat, it's almost always better to carry the trim fully to the top and sides of the nook, even if it means widening the trim. Otherwise, there will be an odd strip of wall (always difficult to paint) between the trim and the ceiling or sides.

over them, I created a lighted stage for a Navajo rug and a Northwest Coast bentwood cedar box (see the photo on p. 182).

The focus of this book is on the inside of houses, but we have to take a quick detour outside, because I designed Ed and Maureen's sun porch as a true room, with variations in ceiling height similar to those in the main spaces of the house. The barrel-vaulted ceiling at the center of the porch focuses attention on the nearby mountains. Flanking either side of the sweeping vault are lower flat ceilings, treated very much like the dropped soffits inside. These flat planes give a sense of shelter to a dining area on one side and a sitting area on the other. Maureen likes to say that no matter where you sit in her home, there's something good to look at. That's true, I hope, whether you're on the sun porch looking out at Mount Mansfield or in the away room looking at the small Hudson River valley landscape painting over the hearth.

## picture this

SIZING A VANITY MIRROR
Whether it's framed or just a sheet of glass, a large mirror looks much better above a vanity if it takes up the entire wall, from one side to the other and from the vanity top to the ceiling. A mirror that's not large enough to fill the wall leaves awkward spaces around it that never feel quite right.

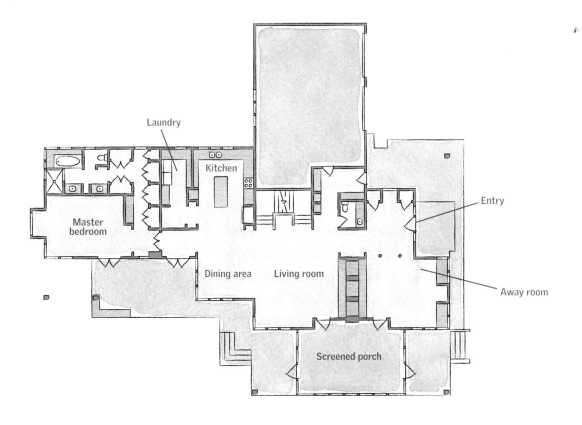

Laundry

Kitchen

Master
bedroom

Dining area    Living room

Entry

Away room

Screened porch

**Master bath** In the master bath, the ceiling is lowered to the window trim line. The trim ties the glass shower stall to the rest of the space and gives it more substance. Wood is okay in a shower as long as it's protected (this trim has a urethane finish) and out of the direct line of water.

**A shared approach to trim connects living room and porch** The sun porch maintains the trim line of the living room, but in this casual outdoor room, the trim is painted white and the dropped soffit, like the ceiling, is paneled in bead board. The cove above the trim line houses lights that illuminate the curved ceiling at night. The plane of the soffit continues beyond the screened windows to become the wide eaves of the roof.

**Of trim lines and soffits** This corner of the away room (on the other side of the hearth from the living room) mirrors the living room with a similar door and a crescent window to the sun porch. The continuous trim line lends order to what's happening both above and below it. Above the line, the crescent window springs from the trim and a boxed area over the display shelf houses a stereo speaker. Below the trim line, as in the living room, there's a dropped soffit. The soffit defines a deep display shelf and the hearth but continues just a few inches wide over the door to bring down the apparent height of the away room.

**A virtual hallway** It's easy to see the floating cherry lattice that helps divide the dining area from the living room. You have to look more closely to notice the beamlike soffit above the lattice (running perpendicular to it) that even more subtly defines a pathway through the living room, a kind of virtual hallway connecting the entry to the master bedroom. Look again at the photo on the facing page and you'll see this narrow soffit defining the pathway back toward the entry.

The interplay between hard and soft, geometric and curvilinear, inside and out are only a few of the contrasts that make this house and landscape so perfect for each other.

# The Landscape of Home

My starter home was a big Victorian on a tiny site in a neighborhood of Boston. With its wraparound porch, turret, and stained-glass windows, it was an exciting house for bringing up a family. But when I ask my children about this period, they describe how they used the landscape, making cascades over the backyard ledges with the hose, building forts in the forsythia bush, and conducting tea parties on the steps of the front porch. Creating these spaces for outdoor living brought us as much—if not more—pleasure as decorating the inside because we were using the outside as an extension of our house. And by extending the house, we transformed the whole property into what I call our landscape of home.

Each of us carries a mental picture of what constitutes our particular landscape of home. It might be entertaining friends for dinner under a grape arbor or roasting marshmallows around a firepit or perching on a parapet looking out to a distant view. Gardens are also part of the landscape of home. A cottage garden greets visitors from the street. A water garden brings sound and visual delight to a corner of the yard. As a landscape designer, I work closely with my clients to wrest these images from them so that I can design gardens that match their inner visions.

**Not So Big** refers to an attitude rather than the size of a house. In this book, we are not addressing just those with a modest piece of land, but those with properties that range from a 10th of an acre to 100 acres. Not So Big refers to houses that don't overwhelm the size of the lot but allow plenty of "breathing room" around it for growing, for entertaining, or for contemplation. Not So Big suggests a way of crafting your house so that it feels like home and crafting your property so that you feel at home on your land. This usually means creating a house about one-third smaller than you thought you needed.

Most homeowners are overwhelmed by the vast amount of information required to know how to organize their space into a coherent whole. Often, they have no idea where to begin. Perhaps it is because, unlike the inside of a house where each room has walls, a ceiling, and a floor, the outside feels boundless, and little but the property line is defined.

And the possibilities seem limitless, bounded only by one's budget, which is usually constrained after the expenses of building or renovating. So the question is: How do we make the outside of our homes as wonderful as the inside? How can we craft places on the land that fulfill our needs and delight our souls? In *Outside the Not So Big House*, you'll find the answers as we break down this new design territory, the landscape of home.

In her earlier Not So Big books, Sarah explained how to make a house into a home. Giving words to spatial concepts that underlie

> **Using framed openings is one way to link inside to outside. Double doors frame a view to the brick terrace, surrounded by flowers that seem to tumble down the hillside.**

our understanding of the built environment, she developed a language of space and form that describes the qualitative experience that people want in a house. As they read her books, many asked for help in thinking about how to approach the landscape from a Not So Big perspective. In this book, we do just that, for we believe that a house is not a home unless it is seamlessly interconnected with the landscape around it.

Imagine a house where you throw open the doors to find an outdoor world in which you can live with all the comforts of home. What would this look like? Just as in the inside, you would have areas of "shelter around activity," such as the grape arbor, where you sit in a protected place looking out onto a larger space beyond. You'd find the Not So Big concept of "layering," in which a series of openings and surfaces break the perceived space into segments, as when sliding doors open out to a veranda that flows down to a series of terraces beyond. And you'd find at least one "away room," such as a cozy gazebo that provides sanctuary. As you'll learn, many Not So Big concepts also apply to outside spaces, helping to connect the inside of your home to the landscape around it.

## A New Definition of Home

What do we mean by the landscape of home? It's not only the gardens, but also the views and vistas, and the walkways and thresholds that let you feel at home on your land. Of course, your house is part of this landscape, too. How do you decide when to use these elements? You begin by realizing that designing your landscape is not so different from designing your house. Each property in the chapters that follow shows a different response to the challenges posed by site and structure, but the professionals who designed the properties used similar tools to create very different landscapes. Giving names to those conceptual

∧ Working outside a house requires a close relationship between designer and client. Here, carefully applied native materials contribute to the impression that this Colorado home is growing right up out of the site.

∧ A bronze water feature echoes the forms of adjacent tree trunks and brings gentle sounds to this sylvan place. Mossy stones are carefully set to make the artificial pond feel natural.

We typically discuss landscaping as though it were something completely separate from the house. If you look at most garden design, you'll be hard pressed to find much connection between inside and out. There might be a screened porch, a terrace, or a deck that provides a gesture at a transition between inside and out. But there's often nothing else.

Like the artistry required in designing a welcoming entrance, there's an artistry required in the design of the interconnections between interior and exterior places. There's much potential to enhance the experience of everyday living when you consider the outdoors as a design element of the indoor space. And vice versa.

Every interior sitting space and activity area offers the opportunity to connect to and participate in a particular aspect of the surrounding landscape, whether that be a view to a beautiful tree, a long vista to a standing stone at the far corner of the property, or a glimpse through a tiny window to a courtyard garden. When inside and outside are designed as one, the results can inspire you on a daily basis, feeding your spirit and allowing you to truly delight in the natural world without having to go outside to do so.　　　*–Sarah*

< The approach to your property sets the tone for the experience of entering the house. Here, a gravel driveway brings visitors to a garden court before they cross the threshold.

tools—i.e., the language of the landscape of home—is the first step in understanding the design process so that you can use them to create your own.

## Site
### Embracing the Habitat of Home

Your site, your house, and your outbuildings make up your habitat: the environment where you feel most at home. When you create the right habitat of home, you set the table for all other design decisions. Every site has a vantage: either a prospect—a view from a high position, as on a mountain; or a refuge—a protected setting such as under a canopy of trees. To create the most favorable setting, it's important to know how the site is oriented, its soils, and existing vegetation. Your house also enjoys a particular relationship to the land, with slopes that face upward, downward, or remain level. Those familiar with Not So Big principles

∧ The vantage of a warm hot tub is perfect for taking in the mountain view.

> From the dining room, the high windows create the feeling of sitting in a terrarium.

< Ground covers and perennials tumble down the hillside, drenching a stone retaining wall in soft textures and colors. The simplicity of the house stands up well to the garden, which is bursting with plants.

will see the connection. Like a home designed for the way we really live, a landscape designed to make the most of its site is more inspiring and more fitting.

One property in the book, a Not So Big House set high in the Berkeley Hills, was designed to take advantage of every square inch of its narrow site. The house nestles into a steep slope and, in every room, high-framed windows and doors bring in views of a flower garden that was lovingly planted by the owners. Brick and stone terraces offer places for entertaining and quiet contemplation, helping make this the perfect habitat for the social couple who live here.

# Flow
## Composing Journeys

Stripped down to its essentials, a landscape is really composed of two elements: paths and places. A path indicates the way you should flow through a landscape—which direction to stroll in and the pace you walk—as well as the mood with which you move.

∧ The water garden is a terminus for one journey on this property.

> This stepping-stone path winds through beds of hosta and underneath the shade of a magnolia tree, linking front yard to back.

Λ A path of flat fieldstone brings the visitor to a curved retaining wall—an overlook and place to sit that invites body and mind to rest a while.

Places are stopping points you encounter along the way, such as spaces for enjoying views inside and outside the house. You can choreograph movement through space, from place to place, through the design of the journey that the path takes. Like a Not So Big house that has a thoughtful circulation pattern that leads us through the entire house, a landscape with a carefully designed journey is one that integrates the inside flow to the outside and vice versa. Whether meandering or straight, a well-designed path links different places, events, or activities to each other around our properties.

The rocky stream that flows alongside one house in the book leads visitors from the cobbled parking court across a bridge to a roofed outdoor veranda. The veranda follows the meandering streambed and terminates in a circular outdoor room that overlooks the water. Sitting in what is a private escape for this in-town house, visitors can enjoy the sight and sounds of the babbling watercourse.

## Frames
### Linking the Inside With the Out

It's wonderful to look out the windows of your house and see a landscape that knits nature and building into one complete design. Your home feels as though it extends beyond the walls of the house.

Who doesn't long to have a stream flowing through the yard? At this home in Colorado, a rocky rill meanders through a narrow side garden, shaded by aspen trees.

Being mindful of framed openings, such as windows and doors, helps you to establish a visual link between inside and out. In addition, building transitional spaces, like decks, porches, or balconies, makes the space between building and landscape more accessible. By enclosing parts of the landscape with walls, fences, or hedges, you create outdoor rooms as pleasing as those inside the house. When you create frames—structures that surround or enclose a particular space—you extend the presence of home beyond your house to embrace the whole property. Of course, this very concept of indoor-outdoor connection is at the heart of Not So Big design.

Λ This framed opening looks out on a lovely garden scene: a pool graced by a grove of bamboo.

< The front porch with its red butterfly chairs looks out upon the neighborhood. A simple tin roof tops the ipé deck, providing needed shade in the Texas heat.

∨ This Chicago garden is crafted from inexpensive materials but planted with a rich palette and a deft hand.

A Not So Big House in Texas displays many ways to link inside to outside. With an open floor plan that maximizes every bit of space, the house features floor-to-ceiling windows that offer views out to the backyard. A deck seems to float over a series of lawn panels that step down to the level yard. The owners are free to live equally inside or outside on their property, experiencing every inch of their landscape of home.

# Details

## Crafting the Elements of Nature

You craft the inside of your home when you choose a window style or a special molding. Each selection reflects your style and displays aspects of your personality, as an individual, a couple, or a family. Similarly, the details that you choose in crafting your outdoor landscape help to anchor the house to its surrounds. This means emphasizing the interplay of materials and echoing forms and patterns to bring consistency to the whole. For example, you can compose a planting palette using colors and textures that

∧ An inveterate gardener planted a wide range of trees, shrubs, and perennials in her front yard and painted the porch columns bright yellow.

delight. Or select native materials that suggest a sense of the history of your locale. By shaping the personality of your home this way, you bring outside into union with inside. And whether or not you're talking about the interior of your home or the area surrounding it, all good design comes down to the crafting of the details.

Every property in this book possesses elegantly crafted details, but one Chicago residence shows how effective using simple building materials with beautiful plantings can be. Carefully edged planting beds harness riots of colors and textures. Each detail fits into the whole; the whole is defined by the personality and aesthetic of the owner.

## Owning the Landscape
As you read through this book, you'll discover new ideas and images that will indelibly change the way you see—and own—your property. Look out your kitchen window, and you'll imagine a host of new possibilities: a wildflower meadow or a deck floating over a lily pond. You'll learn techniques for designing an appealing approach to your home, methods for making a small property seem bigger, and ways to hide views and reveal others. The variety of landscapes and houses highlighted in this book—large and small, located in rural, suburban, or urban settings all around the country—offer ample ideas for every homeowner.

In the simplest sense, the ideas in this book are all about well-being: being well both in your house and on your land. Isn't this what we all want from our homes? Just as my children took delight in playing in spaces we made for them outside our house, so too will you derive joy from creating your own very personal landscape of home.

A screened room sits at a prime location for viewing down the valley to the Vermont mountains beyond. Notice how the local slate under the deep eaves of the veranda matches the gray-green color of the standing-seam roof.

# Playing Up the Corners

It's thrilling to see the elegance and beauty of Sarah's Not So Big principles come to life in this home for a retired couple near Stowe, Vermont. Sited on a large piece of land, the residence sits in a lovely garden and looks out upon a majestic view. The property, a west-facing meadow reminiscent of the former farm community of north central Vermont, is located high up on Elmore Mountain and faces west, looking across to a distant Mount Mansfield. The owners, returning to their Vermont roots, looked to Sarah and landscape designer Cynthia Knauf to design a home with a strong indoor-outdoor connection through a composition of pattern, detail, and scale. Their love of Prairie-style architecture and the Japanese aesthetic supports the design of the house and land to express a harmony between their lifestyle and the natural surroundings.

## NOT SO BIG INSIDE OUT

**Situated on** a beautiful piece of Vermont mountainside, this home is designed to extend its apparent territory all the way to the horizon. Intended to encourage the use of its many outdoor spaces whenever the weather allows, house and land interweave to create a series of spatial layers from interior, to a space I call "beneath the roof but outside," to garden. The sequence of places that connects them makes a continuous necklace around and through the house, and it's this collection that creates the feeling of home. —*Sarah*

The old farm road to the house climbs steadily through a meadow of lupine, daisies, black-eyed Susans, and asters. Designed as a series of horizontal planes, the low-slung structure, with green metal roofs, a massive stone chimney, and an attached garage, sits on garden terraces that ease into the wildflower meadow. A gentle arc in the driveway brings visitors to the front walk. A ribbon of bluestone moves them past a natural stone water basin scooped out to collect rainwater. Here, a transverse path of flat fieldstone interrupts the cut-stone walkway, offering viewers a tempting walk around the garden before entering the house. This path winds through native plantings and past the occasional boulder before ending up at a small Vermont slate terrace at the corner of the house.

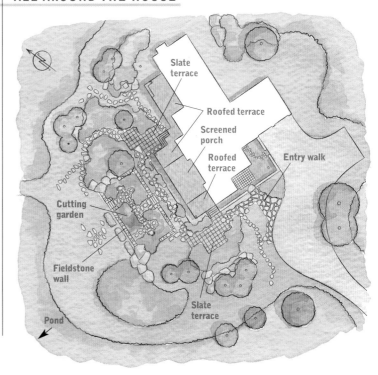

**ALL AROUND THE HOUSE**

Slate terrace

Roofed terrace

Screened porch

Roofed terrace

Entry walk

Cutting garden

Fieldstone wall

Slate terrace

Pond

> A swimming pond reflects the silhouettes of trees and the lights of this handsome home in Vermont.

∨ This natural fieldstone, found on the property, was hollowed out as an "event" along the walk to the front door, perhaps a reference to the placement of *tsukubai*—a water basin along a Japanese tea garden path.

∧ The use of local materials relates this house wonderfully to its surrounds. The front walk interweaves several kinds of stones to help signal which way to go: Take the straight, cut-stone walkway to get to the front door, or follow the irregular stepping-stone path to stroll around the garden.

## Corners Indoors and Out

Both architect and landscape architect play up the corners of this home: Sarah, by placing a bank of windows that wraps around the corner, makes the wall seem to disappear and frames the views so that inside and outside are one. She also placed a window seat that beckons one to sit and linger, looking out to the garden and beyond. By featuring the corners of a space, Sarah makes the space feel bigger than it really is, drawing the eye across the room and to the views.

The same is true outside the house as well. By drawing feet and eyes to the corners of the upper terraces just outside the screened porch, the landscape designer expanded the virtual frame around the house. She also made a place for the corner of the house by creating a void of space that accepts and defuses the corner's energy. Backing up the table and chairs that sit at the outer edge of the terrace with a weeping larch tree, shrubs, and flowering perennials, she echoed the idea behind the window seat, allowing visitors to inhabit the corner of the garden.

At the northern side of the landscape, the designer added another slate terrace, this time as a backdrop for a set of steps that cascade down from the corner of the slate walkway, which unites screened porch and upper terrace. Here, visitors are greeted by a series of offset rectangles that are emphasized by the shape of the teak benches. Stepping-stones, planted on a gravel path that tunnels through soft drifts of plantings, offer a way down to the pond.

## Framing the View

Sitting at the western edge of the house, the screened porch looks out across terraces and pond to the setting sun over Mount Mansfield. The vista unfolds like a Japanese screen, segmented into 12 separate aspects of the same scene: The lower band of four "frames" looks onto the terrace, the middle set focuses on views across the pond, and the top four define the sky. The curving roofline and the upper clerestory also allow for views of the sky; where the window arcs downward, it pulls the eye back into the forest that surrounds the whole property.

From within the house, you have views through interior doorways and windows, so inside and outside continually overlap. An interior eyebrow window lets light into the room, echoed again in the wood fireplace frame. With vistas like these, it pays to "borrow" them, bringing them into your living space by framing each view like the work of art it is.

∧ The view from the screened porch looks across layers of landscape: over a stepping-stone terrace to a cutting garden, across pond and fields and forest to the mountains in the distance. The raised eyebrow window gives unfettered views to the sky.

< Washed pea gravel is the ground cover in this section of the garden, where a layer of landscape fabric has been laid to keep the weeds from cropping up.

∨ Sarah echoed the eyebrow form seen above the screened porch in various places around the house. The curved motif is carried above the fireplace and the clerestory window above the door in the away room.

## A Base of Support

To feel rooted to the ground and promote flow between inside and outside, a house needs a solid and level base of support. The way I think about this is to imagine that the house has fallen forward onto its front façade. The area left by its imprint is about the right amount of level ground needed for a good base of support. This area might be taken up by a

series of terraces that step downhill, as at this house, or by one level space for patio, garden, or lawn in front of the house.

I think of this as the "aura" of the house, displaced onto the land. Landscape designer Cynthia Knauf furthers the idea of the house projected onto the land by echoing the curve of the eyebrow window on the porch in her cobble design on the ground. The base of support for the house steps out and down the slope by the creation of a lower terrace, retained by a handsome fieldstone wall. Here, Cynthia designed a cutting garden composed of annuals and perennials planted for flower arrangements created by the owner.

—Julie

# outside
## p a r a l l e l s

### Blurring the Boundary

**SARAH'S LOW-SLUNG** roofs create a transitional space under the eaves that acts like a porch, a terrace, and a front stoop all in one. Since the roof doesn't have gutters, she provides a drip line of Mexican beach pebbles that sit in a trough formed by the curb that bounds the driveway and the concrete floor of the area under the eaves.

This drip line further defines the aura of the house; its straight lines set it apart from the natural landscape while its contents—the black beach stones—relate to the bluestone walkway that leads you into the house. The massive wooden pillar that holds up the corner of the house sits on a flat fieldstone base, further blurring the boundaries between house and garden, inside and out.      *–Julie*

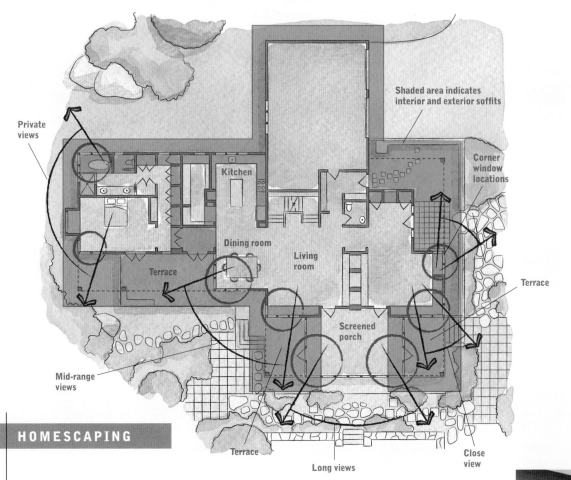

Private views

Shaded area indicates interior and exterior soffits

Corner window locations

Kitchen

Dining room

Living room

Terrace

Terrace

Mid-range views

Screened porch

Terrace

Long views

Close view

**HOMESCAPING**

# Corner Windows

In designing this house, I wanted to give the homeowners the sense, from every major room, that they were all but outside. One of the best ways I've found to achieve this is to "erode" the solidity of the corners so that you are able to look through the part of the house that we most associate with structure and stability. Not only does this increase the view, but it also encourages you to inhabit the corners. A corner, even one that's not wrapped with windows, will provide a sense of shelter for any activity located there. But when there is a series of windows on either side of the corner post, the appeal of inhabiting the corner becomes hard to resist.

The window seat shown here is further enhanced by the lowered ceiling, which, like the kitchen soffit described at right, provides shelter around the activity of sitting and gazing at the view, reading a book, or just daydreaming.

Like the soffit in the kitchen, the eaves beyond the windows are the same height as the lowered ceiling, giving the impression that the boundary created by the windows is only a minimal obstacle between you and the surrounding landscape. Notice that the peeled-log post supporting the roof that extends out over the adjacent terrace aligns with the window mullions as well. This further blurs the distinction between what's inside and what's out.

Looking at the floor plan, you'll see that there are similar sitting places in the living room and dining room, as well as in one of the guest bedrooms on the second floor. The screened porch takes this attitude of the eroded corner to its logical extreme. In a way, the room is all open corners, with no solid wall left at all, yet there's still protection supplied by the roof above. It's one of the reasons I believe people enjoy screened porches so much. There's protection, but only a minimal boundary between inside and out.

*—Sarah*

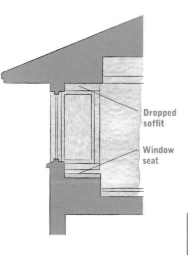

Dropped soffit

Window seat

## Blurring the Boundary

**JUST AS** the wide overhangs give a sense of protection on the exterior, on the interior lots of dropped ceilings over window seats and above countertops help give a sense of shelter to the activity places below. For example, I lowered the ceiling to the height of the window trim above the kitchen sink, so that when working here, a person is not only connected to the view, but also feels protected from above, much as how one feels when wearing a wide-brimmed hat. The eaves are at the same height as the dropped ceiling within, so it appears that the wide brim extends from inside to out. With the extension of the windows all the way to the countertop, the boundary created by the wall is minimized. *—Sarah*

**S**arah has designed a wonderful perching place that feels like part of house and landscape at the same time. A gray slate veranda sits 2 ft. above the garden level, protected under deep eaves. Steps that flow from its interior corner lead down to a red slate terrace, where stepping stones lead out to the natural landscape beyond.

| 1 | 2 | 3 |
|---|---|---|
| 4 | 5 | 6 |
| 7 | 8 | 9 |

**5** **The bonsai trees** are members of the client's collection: one a diminutive Japanese maple and the other a white pine—a miniature of the weeping white pine that towers above it.

**6** **Billowing plantings** of different heights, colors, and textures are carefully pruned to allow views out, yet they create the feeling of an enclosed garden within. Mount Mansfield peeks out over the autumnal colors of maple trees in the near distance.

**3** **The client asked** the landscape designer to make a maintenance notebook that explains what to do with every plant in her garden. Here, the flowering stages for the meadow for spring and summer were documented before it was cut back in the fall.

**One of the delights** of living in a colder climate is enjoying the different seasons. In the crisp fall air, maple trees turn brilliant colors before losing their leaves.

White roses—"Prosperity" on the left and "Ballerina" on the right—stand out vividly against the deep, soft greens of the garden plantings. A brick path flows around the stucco walls of the house.

# Borrowing the Landscape

I magine a charming little house with a private backyard that nestles into a hillside of flowers with a view to a city skyline in the distance. This combination of contemplative remove and vibrant accessibility perfectly describes this sliver of property in the Berkeley Hills in California. Located on a steep hill, this "walk-to" parcel is accessed only by a public pathway—a narrow, flower-strewn lane that ascends through steeply banked retaining walls as a series of steps and landings.

At the top of a set of stairs, a metal gate arches out into the public path announcing the entrance. Two sharp rights and a left-hand turn bring visitors to the front door. The home's close proximity to the public walkway, combined with its circuitous means of access, underscores a delightful tension between nearness and farness; between remove and accessibility.

## NOT SO BIG INSIDE OUT

**Some properties,** like this tiny but delightful California home, have a topography to them that says "shelter," whether you are talking about the house, the land, or both in combination. This one has an archetypal "nestled" quality to it resulting from the shape of the surrounding landscape, a quality that both architect and landscape architect have capitalized upon to make the home a lush, green, and secluded paradise from every vantage point.

—*Sarah*

∧ Visitors pass cascading nasturtium blossoms and bamboo rising against the retaining walls before they reach the beckoning gate and trellis.

Architect Dennis Fox renovated this diminutive home, built in the 1930s, from a tiny 918 sq. ft. to a still-modest 1,084 sq. ft. To take advantage of the views of the landscape offered by the steep hillside in the back, he placed the private rooms—the master bedroom, kitchen, and dining room—on the garden side of the house. Looking from slope down to house, the structure is a stucco box that stands in stark contrast to the flow of the landscape. But when one looks from the inside out, something magical happens: It feels as though all distinctions between house and garden have disappeared, almost like one is inside a terrarium. The architect created this effect by lowering windowsills and doorsills (to better merge with the landscape) and by heightening ceilings in order to include banks of

∨ Roses open to the sun in this exuberantly planted backyard garden—a pleasing contrast to the spare interior rooms of the house.

## ALL AROUND THE HOUSE

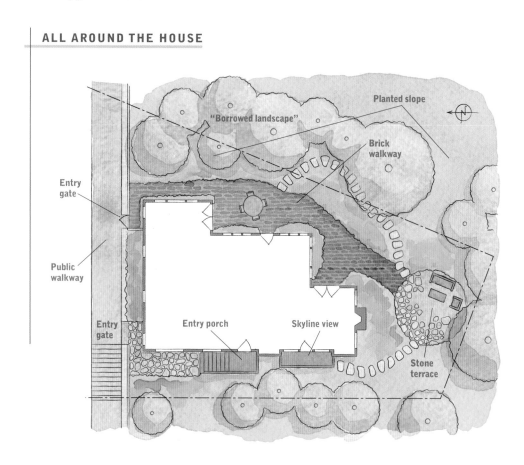

"Borrowed landscape"

Planted slope

Brick walkway

Entry gate

Public walkway

Entry gate

Entry porch

Skyline view

Stone terrace

< Perfectly centered in the frame of a living-room window, these skyscrapers seem to float above San Francisco Bay. The carefully pruned hedge, together with the tall trees, distant mountains, and sky, isolates the view.

clerestory windows above vertical fixed and casement windows. The clerestories open up the view to the top of the hill with tree ferns, rose blossoms, and billowing shrubs that spill down the slope, and the lowered windowsills bring foreground plantings right into the house.

## A Borrowed Landscape
The living room lies on the western side of the property, facing the setting sun and San Francisco Bay. As you enter, your eye is drawn to a single door-way onto a balcony with a view across the neighbor's roof to the distant skyline. Here, the architect employed a Japanese gardening

Λ The architect lowered the doorsill so that the terrace level appears to sweep right in the door. This effect is furthered by the plantings at the threshold and the foundation line of the house.

> Sheltered by the sloping hillside, this teak bench and chair offer a tempting spot for contemplation. The stockade fence, drenched in vines, may define the property line between houses, but it doesn't stop the eye from "borrowing" the neighbor's view.

∨ Tree ferns grow on the slope above the house like a forest primeval. Narrow mulched trails traverse the hillside, terminating in a solitary bench or chair.

technique called *shakkei,* or "borrowing the landscape." Fox called attention to the best vista on the property by erecting a kind of vertical picture frame around it. The door casing borders the top and sides of the picture plane, and a dense hedge and neighboring trees further intensify the view. The distant view within the small frame is a surprising and satisfying visual experience. It also acts as a reminder of this home's relationship with the city: The city feels close enough to "borrow," yet its scale is small enough to give a sense of vast distance.

Landscape architect Heather Anderson chose to literally borrow the neighbor's landscape in her design of this backyard garden. Her planting plan encompassed the mature trees on and adjacent to

< Planting up against the foundation of a house can make it feel as though it springs forth from a garden. Otherwise, a garden can seem like an afterthought. Soft euphorbias contrast with spiky agaves in the afternoon sun.

the site, creating the sense that the property continues beyond its actual boundaries. Concrete-rubble retaining walls were used to make a small cut into the hillside to gain areas for seating. Brick and stone pathways surround the building, opening up to create terraces and, paradoxically, encouraging close-up scrutiny of the voluptuous plantings all around.

## Upward-Facing Slopes

This property sits on the terraced shelf just below a steeply sloping hillside. Thus, the backyard looks directly into the bank of what I call an upward-facing slope. This condition allows intimate views of a landscape, which is seen as a flipped-up plane, like a huge landscape canvas propped up on an easel. What delights here is that every inch of hillside becomes valuable, for it not only makes up the view from within the house but also the enclosure that forms the backyard, while offering secret trails and contemplative perches for solitary strollers. An upward-facing slope turns into a downward-facing one when these vantage points high on the hill become places

to pause and literally reflect on where you came from, or where you're planning to go.

—Julie

< The hillside of flowers seems to cascade right into the wraparound windows of this Not So Big dining room. Clerestory windows allow a view up the slope and into branches overhead.

# outside
## | parallels |

### Sense of Shelter

**IN THE VAST** expanses of the great outdoors, we seek out places of shelter, precincts where we feel protected and secure while being able to survey the landscape around us. We seek a strong "back" to nestle against—such as a hillside—some kind of enclosing arms that harbor and enfold while allowing for a view out.

Landscape architect Heather Anderson placed a teak bench on its own small terrace, backed up against the upward-facing slope of plantings, where it looks out and down to the view beyond. Here, the space is private as well as protected from winds from the San Francisco Bay. The stone steps entice us to ascend, look around, and smell the roses.      —*Julie*

**HOMESCAPING**

## Window Positioning

We've all been in houses in which you are cut off from the surrounding views the moment you sit down. There's nothing more frustrating than knowing there's a beautiful view beyond the window but being unable to see it because the windowsill is too high. The architect for this home has been careful to make windowsills in the dining room and bedroom about 24 in. off the floor so that, as you sit at the dining table or lie in bed, you can easily see out and down a bit as well.

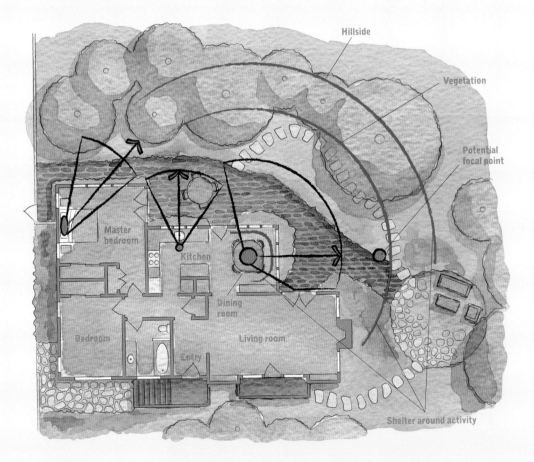

The same is true for the kitchen, but here the sill height must be appropriately scaled for someone standing at the countertop. Here again, the architect has made the backsplash a minimal 2½ in., so as you stand at the sink, you feel very much a part of the outdoor space. As you can see in the doctored image (below, left), a higher sill gives much more of a sense of separation.

Windows can provide a geometrical patterning for interior space as well. Notice how, with the windows in the dining room, our focus is drawn to the larger middle windowpane. This is because the smaller surrounding windows serve as a frame. Although they contain views of their own, they delineate the point of focus for the whole room. For this reason, the place in the garden to where your attention is drawn might also be the spot for a special feature, such as a fountain, a wonderful stone, or a plant. It's this integration between inside and out that really weaves the two into an integrated whole.    *—Sarah*

## Shelter Around Activity

**JULIE HAS DESCRIBED** how the shape of the surrounding hill can give the sense of shelter. At the entrance, below, the slope's presence is comforting. But perhaps the place where we're most familiar with this sense is in the corner of a room. Why else do you think it is that the corner tables and booths in a restaurant are always the most prized spots? We tend to seek out the corners because we feel more protected, and so more comfortable.

As you look at the dining-room corner, you'll see that there's the shelter provided by the hill and its plantings. The nestled feeling you get while sitting here is palpable. You are doubly sheltered, and so doubly comfortable.    *—Sarah*

Rather than follow the usual desire line that leads directly from entry gate to front door, the owners chose to create a strolling path that circles around the garden. For those visitors in a hurry, they added stepping-stones through the garden beds.

# The Attraction of Opposites

Our homes often reflect a particular view of our place in the continuum between the built environment and the world of nature. Frank and Judy Harmon's house in Raleigh, North Carolina, is no different. It's designed to mirror and attract oppositions between inside and out, hard and soft, light and dark, and private and public. Pooling their respective design talents—as architect and landscape architect—the couple created a wonderfully livable home that instructs as much as it inspires.

When they bought a derelict piece of land in a university neighborhood of Raleigh more than a decade ago, Judy and Frank studied the site for a year before sketching out a series of schemes. In order to create the largest garden space possible, they ended up building an elegant boxlike house of concrete, steel, and glass that sits at the back of the property. To counter the noise of student life along

## NOT SO BIG INSIDE OUT

As Julie and I described it in the introduction to this book, our shared vision is that someday all our homes will be designed to integrate interior and exterior, so that they are perceived and lived in as one. When a husband and wife are also architect and landscape architect, there's a wonderful alchemy that takes place, as can be seen in this home—a perfect integration of landscape and building.　　　*—Sarah*

∧ A Mexican hammock strung between trees offers respite in the garden.

the sometimes-busy street, the whole is enclosed by a 6-ft. wall of concrete, colored pale pink to match the interior walls of the house. The setback and the perimeter wall give privacy and allow Judy's plantings to animate the landscape within. Although the garden was originally designed as a perfect oval grass panel, or lawn, bounded by perennial borders, the planting beds have gradually encroached inward so that, today, the grass panel resembles an asymmetric figure eight. The result is a magnificent interplay between house and garden, geometric and curvilinear forms, and hard and soft surfaces.

## Animating the Corners

In a Not So Big House, you're likely to find rooms designed with alcoves or other types of shelter from which to view the main activity of the space. Just like Sarah's principle of shelter around activity, the landscape plan at work here reflects how every square inch is designed for a particular use. With the figure-eight garden occupying the literal and visual center of the yard, each corner takes on a specific role. In the northwest corner

**ALL AROUND THE HOUSE**

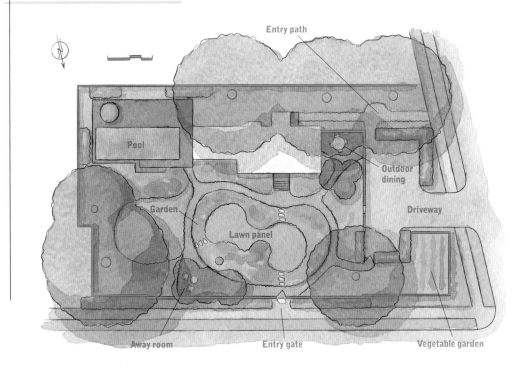

Entry path

Pool

Outdoor dining

Garden

Driveway

Lawn panel

Away room          Entry gate          Vegetable garden

∧ You'd never know that, standing by the vegetable patch, you're just feet away from a busy street corner. Walls and hedges enclose this corner parcel, providing almost complete seclusion.

∧ With so many different places to be—both inside and outside this home—a nearly-empty space provides relief. In this shady corner, the Harmons entertain within the pale pink walls.

< You can place art on outside walls the same way you do inside. A bas-relief panel hangs gracefully on the exterior garden wall.

∧ House and garden are a marriage of opposites: The strict geometry of the floor-to-ceiling glass window walls frames views of the curved beds of the garden.

where two busy streets converge, the Harmons planted a vegetable garden with a plum tree overhanging the wall as an offering to passersby. At the same corner, a Mexican hammock is strung between two trees as an outdoor away room for reading and dozing. And at the southwest quadrant just outside the dining room, a graveled corner of the property is used for entertaining under a canopy of willow oaks, tucked away just yards from the busy street. The Harmon residence is a good example of how, when you

∧ Red, yellow, and blue are considered primary colors because they form the basis for mixtures of other colors. Both red and yellow—like this wall and the metal ladder—are saturated enough to stand up to the bright blue pool.

∨ A Mondrian-like tile design brings together all the colors of the house on the wall by the azure-blue pool.

∧ Divided by an implied walkway, the living room is made up of an intimate, low-ceilinged sitting area around the hearth and a two-story space that fronts on the garden. Looking through a bright red wall, you can see that family room and pool align.

subdivide your property into a series of outdoor rooms with different uses, sizes, shapes, furniture, and plantings, you inhabit the out-of-doors just as you do the different rooms of your house.

## Color Inside and Out

In the southeast corner of the property, the couple built a cerulean blue pool as an outdoor extension of the family room. To set off the family-room wing from the pale pink walls of the rest of the house, Frank Harmon painted the outside walls red. In turn, the red becomes part of the decor of the pool garden, a bright space enclosed by low sitting walls that are decorated with vivid mosaic tiles. Potted plants radiate a tropical ambience augmented by black bamboo growing out of a kidney-bean-shaped cutout in the concrete pool deck.

This vibrant house has formed the backdrop for the busy lives of the Harmons, their two children, their clients, and their colleagues, who gather for meetings and social events inside and outside. Set apart and back from the street, the glassy façade of the house opens up to the landscape—an oasis of delight for all who pass through its walls.

< Different tones of the same color can bring harmony to a composition. Here, the gray-blue succulent plant stands out against the light turquoise glazed pot and the deeper hues of the swimming pool.

## Enclosing the Whole

When you build a wall around your property, you turn it into one large outdoor living room with four walls, a floor (the lawn and garden), and a ceiling (the high tree canopies overhead and the sky). By framing it, you define and protect what lies inside. And with tall-enough perimeter walls, this enclosure helps to hide your house from view, creating a sense of seclusion. The couple encouraged plants to grow on the 6-ft.-high wall to soften its hard surface and offer a more verdant frontage to their neighbors. By enclosing their site, the Harmons protected their home from the noise of the busy street while extending the presence of home onto their land.

The pale pink stuccoed walls that surround the property are punctuated by a main entryway that lines up with the front door. Two round millstones form the landing.

Low grasses knit the stone steps together as a kind of spillway into the street, softening the hardscape at every turn.

—Julie

# outside
## parallels

### Repeated Form

**ARCHITECT FRANK HARMON** punctures walls inside and outside his house to great effect. In order to provide a glimpse into the garden from the driveway side of the house, he cut a square opening in the thick perimeter wall. Your eye is drawn to this porthole of light, softened by

the delicate leaves of a clematis vine that peek through. This simple gesture serves to break down the visual barrier between outside and inside while introducing a design theme that he uses in various ways throughout the house.　　*—Julie*

## Enclosure and Openness

Contrasts heighten our experience of a home. If everything were the same, whether windows and views only in one direction or a single height of ceiling throughout, we wouldn't experience much. But when we add some contrast to the windows and views as the homeowners did here by including long vistas as well as views to places that are more contained, or if we vary the ceiling heights from room to room, then our senses come alive, and we appreciate the qualities of both light and space as a result.

If you look closely at this home, you'll see that inside or out, there is always an elegant interplay of openness and enclosure. Sitting in the living room, for example, you are surrounded by light and windows and view. There's

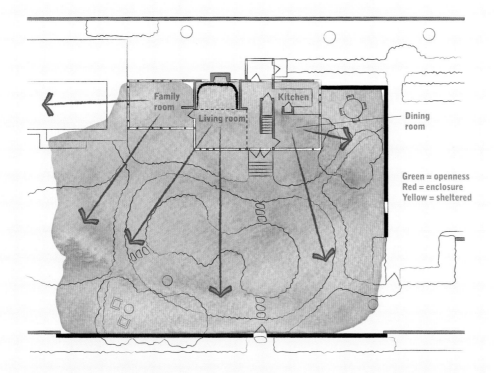

Family room

Living room

Kitchen

Dining room

Green = openness
Red = enclosure
Yellow = sheltered

a real sense of openness. But there is plenty of enclosure as well. The alcove that contains the main seating arrangement is surrounded on three sides by containing walls. Even the ceiling is lower here, giving the space a strong sense of shelter. From this vantage point, it's possible to see a large expanse of garden and sky. The experience is a powerful one because of the contrast between the openness of the view and the enclosure of the alcove.

In the kitchen, enclosure is created by the outside walls—nothing unusual about that. But the openness is far more pronounced than in most rectangular spaces. The windows are a ribbon running the entire length of both walls

and wrapping the corner as well. Seated here, the garden surrounds you like a shawl.

In the bathroom the theme continues. There's enclosure, in this case made by the translucent glass block that allows in light but, appropriately, keeps out view. At the upper part of the wall, where a view presents no privacy problems, the glass block is clear. This is a wonderful example of what I refer to as "view and nonview." Daylight is desirable sometimes even when the view is not.

—*Sarah*

## Repeated Form

**JUST LIKE** outside, inside the house, solid walls define and protect the more private spaces, such as bedrooms, bathrooms, and utility spaces. The opening in the photograph above bears a striking resemblance to the square opening in the surrounding exterior wall (at left). Here again, it is a single puncture in a monolithic surface, giving a glimpse of what lies beyond. Its perfectly square shape is an example of a repeated form. Using a repeated form is one of the easiest architectural tricks for tying inside and outside together, even when the characters of the parts are very different.                     —*Sarah*

The Harmons decided to locate their house along the south side of the lot in order to give Judy the largest possible area for building a garden. As seen from the outside, the house is composed of two parts: the red-hued family-room wing that abuts the pool and the pale pink main living space—in glass, steel, and concrete—that opens out onto the entry garden.

| 1 | 2 | 3 |
|---|---|---|
| 4 | 5 | 6 |
| 7 | 8 | 9 |

**2** | **Simple organic forms** contrast wonderfully with geometric shapes. This kidney-bean-shaped planting bed cut out from the pebble pool deck isolates and accentuates the slender verticality of the black bamboo growing there.

**3** **6** | **Outdoor accessories** bring balance to the garden's palette. The planting tray that rests on the balcony above the front door contains purple plantings that echo the color of the front door and the purple iris nearby.

**4** | **The oval lawn** appears as a larger version of this little fish pool, since both are bordered by billowing perennials. Allowing plantings to spill over geometric forms and crisp edges makes a space feel inviting and informal, even injecting a sense of romance or mystery that might otherwise not be present.

**5** | **Hues that are adjacent** on the color wheel—called analogous colors—look harmonious when planted next to each other. Here, yellow yarrow (*Achillea x* 'Moonshine') and sedum flowers match the yellow and green spikes of yucca leaves.

Though a neighbor's home sits just beyond the fence, this house feels secluded, thanks to the cobblestone drive, the native aspen groves, and the entry pond that provides year-round beauty.

# A Stream of One's Own

It is rare to discover an available in-town site on the banks of a river and, though local ordinances bar it, very tempting to build a house that faces onto it. The clear challenge of this narrow Aspen, Colorado, site on the Roaring Fork River was to create a unique and functional landscape of home in the space between the property lines while respecting the protective covenants that govern riverfront development here. So landscape architect Suzanne Richman chose to build her own stream.

Suzanne uncovered an existing irrigation ditch and reworked it to become a meandering stream that flows right next to the house. Highlighted with large boulders and small pebbles, flowering perennials, and recirculating water, the stream is punctuated with several pools, each treated as a feature in itself. The resulting woodland rill delights her clients, captures the changing qualities of light

## NOT SO BIG INSIDE OUT

Although this home is hardly Not So Big in scale and square footage, the site on which it sits is relatively small. The way the landscape has been crafted to give the impression of a woodland sanctuary is masterful, and it holds many lessons for those of us with smaller dwelling places. The numerous layers of structure, paths, streams, and plantings give the home a sense of both seclusion and expansiveness. It beautifully illustrates how an integrated approach to inside and outside design can give the impression of more territory than there really is. —Sarah

**V** Light cast through aspen leaves makes dappled shadows like a pointillist painting across the stream, creating the effect of a natural woodland.

in the reflections on the water, and has truly come to be their landscape of home.

## Entering the Realm

At its heart, the landscape of home should be thought of as a realm, a kingdom in the world, and as such, every corner is worthy of thoughtful design. On this property, it's clear from the beginning. Your first view of the striking Arts and Crafts style home comes as you drive down a cobbled lane. Aspen trees narrow the space alongside the drive, and a garden path beckons you under the arched roof of the entry porch. You pass by the first of the water features: a rocky pond occupied by a massive boulder that has been hollowed out to create a basin from which a tiny stream trickles.

On a long, thin site like this, spatial layering, or adding detail at various tiers, helps create a sense of depth along the property line. This third-of-an-acre site has two faces, with the west side speaking to the comfortably scaled east-end Aspen neighborhood and its older homes, and the east side addressing the neighbor's house and

**>** The posts of the wooden gazebo frame a view of the streambed as it circles around this conical form.

∧ Native cobbles on the driveway provide more than a handsome look; they transport us to a quaint and charming village. The architect chose to hide the garage on the north side of the house.

> Unusual jewellike inserts of glass under the porch rail form a counterpoint to the naturalized plantings along the watercourse.

## ALL AROUND THE HOUSE

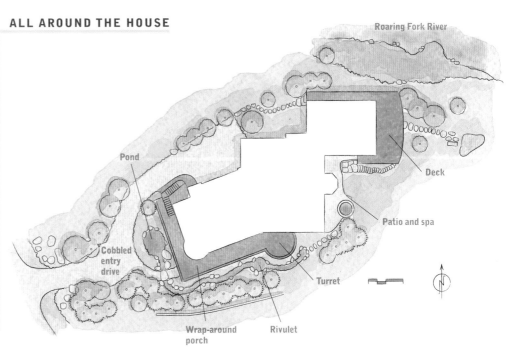

Roaring Fork River

Pond

Deck

Patio and spa

Cobbled entry drive

Turret

Wrap-around porch

Rivulet

∧ Skylights cut into the porch roof throw light onto the walking surface in rhythmic patterns. Notice that the same stone that forms the shores of the streambed appears in a foundation wall.

the river with its densely planted slope. At the top of the garden, Suzanne built 6-ft.-high walls and layered in aspen trees to screen the walls so that the close physical boundaries of the site vanish among the vertical layers of leafy vegetation. In front of the aspens, she planted billowing perennials that act as an informal shoreline for a narrow, rocky rivulet.

This little river, a smaller version of the Roaring Fork River, meanders alongside the formal porch with its long sandstone steps into the garden. From a schematic perspective, it's easy to see how these various garden elements add up to a series of parallel lines that move from the built edge of the house outward, becoming ever more natural until they reach the property line. These layers hide and reveal the narrow garden in front of the wall, making it feel more spacious than it actually is.

∧ Massive steps made from ledge rock provide an organic transition from house to site. Setting such large, flat stones often involves using shims, or thin wedge-shaped stones, which are tamped in underneath.

< A hot tub occupies another outdoor room, its walls made up of the same pieced stone as the foundation walls. A rounded boulder next to it serves as a pleasing perch.

## Creating a Focal Gathering Place

An unusual copper-covered turret room juts out into the garden to form a place to sit, acting as a terminus to both the porch and the streambed. This focal gathering place encourages viewers to step down to the streambed level, where plantings spill over the limestone tread and water. An outdoor away room, this spot frames views of a shady section of the garden and is kept bright by sunlight that pours forth through a small oculus in the roof.

Continuing around the garden, stepping stones take you to an intimate patio with a spa tucked into a stand of aspens and flanked by a round sitting rock. This leads to a large deck and a breakfast nook set in a bay window that overlooks the rushing river. A set of ledgerock steps leads you down to a streamside patio and the shore, where you can glimpse views of the mountainside beyond. Using the strategy of organizing your landscape's design around a nearby natural feature provides one satisfying way to relate your site to its surrounds.

THE LANDSCAPE OF HOME

### Echoing Nature

The best way to learn how to design an artificial stream is to study how Mother Nature does it. Find a nearby river or brook and take note of how rocks line the shores, where deposit and erosion occur to create bends in the streambed, and how sand and small stones build up to form islands. Be aware of how differently water moves in a deep versus a shallow channel, and notice how many types of waterfalls form along a natural watercourse.

When you are ready to create a brook in your own backyard, don't align your rocks like a string of pearls. Instead, intersperse rocks with patches of moss, ferns, or grasses to break up the stone shoreline; intermingle large boulders with smaller stones; or create small pockets just off the main flow where eddies can occur. By going to the source, you'll end up with a rock grouping, a pond, or a brook that feels like it's always been there.

—Julie

# outside

## [ parallels ]

### Archetypal Form

**ONE OF THE** most satisfying ways to create a seamless landscape design is to repeat an archetypal form in different guises. Landscape architect Suzanne Richman chose a circle, echoing the geometry used inside the house. You first encounter the circle underfoot, as you walk across a metal

grate that hides the mechanical system of the stream.

In the railings that protect the porch, jewellike spheres of glass dazzle the eye as light plays across them. In the away-room turret, the roof is circular, and the oculus—a circular opening— washes light across the interior copper shingles. These small but significant repeating forms act like signposts that carry you through the property and into the house.                 *–Julie*

HOMESCAPING

## Layering

Julie has described how layers of plant material, such as aspen trees, have been used around the edges of the property to create a secluded environment. But if you look closely, you'll discover that the same principle of layering has been applied throughout the design to create a gradation of interior to exterior places. One of the most obvious of these layers is the wraparound porch, which creates a covered outdoor realm in which to sit or stroll. Although it is outdoor space, it is a part of the house. Does that mean it is landscaping or architecture? It's both.

A seat in the living room provides a view through large windows defined by a distinctive pattern of muntins (the small dividers in each window). The pattern establishes the windows as a layer of see-through structure. And beyond this is the outdoor realm of the porch covered by the wide eaves above. The vegetation beyond this is the final layer in the gradient from inside to out.

The benefit of creating such layers is that while one space is only partially obscured from the next, each is clearly defined by its respective material, whether that be muntins, eaves, or plantings. Just as punctuation is used in a sentence to make it more comprehensible, layering allows your eyes to understand more easily what they are looking at, and it creates the perception that there is more to see. If you were to remove the muntins, lop off the eaves and porch, and remove the stream and the aspens, the property would actually seem much smaller and a lot less engaging.

—Sarah

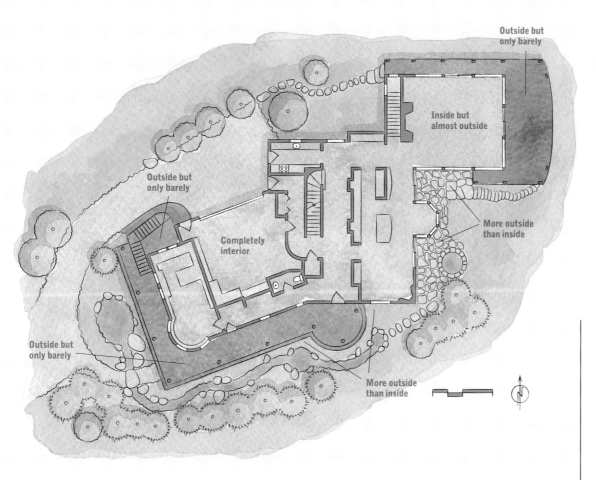

Outside but only barely

Inside but almost outside

Outside but only barely

More outside than inside

Completely interior

Outside but only barely

More outside than inside

## Archetypal Form

**THE EYEBROW** window that plays a dominant role from the outside has an equally essential role on the interior. After parking in the garage, the homeowners are welcomed inside by this view, giving them a glimpse of the living space. The wing wall seen to the left of the opening obscures the kitchen but allows the eye to take in the complete form of the eyebrow.

When you are using an archetypal form, it's not always necessary to use the entire form to establish a sense of connection to other parts of the house. Whereas outside the complete circle is used, inside the form is subtle, as in the eyebrow and in the second-floor balcony.

—Sarah

# Shelter and Embrace

When visitors first spot this Santa Fe, New Mexico, residence, it looks like a classic adobe structure in a neighborhood of similar homes baking in the brilliant desert sun. By ordinance, much of the area around the house was relandscaped to match the juniper savanna ecosystem that surrounds the site, asserting the natural dominance of the desert with its low rainfall, exposed and windy setting, and low-humus soils. But move closer to the house, and the differences between this property and those around it become apparent. The "choreography" of the entrance, or the sequence that visitors are meant to follow—the portals that protect, the walls that embrace, the interplay of light and shade, and the beauty of the setting—all contribute to what makes this a special place.

## NOT SO BIG INSIDE OUT

**In very flat** country, many houses look as though they've landed on their sites from outer space because there's little or no integration between house and site. This New Mexico home is, by contrast, beautifully integrated into the land, despite the challenges presented by its location. Julie and I love its connection to the terrain, as well as its sophisticated development of exterior and interior living places.     *—Sarah*

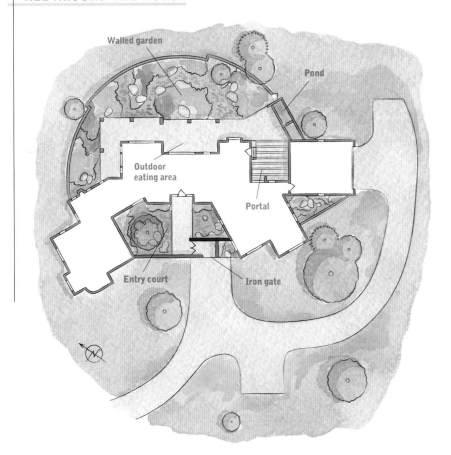

Walled garden

Pond

Outdoor
eating area

Portal

Entry court

Iron gate

∧ The low-slung house, reminiscent of a traditional
adobe, seems to grow right out of the desert landscape.
The swooping curve of the driveway reminds us of the
curved garden wall that embraces this home.

∧ Thick walls stand up to the harsh conditions. Once inside
the iron gates, visitors are greeted by a landscaped courtyard
that offers a more benign setting.

Move inside the walls of this residence, and you begin to
experience space as it unfolds in layers. From the guest parking
area, a pair of freestanding stucco walls reminiscent of traditional
adobe beckons. Like two arms reaching out, the walls are offset
from each other, creating an entry portal, a feature typical to south-
western architecture, two steps up from grade. Full-height openwork iron gates lead to an inner courtyard where a surprising thing
happens: What had been adobe-colored walls on the outside are a
deep and satisfying red stucco on the inside. This entry courtyard is
spare and open, with a single Russian olive tree, a few clumps of
ornamental grasses, and a sculpture of a cactus. A wide path bisects
the space, leading directly through a full-size door on pivots
into the center of the house. From here, there is a view through
the house and into a walled garden full of flowering perennials.

< The front door pivots inward to reveal a view clear through the house out to the garden and beyond. The unadorned opening is a solid version of the almost-frameless windows that adjoin it.

∧ Color has been subtly modulated in the entry courtyard. The rusty hues of a cactus sculpture are picked up in the far wall and contrast with the near wall, a deep vermilion.

## Portals that Protect

With its dramatic views to the surrounding mountain ranges, the native landscape is breathtaking. Here, outdoor living can be enjoyed throughout most of the year, especially when protected from the high-altitude sun and southwesterly winds. One way that the designers chose to set off the distant views from within the house was to use a porchlike transitional area between house and garden. This portal replaces traditional wooden porch posts with modern pillars clad in stucco. Their depth, combined with the heavy roof, shades the generous sliding glass doors. The portals help bring nature into the house and draw people into the garden.

∨ Good design often depends upon the deft use of transitional spaces, offering protection from the elements and opening to significant views and the intimate landscape. Here, a wide masonry post supports a deep beam to form the portal.

∧ Where the portal ends, the geometry of the terrace changes, creating a transitional path to the pond by the kitchen patio. The square frame of the window acts like a porthole in a ship, focusing the view from within while reflecting the sky.

## Embracing Walls

A curved courtyard wall gracefully encloses the garden on the northeast side of the house, creating a private space that harkens back to the architectural traditions of the Southwest. Inside, a brilliantly colored xeriscape—a landscape of plantings that need little water in order to survive—includes bold combinations of perennials and ornamental grasses arranged in naturalized drifts, with the occasional river-washed boulder placed as an accent in the rock mulch. Splashes of color, including the yellow black-eyed Susans and the mustard-colored walls, play off against the complementary lavender hues of the Russian sage.

The same light purple colors the outer wall by the kitchen, a mediating shade between water and sky. Water pours out from a metal channel into a long rectangular trough; the sounds and sight of the silvery liquid add a sensory accent to the outdoor eating area under the wooden pergola.

## Solid and Translucent

In the desert, solid walls surround a house to keep harsh light, wind, heat, and cold from penetrating within; they are punctured only when special sensory effects are desired. Here, the architect played the thickness of walls against the transparency of glass. The thick rim of stucco that borders the square kitchen window, for instance, turns the see-through glass into a framed picture. Seen from the outside, the picture becomes a mirror of walls and sky; from the inside, the glass becomes invisible, bringing the sunlit garden right into the dark, cool kitchen. Dramatic night lighting turns the house into a lantern, the interior contrasting effectively with the solidity of the building's walls and portals. In this harsh environment, the landscape of home thrives best within the shelter of embracing walls.

< The landscape was thoughtfully planted, with the soft curves of distant mountains repeated in the rounded shapes of the shrubs, grasses, and perennials.

### THE LANDSCAPE OF HOME

## Oasis in the Desert

In dry landscapes, the appearance of water can feel like a miracle. Here, this silvery elixir of life falls from the mouth of a simple metal scupper, its source unknown. This little rectangular pond turns this garden into an oasis—literally, a fertile ground in the desert where the existence of water allows plants to grow and travelers to replenish water supplies. For the homeowners, it brings visual, sensory, and thermal delight, with the lavender-blue walls adding a sense of calm.

Bringing water into our backyard landscapes always stimulates and soothes. We are captivated by the reflections of clouds on a still reflecting pool and mesmerized by the ripples of a bubbler. Jets enthrall by the upward thrust of their sprays, and waterfalls fascinate as they cascade into a waiting pool. Even the simplest birdbath offers hours of enjoyment, as birds chirp and flitter, enlivening our landscapes and our enjoyment of them.

—Julie

### Light Intensity Variation

**A PLACE** with intensely bright sunlight shows us how to use the contrast between light and shade to bring an extra dimension to our landscapes. On clear days, you can find four different light conditions in the garden. Unobstructed sunlight highlights and defines forms, such as this white rock.

Deep shadows caused by obstructions such as buildings, walls, or trees

provide thermal relief in desert climates. Broken light is the pattern of sunlight and shade created by light passing through objects such as latticework, trellises, or tree branches. Here, openwork beams cast diagonal stripes across an outdoor eating area. Dappled light through trees makes patches of light.　　　　*—Julie*

---

# Almost-Frameless Windows and Doors

One of my favorite techniques for blurring the boundary between inside and outside is to employ a technique that I call "almost-frameless windows and doors." By minimizing the frame of an opening in a wall, ideally stretching it all the way to each of the adjacent surfaces—the floor, the ceiling, and the sidewalls—our eyes are led to believe that there really is no window there at all.

In this home, you can readily see just how effective the technique is. Because the windows and door fill each opening, it appears that the space flows out into the courtyard beyond, unobstructed. The ribbonlike black frames all but disappear, making the inside and outside spaces seem like parts of a single whole.

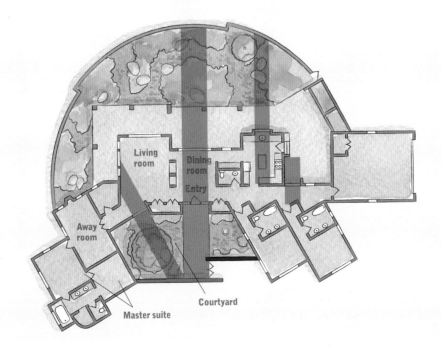

## Light Intensity Variation

**A HOUSE** that lets in a lot of sunlight in a hot climate can be extremely uncomfortable. But here, the architect has allowed only occasional brilliance amid a more measured approach to letting in the natural light. Notice the difference in light quality between the brightness of the bookshelves, lit from skylights above; the brilliant light entering through the small, unprotected square windows at the top of the room; and the more subtle daylight provided by the sliding door, protected from direct sunlight by the overhang above. There's even daylight reflected on the ceiling coming in from the glass door. In combination, these sources give a wide range of light intensities that make the space a delight to experience.     *—Sarah*

Another place you can use this effect is at kitchen countertops. By bringing the window all the way down to the countertop surface, so there's no backsplash, and by extending the side window all the way to the adjacent perpendicular wall surface, the window itself is played down, while the connection to the outside is played up. Once again, there is the illusion that you are completely connected with the exterior surroundings. Add even a small backsplash, however, and the experience disappears. It's the unobstructed flow of space that makes it work.     *—Sarah*

The way we perceive color is affected by many factors: time of day, latitude, altitude, season, and cultural conditioning, to name just a few (night lighting is an art in itself). Here, warm interior lighting filters through the glass sliders into the portals, where ceiling fixtures add a soft glow in the twilight.

| 1 | 2 | 3 |
|---|---|---|
| 4 | 5 | 6 |
| 7 | 8 | 9 |

**4** **In sunny climates,** it pays to use vivid colors in the landscape, since bright light tends to wash color out. From the cool shade cast by the broken light across the teak table and chairs, the lavender wall seems to match the sky.

**5** **Sandwiched between** the earth-tone garden wall and the muted interior, the brilliant purple Russian sage focuses the eye on the middle distance.

**6** **9** **Notice how,** in full sun, bright colors fade out but the detail of dark greens pops out. In full shade the opposite is true: Bright colors tend to stand out, and dark colors lose their detail.

**9** **Ornamental grasses** combine with just a few hardy perennials—Russian sage (*Perovskia atriplicifolia*) and black-eyed Susans (*Rudbeckia fulgida*)—to vivid effect.

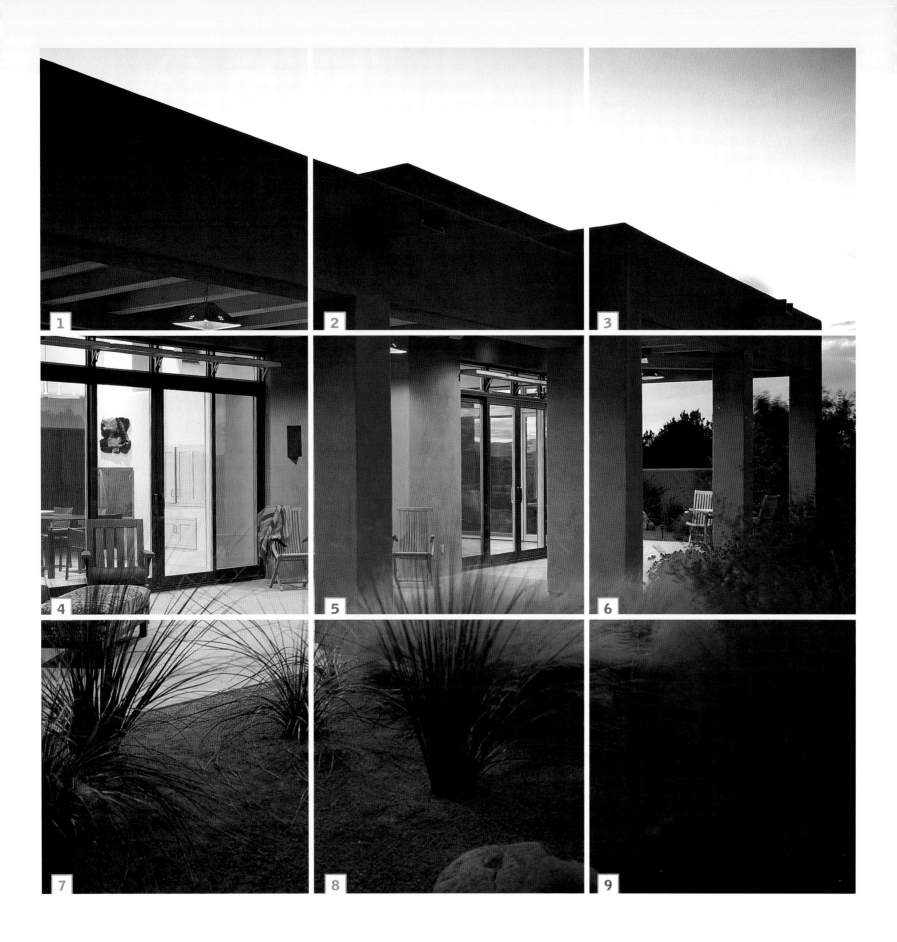

A threshold of cut bluestone pavers offers a pausing place along the stepping-stone path, where a gateway is adorned by clematis vines. The large, diamond-shaped stone signals this temporary stopping point.

# Variations on a Theme

The Fox residence is a tiny, seemingly modest property that is full of magic. People who visit this Berkeley, California, home are drawn from the unassuming front yard down a path along a side yard and into a secret garden in the back. Landscape architect Charles McCulloch choreographed the design of the property of his clients, Berkeley architect Dennis Fox and his gardener wife, Mary. Using one material—bluestone—in a variety of shapes, sizes, and finishes, McCulloch organized an elegant journey from street to backyard, with many horticultural pleasures and other special "events" along the way.

The neat front yard with its slate walk, lawn, and foundation plantings offers few clues about what lies beyond the gray stucco walls. The first surprise is that where one might expect to find the side driveway, a garden has been made. Here, stone is the theme.

## NOT SO BIG INSIDE OUT

Just because you have a small house and an equally small yard, it doesn't mean that you can't make a very beautiful and secluded haven. As you'll see in this California home, every space both inside and out has been designed to make the entire composition a delight. Woven together with an underlying geometrical order, it beautifully illustrates how the application of a few simple tricks can transform "too small" into "just right."                                          —Sarah

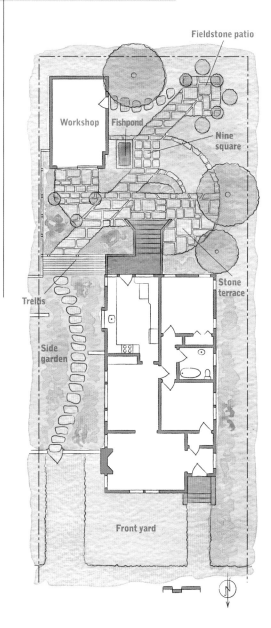

Fieldstone patio

Workshop    Fishpond

Nine square

Stone terrace

Trellis

Side garden

Front yard

> Flat fieldstones wander their way through this side garden—an elegant replacement for a former driveway.

∧ The sloping backyard of the Foxes' house has been terraced into three levels. The sophisticated path system moves visitors through the spaces to a terrace built for two at the bottom of the garden.

< A long gateway stretches from the railing of the upper deck across the entry to the backyard, forming an arbor that is covered in clematis and rose vines. The latticework on the deck continues as low fencing by the gate, allowing a glimpse through.

Low stone walls separate landscape from street, and flat fieldstone stepping stones meander their way through the plantings where the driveway once was. Tall trees give privacy and intensify the experience of the path by narrowing down the width and lengthening the spatial experience.

## A Gateway at Home

At the back corner of the house, a framed opening extends the wall of the house into the landscape, beckoning you to walk through to the secret garden beyond. But even as you are drawn to this clematis-covered gateway, a cut-stone threshold, what I call a "pausing place," makes you stop a moment before moving on (see the photo on p. 250). A square of bluestone, rotated so it looks like a diamond, occupies the middle of a small terrace of oblong stones, making it feel like a welcome mat. Here, we are introduced to a shape that will dominate the pathways in the Foxes' backyard garden. The diamonds continue as stepping stones along a diagonal axis into the backyard.

## Laying Down a Grid

As he planned the garden, Charles McCulloch divided the backyard schematically into nine large squares, then drew a diagonal pathway across this implied grid to create a long line of sight. He arranged distinctly different landscape elements within the three rows created by the grid (see p. 256). By the house, he designed a stone terrace that overlooks the garden, which acts as one of several destination points from which the garden can be viewed. Charles designed the second row of the grid as a panel or section

∨ Looking at the front yard of the Foxes' house, you would never know that beyond it lies a flowery paradise.

of grass terminating in a fishpond. The lowest terrace—the last section of the grid—sits at the back property line and is planted with various woodland plant species to screen the neighbors and add privacy. A small fieldstone patio nestles into the plantings, offering intimate seating and views back up the slope toward the house and garden. Combining this nine-square grid and the diagonal path is a master stroke that makes the tiny space feel larger by subtly organizing the space into parts that are linked by the strong linear journey through them.

∨ You can decorate the landscape just as you might your interior. This small pond contains fish and water lilies alongside creeping ground covers. The obelisk-like stone provides a strong vertical focus at the head of the pond.

< A pad made up of nine concrete squares acts as a terrace as well as an orienting device in this backyard landscape.

∧ Collections can form the backbone of your garden. Homeowner Mary Fox, a talented gardener, loves succulent plants. At the edge of the stone terrace, her collection spills out of planting areas built into the wall.

## Knuckles in the Landscape

What designers refer to as a "knuckle" is the place where things come together in a space: nodal points or pivot points where special events happen. Here, these knuckles occur at the intersections of the grid lines and the diagonal path. Plants, pavements, and the small pond were all placed within the grid or at significant intersections of grid lines and the diagonal path. The most obvious knuckle that draws the eye and gives order to the whole composition is the nine squares of paving that rest in the very middle of the garden space. These paving squares stand for the implied grid, which viewers never see, but intuit as an organizing device in this elegant landscape. The large square pavers are parallel to the woodshed and the house, and they move the visitor through the site and over to the far corner of the garden. Designing a knuckle that interconnects all the parts at once can be the trickiest part of a landscape to design, but it's also the most satisfying. It's like fitting the last piece of the jigsaw puzzle into place; the whole design suddenly pulls into focus.

### Intimate Immensity

Playing with the scale of the features in your landscape gives added visual interest. I find that objects that are tiny or huge in relation to me tend to hold my attention longer than something scaled to my size. Part of this enchantment lies in a paradox: When I look at the presidential faces on Mount Rushmore, am I petite or huge in relation to them? My body is much smaller, but my mind is immense as it rushes to examine President Roosevelt's face close up. When it comes to understanding scale, imagination may be more compelling than reality.

At the Fox residence, the small pool with its standing stones next to a fairy statue acts as a miniature landscape next to the nine overscaled paving stones. The owners planted these focal points with small-leafed perennials and placed miniature water lilies in the pool to preserve the sense of an intimate scale in this already tiny garden. On the terrace, Mary Fox, the gardener in the family, planted a collection of her favorite sedums, which add a delicate size and texture to a relatively large expanse of pavers.

—Julie

# outside
## p a r a l l e l s

### Pattern and Geometry

**USING REPEATING** patterns in a landscape helps make it intelligible to a viewer. The nine-square pattern that forms the focal point focuses your attention and organizes the space into components. The ironwork pattern of the stair railing—three rails and a space—is repeated in the rails of the fence at the back. As you look at the photo, notice how your eye follows the

pattern of dark verticals spaced in threes around the garden.

Mary Fox also uses container plantings on the stairs in a repeating pattern. These use the same textures and colors found in her sedum collection on the terrace. Using pattern to reveal underlying design themes brings a level of sophistication and coherence to your landscape. —*Julie*

## Organizing Strategy

In discussing the layout of the garden, Julie describes an imaginary grid over the entire backyard to give an underlying order—what I call an "organizing strategy"—to the design. Organizing strategies, while not always obvious to a home's inhabitants, can help give it a sense of balance and meaning.

The basic organizing strategy for this house is a simple rectangle, covered by an equally simple hipped roof with a front gable. Looking at the floor plan, you can see that there are no extra corners, bump-outs, or cantilevers, which would have added to the construction cost.

But just because it's simple in form doesn't mean it has to be boring. Often these constraints provide the catalysts for creativity. While in the back garden the nine-square pattern provides a point of focus, on the interior, the informal eating area is the focal gathering place. If you look closely again at the plan above, you'll see that the eating area is almost exactly at the center of the property. It's one of the most comfortable places to sit, and its placement, at the center of the land and at the boundary between inside and out, makes it feel like the most important and connected place in the house.

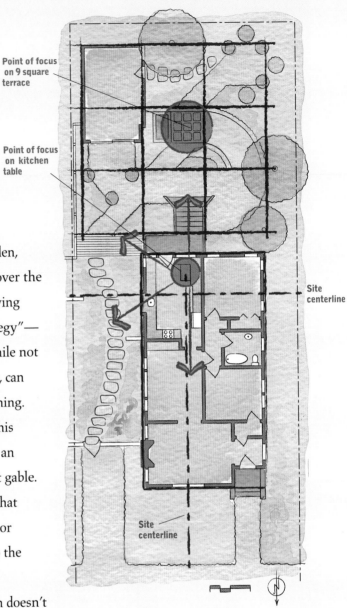

Point of focus on 9 square terrace

Point of focus on kitchen table

Site centerline

Site centerline

## Pattern and Geometry

**WHILE OUTSIDE** the house, the geometric pattern of nine square pavers attracts our attention; inside, the application of pattern is less noticeable. Yet the role it plays is very much the same. This home, like many older homes, has windows with dividers, or muntins, to break up the view. The muntins are a simple pattern overlaying the window. They give us something to look at in addition to seeing what's beyond. Although in modern houses this is less common, many homeowners enjoy the feeling of intimacy that muntins give to the interior. Smaller segments of anything create a more approachable scale. If they were to be removed, the house would lose its cozy feel. *—Sarah*

The eating-area window is aligned with the outdoor stairway leading down into the garden, which in turn is roughly aligned with the nine squares, so as you move through the house, from living room to dining room to kitchen, there's a strong axis, and a long view through the house, that's aligned with the pathway into the garden. Alignments like this can give a subliminal but powerful sense of order to a home.

The original house had double-hung windows with a six-over-six-pane and four-over-four-pane pattern, but in the remodel, architect Dennis Fox used casement windows with a four-pane pattern. He brought the windowsills all the way down to countertop height so that someone standing in the kitchen has more connection to the garden. *—Sarah*

This **Not So Big House** on a small lot is packed with opportunities to learn about good design. Inside and out, landscape and architecture are brought into harmony along the home's carefully crafted paths and places.

| | | |
|---|---|---|
| 1 | 2 | 3 |
| 4 | 5 | 6 |
| 7 | 8 | 9 |

**3** **This flower vase,** filled with roses from the garden, embellishes the corner window in the kitchen. Wherever you look, blooms bring the outside in.

**1** **Homeowner Mary Fox's** nosegays adorn different areas of the house, including a niche in the bathroom.

**9** **Mary's collection** of succulents is augmented by many species, including the genus *Sedum*, *Sempervivum*, and *Crassula*. The owners left small planting pockets in the stone steps leading to the middle terrace.

**6** **An Australian** plant called "Kangaroo paw" (*Anigozanthos* "Bush gold") adds a vivid hue as well as texture to a garden palette.

Two stones occupy a circular "pool" of gravel in my clients' front yard. Every inch of the raised ranch and its environs has been altered and improved.

# Japanese Journey

Drive past this renovated raised ranch in a Boston suburb, and you just may have to pull over and gape. The front yard has been turned into an otherworldly landscape—a verdant terraced garden centered around a circular "pool" of gravel. Two stones—one standing, another "floating" upon the gravel's surface—focus the eye. I designed this garden for the homeowners, who, to my good fortune, had a strong artistic bent. The garden forms the beginning of a landscape journey that encircles the house from front to back and feels like a geometric version of a Japanese garden.

Redesigned by architect Linda Hamlin, the house is now a glassy, open structure that allows views from the front yard through to the back. Double doors and casement windows open out to the front garden; floor-to-ceiling sliders extend the living room out onto the

## NOT SO BIG INSIDE OUT

This ordinary ranch house has been transformed into an evocative metaphorical landscape in which the views from inside, as well as the paths and places contained by the home's surroundings, connote a journey of wonder and delight. With gravel symbolizing water, stepping stones for islands, and a teahouse standing in for a foreign land, there's exploration and discovery possible with every glance and in every step.
*—Sarah*

back deck, obscuring the distinction between inside and out. Sitting above the street, the house lights up like a lantern at night.

## Geometric Japanese

At its most basic, the landscape outside a house should be like this one—a series of paths and places that owners can choreograph as a journey through space. Here, the garden journey is made up of a simple palette of bluestone squares and oblongs that travel over gravel, grass, and plantings to end up at a little teahouse on a hill in the backyard. While Japanese in spirit, the garden is designed using distinctly un-Japanese forms: circles, squares, and S-curves.

A path of cut bluestone takes you around the side of the house to the backyard, where large perimeter trees and an upward-facing slope create a bowllike feeling from the ground. To organize this space, I used a traditional Japanese technique called *karesansui* or "dry mountain river" style. Such gardens feel like an abstracted— and dry—version of a natural landscape, often including miniature hills, islands, and watercourses without water represented by raked patterns in gravel or sand. With this technique in mind, I created a large circular "pond" made up of chunks of gravel and placed a

∧ "Mouse-hole" entries like this low gateway increase the sense of anticipation about what's ahead on the landscape. Here, a pruned beech leads to a Japanese teahouse.

< Inside and outside converge at the living-room sliders that lead directly onto a wooden deck. An openwork trellis structure overhead is covered with vines in summer, adding a "ceiling" to this outdoor room.

**V** The owners altered every surface in the front yard, including their driveway, where they used square concrete pavers. Against this, a concrete retaining wall is softened with billowing Japanese juniper.

## Pools of Space

In keeping with the idea of creating a geometric Japanese-style garden, I designed a circular "pond" of gravel in the front yard and placed in it two large granite boulder "islands" hand-selected from a local quarry. Echoing the species, texture, and color of the white pines that edged the property, I brought in dwarf pines and Japanese juniper, making an abstract evergreen shoreline surrounding the pond.

Designing the open space of a landscape as a pool—whether of actual water or gravel, sand, or even plantings or turf—allows you to create a pleasing form in an otherwise amorphous landscape. A pool needs a clean edge for the shoreline, so it's important to use different materials, such as steel or wood on end, or create a line of cobbles, brick, or stone. The best way to make your pool look natural is to use

different-size stones and leave spaces for plantings, just as Mother Nature does. Also, I shy away from using plastic or other manmade materials as edgings, because they tend not to lose their sheen or develop a natural patina.

—Julie

**<** I organized the landscape as a journey from front to back, in to out, down to up, and closed to open. Here, the deck's stair railings lead eye and foot directly into the garden.

square of grass that seems to float like an island over the "watery" landscape.

Used at the time by the homeowner's young son as a play space, the square of grass lies at a 45-degree angle to the house. Its diagonal placement brings energy into the otherwise circular design of the backyard. On a slope at the upper corner of the garden, a wooden teahouse looks back onto the house, set almost perfectly parallel to the diagonal lawn. It is, of course, the destination point of this garden journey. Along the way, a path of thick bluestone stepping-stones takes visitors on a journey around the garden, with smaller squares designed for one step each and large squares set as pausing places. Here, there's room to plant both feet and let your eyes

∧ Using cut bluestone squares and oblongs of different sizes as path material, I linked the whole together as a design of stepping stones and raised stone "bridges," as pleasing to look at as it is to walk along.

∧ The lovely perennial known by its less lovely common name, Toad lily, accentuates the elegant structure of the garden.

< The teahouse peeks out over a hillside of mountain laurel, its diagonal placement chosen to give the longest view across the garden. Placed on a 45-degree angle to the house, it lines up with the square of grass.

> A "watercourse" cascades down the hill from under the teahouse to culminate in swaths of washed pea gravel, grass, mulch, and gray river stone just past low-growing bamboo that edges the "shoreline."

## ALL AROUND THE HOUSE

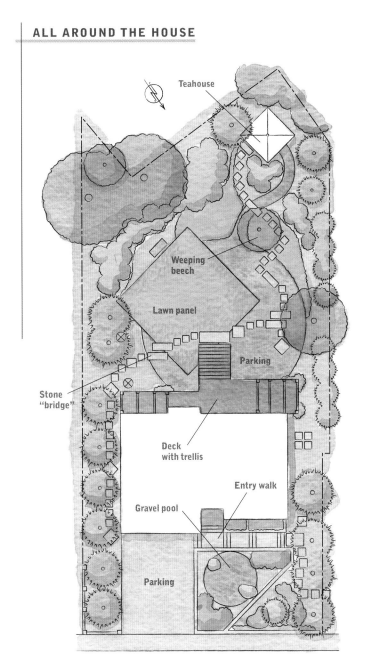

Teahouse

Weeping beech

Lawn panel

Parking

Stone "bridge"

Deck with trellis

Entry walk

Gravel pool

Parking

wander upward and into the garden. I also raised long slabs of bluestone up on foundations as "bridges" that allow a slightly higher vantage onto the garden.

Stepping-stones move through "water" and "shoreline," ducking under a gateway formed by the bough of a weeping beech tree, and finally wind their way up the hillside to the teahouse above. A "stream" of gravel pours down from under the teahouse to the pond in an elegant S-curve. At the top of the hill, you can finally stop and take stock of where you've been, retracing the path of your allegorical voyage through time and space. It helps to think of your landscape as a spatial journey through your property, linking different events along a continuously changing path. When you voyage forth into the nature of your own backyard, it's likely you will find yourself somewhere along the way.

# outside
### p a r a l l e l s

## Framed Openings

**IN THE NATURAL** landscape, you can find framed openings everywhere. Tree trunks act like upright borders, or a break in a hedge line serves as gateway. At this property I designed, framed openings abound. For example, the teahouse at the top of the hill is

structured so that one person or an intimate twosome can look out at the garden. A built-in bench nestles next to an alcove in a stucco wall. Wooden posts do double duty, supporting the roof structure as well as framing the views to the landscape below. Set into the sidewall, a circular window and two triangular clerestories bring the forest into the small building.

*—Julie*

## Openability

Although in this country we like to use the occasional sliding door to connect us to our surroundings, it's rare that we will use multiple sliding units "ganged" together, as in this home. The effect, when done well, is to minimize the boundary between inside and out and to allow passage to the out-of-doors wherever your heart desires. With the long platform deck that extends across its entire back face, the whole house feels like a screened porch—you're almost outside, no matter where you are. When the surroundings are beautiful, this can make the house seem much more engaging. You are borrowing the character of the outside to provide animated and colorful "wallpaper" for the home's interior.

If you are familiar with traditional Japanese architecture, you'll know that translucent shoji screens and solid sliding screens called *amado* substitute for solid exterior walls, so there's always a strong interconnection between inner and outer worlds. When the boundary is movable, it's easier to see that both in

and out are states of mind as much as they are locations. When interior and exterior are woven together as one in a home, the experience of the interior world feeds that of the outer world, and vice versa. I often think of interior space as simply a sheltered position from which to experience the outer world.

*—Sarah*

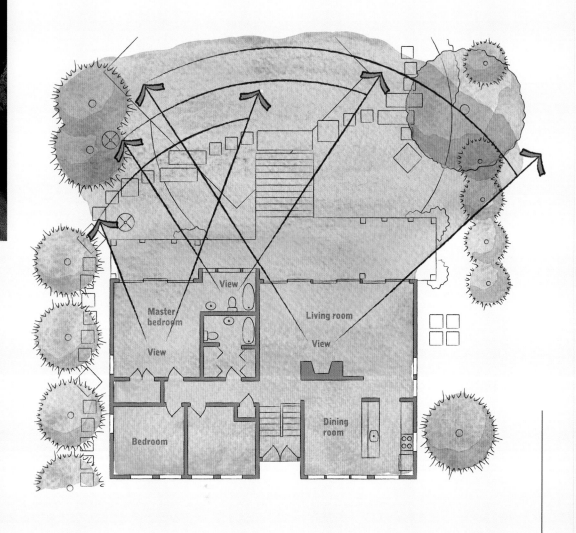

## Framed Openings

**A WIDE DOORWAY** or archway is a lot like a picture frame. With doors wide open, it literally frames the view beyond, drawing attention to it and making it a sort of canvas. It takes a designer's eye to recognize and work with a framed view, as Julie has here.

Notice that although the gravel "pool" is not centered on the framed opening, the boulder is. It becomes the point of focus from the front entryway out to the street. Imagine how much less inviting this view would be if there were only a front lawn beyond the retaining wall and the steps. There would be nothing to draw your attention outward, and the retaining wall itself would become the focus. *—Sarah*

This home is a study in the differentiation of materials and elements.
For example, the downspout, a special and separate form, becomes
a surprising point of focus on the façade.

# Parallel Paths

Architect George Suyama's dream was to design a house on his narrow beachfront property located in an old summer getaway community on the Puget Sound in Washington. On the site there existed two structures: a bunkhouse and a one-bedroom log cabin, which sit just steps from the beach. Designed to respect the fragile nature of the site, the minimalist house George built perches back up the hillside, standing in stark contrast to the older rustic cottages.

Built on a sliver of a lot, the house follows the grade from a high point at street level, moving down a full story as it makes its way toward the sound. The house is designed as two parallel journeys: one for people, the other for water. Entering the house from the street, visitors pass through a series of cast-concrete walls as they walk along a floor of polished concrete. To the right lies a

## NOT SO BIG INSIDE OUT

What struck Julie and me about this home is the amazing integration of indoor and outdoor spaces. So blended are they that the terms don't seem to make much sense here—a remarkable achievement on so small a piece of land with so small a house. Landscape and building are components in a singular sculpture for living in. It's truly a remarkable illustration of what *katei*, the all-encompassing Japanese term for "house and garden," can really mean.     —*Sarah*

> A watercourse brings movement into an otherwise static space. Hidden from the street by a cast-concrete wall, a channel is fed by a small weir—a dam that holds the source of the water.

Λ From the street, it's clear just how narrow waterfront properties can be. The house, buried behind the garage, is hidden from view.

watercourse that flows as a series of stepped terraces alongside the house. It begins as a small reservoir by the front door, turns into a long narrow canal that runs under a cantilevered wooden deck, and disappears for a time until it reemerges at the lower level of the house.

## Unadorned Details

On the left, along the implied corridor, lies a series of rooms—indoor and outdoor—that are protected by one long roof structure. The first is an outdoor living room centered

< Two cottages face the water while the Suyamas' new house gazes out from above.

on a hearth, providing warmth and visual delight to an otherwise austere space under a ceiling of open roof joists. You begin to read a particular design ethic in the crafting of each material, each connection, each detail. Walls are unadorned, posts rise from the simplest of bases, rafter tails are sawn straight, unchamfered.

## Stroll and Mind Journeys

What I term a "stroll journey" is a physical voyage you take on foot around a landscape; a "mind journey" is the mental voyage that occurs when your body is at rest and your mind is engaged by a scene, view, or focal point. Both journeys occur at the Suyamas' house. You take a stroll journey as you move past glass walls into the heated living area, entering the combined kitchen and dining room. The long, narrow nature of this space is emphasized by a series of lines: A bank of cabinets runs the length of the south wall, lit by a long, narrow window set over the sink. Across from the dining table that stretches down the middle of the room, a band of high windows encourages views of the tree canopy along the side of the property. As you

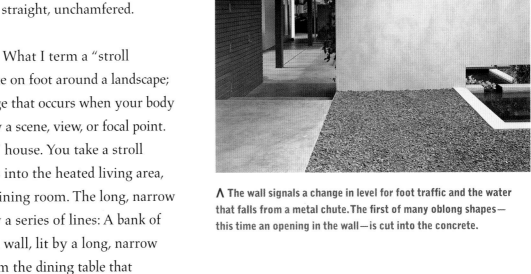

Λ The wall signals a change in level for foot traffic and the water that falls from a metal chute. The first of many oblong shapes— this time an opening in the wall—is cut into the concrete.

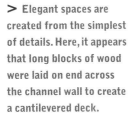

> Elegant spaces are created from the simplest of details. Here, it appears that long blocks of wood were laid on end across the channel wall to create a cantilevered deck.

Water
garden

Bedroom/bath

Watercourse

Puget
Sound

Wooden
deck

Outdoor
living room

Garage

Street

Roofed
balcony

Kitchen/dining

∨ This plant seems to dance in its pot, bringing a sense of movement and playfulness to the handsome vessel in which it is planted.

∧ Vertical shapes demand our attention, whereas long, horizontal shapes feel restful to the eye. Oblongs abound in the furniture, cabinetry, and decor of the entry terrace.

<Floor-to-ceiling windows are used as transparent walls that seem to disappear amid the weightier materials around them. This balcony space, with its potted Japanese maple bonsai, enjoys wonderful views.

∨ The location of the lights has been carefully calibrated to great effect. Candles march across the long dining table, spaced between dinner partners. Above, twinklers have been set between every other rafter.

move to the end of the room, toward the light and views of the sound, you leave the interior space to stand on a roofed balcony. You've reached a destination point of the stroll journey, what I call the "mind journey." Here your body is in repose while your mind is engaged with movement on the water, enjoying views of ferries, fishing vessels, and distant islands.

The journeys continue as you venture down a flight of stairs to the private realm of master bedroom and bath. Here, the watercourse reemerges as a sluiceway that cuts through a thick wall, pouring into a perimeter pool that borders two sides of the

∧ Water and light interweave in the master bath, half a floor below the street level. Tracks in the floor, wall, and ceiling allow glass doors to roll shut, providing shelter from the elements.

∧ Look through this concrete slot, and you will see the metal sluiceway that bridges entry pond and bathroom pool. A smooth stone sits just above the mouth, dividing the water enough to create patterns as it streams.

∨ A water garden forms the terminus for the watery journey. Here, floating leaf aquatics, like the water lilies pictured here (*Nymphaea spp.*) and lotus (*Nelumbo spp.*) usually have roots at a depth of 1 ft. to 3 ft. below the surface of the water.

∧ A basement window opens out to the water garden, reflecting the bamboo, ferns, and iris planted to soften the perimeter fence. The windows, walls, fences, and vegetation are carefully placed, making the narrow lot seem much more expansive.

bathroom. Once again, the boundaries between inside and outside almost completely disappear. Open to the sky, the narrow watercourse can be closed off by floor-to-ceiling glass sliders. As it moves through the bedroom, the watercourse again disappears, surfacing outside the walls of the house as a water garden before it circulates back to the start of the journey once more. This simple yet elegant home is crafted with an astonishing level of care. Outside dissolves into inside; stroll journeys parallel mind journeys; the whole is a habitable work of art.

## Animating Influences

Architect George Suyama's house is a study in careful control; everything seems exactly right. Yet in the deepest, most inward-looking place—the wine cellar in the basement—a surprise awaits: a pair of old glassy French doors, elements that are clearly not of George's fashioning. Japanese masters speak of creating something imperfect within the perfection of their gardens; these gates speak to memory and the surprise of the accidental in this otherwise immaculate environment. Their patina also recalls the beginning of the journey: the rustic cabins perched at water's edge, which predate the house itself.

Upstairs, in the kitchen/dining room, another surprise awaits the visitor, an element quite different from the otherwise perfect order and control. An antlerlike branch sprawls over the long dining table, its curves and rough edges disturbing the geometric perfection of the room. Without it, the room might feel too serious, self-conscious, even staid. Instead, it lives and breathes. The "accident" enlivens the whole.  —*Julie*

## Differentiation of Parts

**ARCHITECT GEORGE SUYAMA** crafted his home by clearly differentiating its parts. Each building element—wall, beam, sluiceway, roof edge—is made of a different material and treated separately. For example, where the gravel drip space abuts the wooden border of the flat roof (below), it lies separated by a metal edge.

Plantings here work in the same way. Bamboos, ground covers, and water plants are massed separately so you can see the color, texture, and form of each type of plant.   *—Julie*

# Blurring the Boundary

The aspect of this house that delights me the most is the ambiguousness of what's outside and what's inside. In previous chapters, I describe how almost-frameless windows can help to minimize the separation between interior and exterior, but this house takes this concept to a new level. For example, at this entry door, the wall all but disappears. It's made entirely of glass with the most minimal of frames abutting the rafters above. This transparency stands in stark contrast to the solidity of the adjacent stucco wall, which continues into the house on the other side of the door. In the same way, the sturdy beam supporting the roof structure above the courtyard continues

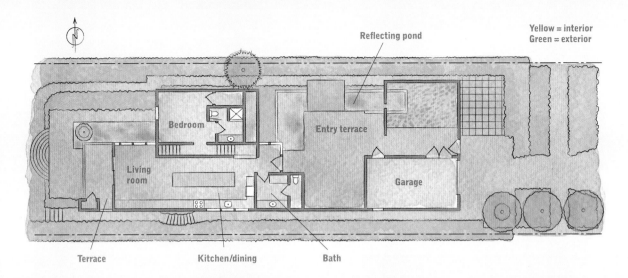

Reflecting pond

Yellow = interior
Green = exterior

Bedroom

Entry terrace

Living room

Garage

Terrace

Kitchen/dining

Bath

## Differentiation of Parts

**THE CONCEPT** of differentiation of parts in design is analogous to the type of fine cooking where each ingredient is separately prepared and displayed on the plate. Each element is strongly stated, but connected by placement rather than intermingling. The platform (below) is a separate plane, accessed by a separate folded black metal plate, a stairway. Even the railing is pulled away from the steps to differentiate it as a separate object.

Now look at the objects on the center table, and you'll see the same attitude applied to the accessories in the space. Each "part" sits serenely on another simple part that we call "table." The whole design, a perfect example of the differentiation of parts, is nearly archetypal in its simplicity. —*Sarah*

inside without interruption, supported by a simple post that also serves as the door jamb on both sides of the door. There's a complete blurring of the boundary that we would normally call the exterior wall.

Several other blurring mechanisms have been used by the architect to bring the outside in, like the water feature that runs through the house. Though each space is completely enclosed on each side by solid walls, there's always light from above, giving another reference to the outside.

In a tiny pocket garden off the master bathroom (left), the deep soaking

tub also serves as a pool that is visible from the bed. Natural light from the skylight above cascades down the wall. A reflecting wall surface like this makes an otherwise dark side of the house radiant and inviting.

All of these elements combine to create an environment for living that's so dramatically unlike our normal understanding of house and garden that it may not strike you as a house at all. But it's the essence of the Japanese term *katei*—wonderful architecture, wonderful landscaping, and in combination, a wonderful place to live. —*Sarah*

# The World behind the Walls

When they were married some 40 years ago, these homeowners bought a 1920s hunting lodge set on a wooded lot in a Boston suburb. Like so many structures of its day, the house, unfortunately, turned its back on its setting, here one overlooking a lovely pond. In 1995, inspired by the villas of Tuscany, the couple hired architect Abigail Campbell-King to open the house up to its view of the pond, add more space, create a sense of flow, and allow for entertaining with ease. She designed a garage with an office suite above and a new kitchen and dining room oriented to face the pond. As construction began on the addition, I was brought on board to design the landscape. Together, the owners and I worked to anchor the house to its site and knit its parts into a coherent whole.

## NOT SO BIG INSIDE OUT

So many homes sit on beautiful pieces of land, but neither the house nor the landscape is designed to take full advantage of the site's potential. That was the case with this home until the homeowners hired an architect and landscape designer—Julie—to help them reveal the beauty that lay hidden by walls and tree limbs. Today, the home is an extraordinary example of what's possible when designers collaborate to make the most of what's already there. *—Sarah*

> The couple added natural light to their new living space with a skylight. Here, the dining room feels brighter than the shady hemlock grove it looks upon.

∧ The focal point from the dining room is a serene pond where autumn colors reflect across its surface. This view is a surprise that can't be seen until one moves through to the back of the house.

Today, the couple's home feels as though it's bursting forth into the landscape through each of its many openings. Reoriented to face the water, windows cover every wall along its L-shaped perimeter on the pond side. The renovated kitchen and dining room nestle in the center of the addition, where a skylight illuminates an oblong banquet table. French doors open onto to a grove of hemlock trees that have been carefully pruned to allow views through to the water below. The many glass doors along the perimeter of the house allow the couple generous access to the outside—to walk along paths, entertain on the overlook, or sit at the breakfast terrace—or to feel connected to the outdoors by borrowing the views from their dining room-window wall.

## Overlooking the World

We are drawn to overlooks because they feel both exhilarating and dangerous. Here, I created three important overlooks: the threshold stones that look out on the pond from the kitchen/dining-room addition; the party terrace that looks across a sloping garden of ornamental grasses behind a semi-

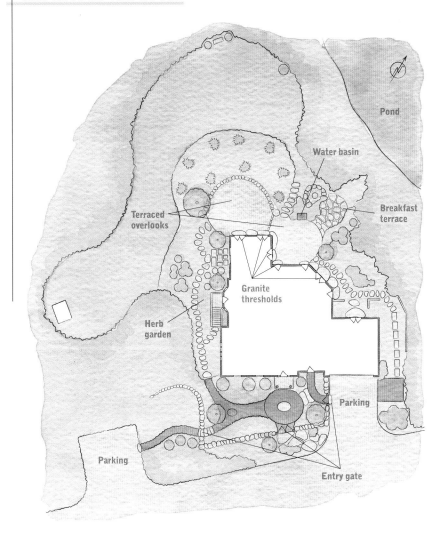

▼ A breakfast terrace of quarried granite stands poised above the pond that is spied through carefully pruned hemlock trees. Stone in many forms was used as the unifying material around this European-style home.

circular sitting wall of stone; and the breakfast nook that sits just above the pond, large enough for a teak table and two chairs. In order to lend a feeling of safety to a high overlook, it helps to create a parapet, or turned-up edge, like the sitting wall of stone we built at the terrace. The couple enjoys looking down from their high prospect, an important part of creating their particular landscape of home.

## ALL AROUND THE HOUSE

> Granite thresholds take the place of foundation plantings around the base of this home, acting as a step between building and landscape. Beyond, a terrace of bluestone set diagonally to the house unites the different outdoor spaces.

∧ Two water features are in view at the same time: the neighboring pond and a carved granite basin. The latter provides an architectural counterpoint to the rounded boulder that flanks it.

## On the Threshold

Large granite chunks act like mini overlooks at each entry. These thresholds sit a half foot above the garden level, rooting the house to the ground. Looking out from the den, your eye tumbles from the threshold of granite to the bluestone overlook, to the granite breakfast terrace, and to the softer pine needles, the shoreline, and finally the dark liquid expanse of pond. This waterfall effect is just one of the ways that the house and additions welcome the lush gardens and views.

< Large granite stepping stones lead through a garden of sensory pleasures: the owner's herb and cutting garden. Here, the south-facing slope offers a place for roses, Russian sage, oregano, rosemary, and even tomatoes to flourish.

Using one material in a variety of different shapes and forms brings coherence to a design, both inside and out. I used the granite thresholds to link indoor and outdoor spaces. The same threshold stone is also used as the paving stone for the breakfast nook, for all the landscape steps down the slope, and for stepping stones through the herb garden. A further variation combines granite with brick pavers in the front courtyard and granite with bluestone pavers on the party terrace.

## Embracing the Realm

The land is surrounded by masses of mature rhododendron bushes and giant hemlock trees, giving it privacy from the adjacent roads that border two sides of the site. To give them even more privacy, I decided to build walls around the front entrance to the house, hiding the beauty within. Walls cascade in curving steps along the roadway and around the corner of the driveway, bestowing a lyrical quality to the solid structure. Inside, I created an oval-shaped courtyard of brick and granite. An American dogwood tree graces the corner; its blossoms are replicated in the wrought-iron window carved into the high wooden entry gates. When you embrace your land, or realm, by enclosing it with a wall, fence, hedge, or plantings, it effectively makes a home feel private, secure, yours.

## THE LANDSCAPE OF HOME

### A Continuously Changing Path

Every successful garden journey links different events along a continuously changing path. Here, the spatial journey allows the house and garden to be revealed in sequence. Underfoot, brick becomes granite, granite becomes bluestone, and bluestone changes from a random rectangular pattern to a diagonal pattern as it modulates out from inside the house.

A granite "welcome mat" facing the entry vestibule forms the center of a series of concentric bands of brick radiating outward (see p. 285). At the end of the same courtyard, a circular pattern in brick marks the spot where three paths come together. One links this brick circle to the oval granite welcome mat. Another path leads off to an herb garden around the south side of the house, where the large granite chunks reappear, this time as stepping stones. The last guides you up some steps and through an arch of wrought iron that directs

you to the street. Paths, like gateways, can help guide us on our garden journeys, making sense of the landscape of home.    —Julie

# outside
## p a r a l l e l s

### Gateways

**A GATEWAY**, by its formality, materials, heights, and location can help visitors find their way. Here, three gateways stand out. The main gateway is an 8-ft.-high set of wooden doors with a curved top that echoes the curved steps in the wall. A wrought-iron window is carved out at eye level so visitors can look through and see the front vestibule, which is on axis with the centerline of the gate. A shorter antique iron

gate swings open from the driveway—the "back door" entry off the main courtyard. The third—an old wrought-iron archway—links the overflow parking area with the front entry court. —*Julie*

## Psychological Breathing Space

Have you ever noticed how awkward the transitions between inside and outside are in most houses? There's typically a poorly designed step, ranging from 3 in. to 8 in. in height, and there's no thought given to the experience of moving from inside to out. Just as with the process of entering, where a "receiving place" is desirable to allow a shift of personality from public to private self, the same is true as we move out into the landscape. We need a place to stand for a moment and appreciate the qualities of this new realm we're moving into. Such a place provides us a "psychological breathing space."

The large slabs of granite at each doorway provide delightful breathing spaces, almost like miniature balconies, from which to survey the garden before committing to exploring it further. Their uneven shape associates them strongly with the natural world beyond the walls of the house, but their broad, flat surfaces invite people to move easily from inside to outside realms and back again. Collectively, they also provide a base for the entire addition, grounding it and giving it an organic, natural feel, as though the house were built on bedrock.

In a similar way, at the front entry, there's a palpable sense that you are entering a special place as you step through the gate connecting inner and outer worlds—street on one side, inner courtyard on the other. Directly aligned with

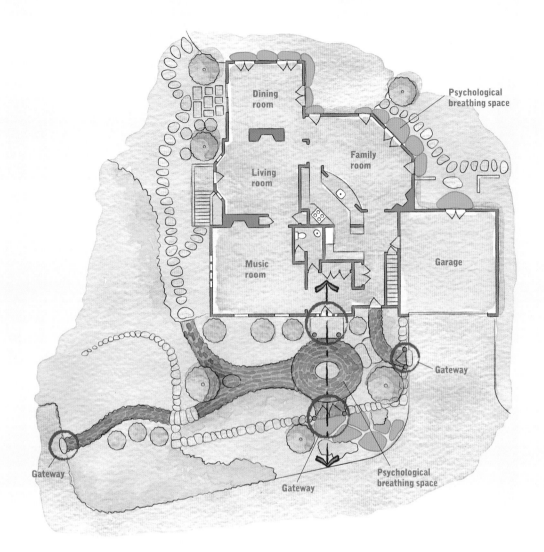

Dining room

Living room

Music room

Family room

Garage

Psychological breathing space

Gateway

Gateway

Gateway

Psychological breathing space

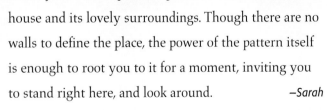

the front door, one's gaze is drawn inevitably to the granite circle ahead, surrounded by its radiating crown of brick. The entire composition centers and grounds you, and, as a visitor, you can't help but stop here and take note of the house and its lovely surroundings. Though there are no walls to define the place, the power of the pattern itself is enough to root you to it for a moment, inviting you to stand right here, and look around.   —*Sarah*

# inside
## parallels

### Gateways

**A DOORWAY** or framed opening is the interior equivalent of a gateway, and just like its exterior counterpart, it designates and celebrates the transition between one place and the next. The front doorway is the most important gateway of all because it provides the primary point of access between inside and outside realms.

In this home, the front door, with its flanking sidelights and covered stoop, is aligned with the front gateway at the entrance to the property,

so the sense of entering is accentuated and made a little more formal. On departure, the alignment draws attention to the entry to the outer world. In conjunction, the two gateways heighten the powerful experiences of coming and going.   —*Sarah*

**A**n openwork wrought-iron gateway breaks the solidity of the handsome granite walls around the house. Beyond, the path is windy, narrow, and more informally planted than the entry that sits a few steps above it. These clues all indicate which door to go to: friends and family to this casual "back door," and newcomers to the front gate.

|   |   |   |
|---|---|---|
| 1 | 2 | 3 |
| 4 | 5 | 6 |
| 7 | 8 | 9 |

**5** **By creating a pivot point** at their center, these three paths were brought together in a subtle but recognizable way. This circle of bricks acts as a point of decision, no matter from which way you come.

**4** **These superbly crafted** granite walls were built by an Italian stonemason to match an older existing wall nearby. An orange-berried scarlet fire thorn (*Pyracantha coccinea*) has been espaliered, or trained, to grow flat against this upright wall, enlivening it and giving the entry court a European feel.

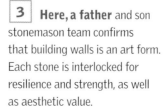

**3** **Here, a father** and son stonemason team confirms that building walls is an art form. Each stone is interlocked for resilience and strength, as well as aesthetic value.

287

Designed to extend the presence of the house into the landscape, this deck seems to float above the lawn. Even the vines look like they're barely touching the nearly invisible wire fence that supports them.

# Living Lightly on the Land

If there were a corollary to "Not So Big" in landscape design, it would be what I call "living lightly on the land." This principle can be translated as design in several ways: You can downsize the amount of space you use for living and gardening, use sustainable materials and techniques, or design with an eye for economy and simplicity. Architects John Maier and Ulrike Zelter chose to live lightly in their 1,300-sq.-ft. duplex in Austin, Texas, taking a 1950s house with a big yard and creating a home that is small, simple, and sustainable.

Built in an area of cottages and bungalows, this modest home contains two living units. Originally, a path led to a centered, gabled stoop that provided shared entry. This bisected lawn seemed meager to the new owners, who decided their tenants should have the front yard for their use. The couple then built a generous porch along the

## NOT SO BIG **INSIDE OUT**

**This house** is a great example of using a simple, limited, and inexpensive palette of materials to accomplish a sense of serenity and delight without having a lot of space inside or out. Like several of the houses in this book, it's no accident that this is an architect couple's own home. They know the value of good design and understand how to implement it to maximum effect.　　　　　　　　　*–Sarah*

front of the house that was shifted toward the tenants' unit. The front walk remained aligned in the center. This overcame the "duplex symmetry" of the house, giving it a more homelike appearance. It also gave the rental unit another 200 sq. ft. of living space. Large concrete slabs, lined up with the side-by-side front doors, provide a playful front walk for both units. The whole is as carefully composed as a Japanese garden, but created out of modern materials.

## Back to the Front
Choosing to locate their entry at the rear of the site gave the architects privacy from their tenants and neighbors, an expanded backyard, and immediate access to their carport. Desiring more connection between inside and outside, they located two pairs of glass sliding doors that open out onto an ipé deck. Echoing the planter box detail that they used in the front, the couple built two steel boxes that terrace down from the deck onto a lawn bounded by a wide strip of knippa stone—a local gravel. The simplicity of these materials brings presence and design clarity to the form of the house.

∧ Two doors greet visitors as they pick their way up the front walk of concrete slabs. The very first pavers indicate by their placement that two families live there.

< At first glance (far left), the front yard looks like others nearby, but closer inspection reveals a thoughtfully designed juxtaposition of materials. This couple peeled back the lawn to expose a sidewalk of gravel and composed their welcome path of sidewalk-size slabs of concrete. A closer look reveals a sheltered retreat: Red canvas butterfly chairs sit on the front deck (left), which is covered by a corrugated roof and supported by the slimmest of columns bringing a tropical flavor to this comfy hangout.

> **This architect couple designed their home to reflect their desire for economy and sustainability. The carport/workshop roof floats with only the barest of supports, and a wide wooden wall moves on rollers across a track.**

## ALL AROUND THE HOUSE

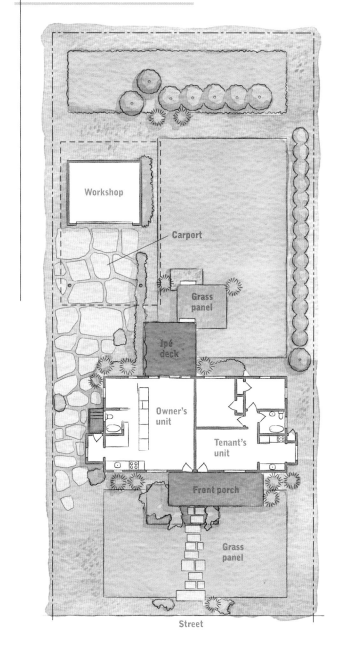

Workshop

Carport

Grass panel

Ipé deck

Owner's unit

Tenant's unit

Front porch

Grass panel

Street

## Privacy Without Walls

While constructing masonry walls or high fences at the property line gives a feeling of seclusion and privacy from nearby neighbors, you can create a similar feeling of sanctuary by the use of screens, borders, and buildings. At the edges of their gravel border, John and Ulrike planted tall evergreens to give privacy to the yard without having to build a fence. Enclosed by steel mesh panels, the workshop is further integrated into the garden by allowing the panels to rust and covering them with passionflower vine. A similar screen is used to give privacy at the back deck, where evergreen clematis grows on horizontal wires that allow air and light through.

## Inside Out

The owners designed their unit from the inside out. They wanted a more spacious living area with better light and a stronger connection to their backyard landscape. So they removed all the walls except those surrounding the bathroom and divided the living areas with large, multifunctional cabinets. They also chose to repeat certain colors throughout: spring green walls that echo the grass and plantings outside, complemented by a rich red that washes walls and door frames and is found outside on the canvas seats of the butterfly chairs.

< The design vocabulary inside is consistent with the outside. An interior door, painted red, seems to float in space with no obvious hinges attaching it to a frame.

The couple's choice to live lightly on the land is supported by design details that create the sensation of levity. Each different material or element seems to float separately in space. As seen from the back corner of the property, the lawn floats next to a plane of gravel bounded by steel edging. The carport roof floats out over the lawn, seemingly supported by only the slimmest of steel columns. A grass panel floats above the lawn, edged by a band of black wood to form a turf step down into the landscape. A single rectangle of concrete—the first step off the cantilevered deck—seems to float upon the grass panel. This home shows just how one might execute a sustainable, economical design that's also a thing of beauty.

< Everything in its place: A picnic area at the rear of the property offers a long view across the lawn to the house.

## Recycling Materials

The Maier-Zelter home demonstrates ways that house and landscape design can be elegant and sustainable. The couple sought to reuse existing materials wherever possible. They built with refurbished steel casement windows and cedar sidewall shakes, and they constructed a new table and benches from Douglas fir framing material. Outside, they cut concrete walkways that surrounded the house into tile-size chunks for stepping-stones. From the badly fissured concrete driveway, they created a new oversize "cracked ice" patterned driveway that lies in a bed of knippa stone and plants.

Landscape designer Jon Ahrens and the owners also chose to create a low-maintenance garden using xeriscaping principles, which involve creating sustainable landscapes that conserve water and protect the environment. In urban areas of Texas, about a quarter of the water supply is used for landscape and garden watering. Good planning and design, careful soil analysis, limiting turf areas or using drought-tolerant grasses that don't need irrigation, along with appropriate plant selection, efficient irrigation, use of mulches to hold in moisture, and appropriate maintenance, all help preserve water in arid states.

—*Julie*

∧ The raised panel of grass projects above the lawn and connects the deck to the backyard. A third raised rectangle is seen in the roof of the carport/workshop, completing the composition.

# outside
## parallels

### Floating Objects

**IN THIS HOME,** each material—metal, wood, concrete, plant, or grass—looks as though it is floating or weightless, hovering above the surfaces around it. At the owner's entrance, a metal roof floats above the walls, its structure invisible from the garden. Below, the ipé deck drifts above the ground plane, seemingly attached only at the house and cantilevered far into the garden

space. Two poured concrete slabs, their white color standing in stark contrast to the dark stain of the deck and steel planter adjacent to them, seem to hang above the grass and gravel plinths on which they sit. Even the planters, separated from other materials by color, texture, and edging of steel, seem to float above the lawn panel. —*Julie*

## Doing Double Duty

**D**ouble-duty function is at the core of what makes this home work so well with such limited spatial resources. Julie has described how the carport not only provides a place to shelter the cars from the elements, but also helps enclose the garden, protecting it from neighboring properties and even from a view to the cars themselves. This is a perfect example of one element doing double duty.

So, too, is the front porch design. It does double duty by creating a sense of entry for the house as a whole while quietly offering the tenants of the second unit a bit more space to call their own. Had the design of this porch been considered only as a shelter for the entry doors themselves, there'd be no double duty. It's the extension of the porch in front of the tenants' living-room picture window that makes it work. This is clearly their territory, and not that of the primary unit.

On the interior of the house, you see the same attitude brought to bear in the design of the pod of space described at right. When the doors are closed, it looks like a piece of boldly colored furniture. But when it's open, it adds alcoves of activity space that you don't always want to have visible, but which are very

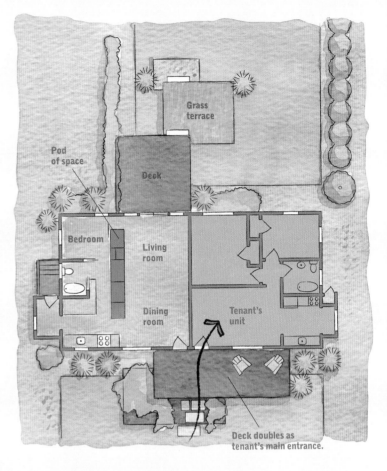

Grass terrace

Pod of space

Deck

Bedroom

Living room

Dining room

Tenant's unit

Deck doubles as tenant's main entrance.

## Floating Objects

**INSIDE A HOME,** you can use "floating objects" to make a space look significantly bigger than it is. Instead of separating rooms with walls that extend to the ceiling, you can create what I call a "pod of space"—an object that contains storage, or a small activity place or utility area. If you look at the floor plan on the facing page, you'll see that instead of a dividing wall between the bathroom and the living area, the couple has employed a pod of space for storage. The ceiling plane extends over top of the pod and beyond the edge of the "room." Your senses perceive that the room you're in is larger than it actually is. The same effect is accentuated by the sides of the pod, which is finished to resemble furniture, rather than a wall.                    —*Sarah*

much needed in a house of this size. In addition to its room-dividing functions, it is also chock full of creative storage. With the sliding panels open, the living area now includes a desk space, the dining table serving as extra layout area. Also hidden behind the sliding doors is storage for stereo equipment and CDs, as well as bedroom closet space, which is accessed from the other side of the pod.

—*Sarah*

Extending the presence of home into the out-of-doors allows us to witness the elements without actual contact. On still summer evenings, any movement of the air, enjoyed from the back-and-forth rhythm of a rocking chair or porch swing, is refreshing.

# Easy Living

Down South, people just know how to live out-of-doors. To take advantage of a warm and humid climate, they have created a network of indoor-outdoor places for enjoying their family, their neighbors, and their environment. Porches, screened rooms, arbors, and formal gardens are among these spaces— attached to the house yet part of the landscape. They are transitional places that combine home with garden and encourage privacy or sociability, depending upon one's mood.

Husband-and-wife designers Ken Troupe and Cally Heppner got the mood just right on their property in Beaufort, South Carolina. Sitting out on their covered front porch on a sultry summer evening, the couple can stir up a breeze in their side-by-side rockers or on their hanging porch swing. From their perch 4 ft. above the street, they can nestle back against the house or call out

## NOT SO BIG INSIDE OUT

This house exhibits such a beautiful integration of landscape and building, with the two aspects interconnecting throughout the property, that Julie and I instantly knew it belonged in this book. Its parts extend out into the site, where plantings grow abundantly over and through them to create a sense of cloistered sanctuary—proof that you don't need acres to attain a sense of seclusion. —*Sarah*

< When the source for this charming bronze statue is turned off, the central water feature becomes a reflecting pool, complete with water lilies floating on the surface.

to a neighbor passing by—it's a perfect vantage point that offers both prospect and refuge at the same time. The porch also acts as an outdoor entry vestibule. It's the place where a visitor might dust him- or herself off before knocking. Secluded and secure, it is a special transitional space that makes occupants—whether inhabitants or visitors—feel completely comfortable.

## ALL AROUND THE HOUSE

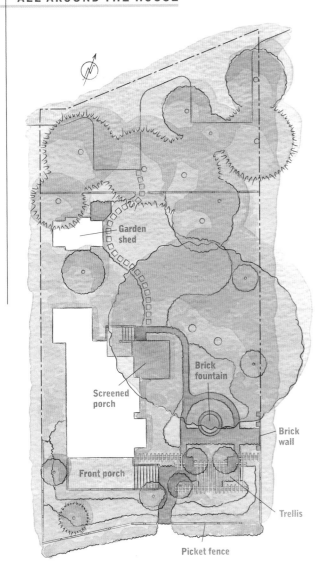

Garden shed

Brick fountain

Screened porch

Brick wall

Front porch

Trellis

Picket fence

## Serene on the Side

Another porch, this one screened, wraps the side and back of the house and fronts on the formal side garden. Designed to extend an insect-free indoor-outdoor living space into the landscape, this screened room adds a special dimension to everyday life. The high-gabled roof and ganged window screens veil and soften the eastern morning light. Jutting out into the landscape like a dock over water, the screened porch, along with a pair of towering live oaks, serves to break down the side garden into two parts.

A formal garden, complete with circular brick fountain and semicircular matching path, occupies the side yard. Its strong geometries focus the eye, creating a literal center with a dynamic focal point—a fountain of water that occupies the center of the brick pool. Traditional southern plantings like boxwood trees, azaleas, and dogwood trees soften the edges of this landscaped outdoor room.

< The couple chose their lot for the two majestic live oak trees that shade the whole backyard.

< Here you can see how to literally extend the presence of home by building a framework of trellising and screens as part of your landscape.

< *Verbena canadensis* "Homestead Purple" sews itself freely in front of the picket fence along the lane. Behind the fence, confederate jasmine vine blooms white to form a dense hedge.

## Screening Out the Public

Since the house is located within yards of two public streets, privacy is a major concern. A sense of separation between the public space of the sidewalk and the private yard has been created with a 4-ft.-high picket fence. Dense plantings on each side of it add another layer of screening at the base of the house.

To wonderful effect, the owners carefully echoed details, colors, and forms throughout their property. For instance, the pickets in the fence are repeated in the railings that encircle both porches. A tall, carefully pruned pine tree creates privacy on the second-floor porch, playing up the contrast between the stark white building and the soft green plantings that surround it. A decorative trellised gateway and picket fence provide privacy for the back yard, and a brick wall and another fence along the side property line define and enclose the low-maintenance courtyard. With so many delightful sitting places to choose from, this study in gracious Southern living is a place for all to emulate.

< In this neotraditional community, architectural and planning review boards determined that the lots should be small and the façades close to the street to create a close-knit community.

## Open Enclosures

When you reside in a neighborhood setting, it's hard to feel good about walling yourself off from others. Cally Heppner and Ken Troupe used what I call "open enclosures" as a means of screening but not separating themselves from view.

Along the street edge, they erected a hall-like wooden post-and-beam structure on which vines grow, and they fastened openwork trellis panels between columns to screen out the street. The couple left out panels to either side of the central trellis, creating windows into the garden. This composition keeps the sense of neighborliness while firmly defining private from public space.

Cally and Ken also erected handsome piers and in-filled them with a high solid wall flanked by lower openwork screens, all made of the same brick used for the fountain. This solid-open-solid pattern echoes the wooden trellis structures along the street edge, offering privacy yet allowing controlled views in.

*—Julie*

< **Furthering the traditional feeling of this neighborhood is the rear laneway, which means that cars are kept in back. Here, the couple screens the driveway area with a charming trellised gateway and picket fencing.**

# outside

## parallels

### Moving Toward the Light

**OUTSIDE YOUR HOUSE,** you can use plantings and built form to lead eye and foot along a path from darkness toward light—a wonderful way of drawing people through a space. Here, Cally and Ken built a pergola that feels private despite its location next to the street and sidewalk.

The long, linear trellis creates a hall-like enclosure to bring privacy to the

side-yard garden. The structure's roof makes a crosshatched shadow on the brick floor. A panel of wooden trellising also creates dappled light and air circulation in this "hallway." At its terminus, the structure is open to the sky and to the street, allowing shafts of light to lead you forward to enjoy the plantings that mark the destination. *—Julie*

## Sequence of Places

Whenever I'm designing a house, I like to think of it not as a set of rooms, but as a sequence of places for the activities of daily life. When I first sit down with clients, I'll ask them to describe for me their mornings, daylight hours, and evenings. This helps to liberate us from the limitations that come with individual room names. A dining room doesn't always have to be for dining, for example. The same thing holds true when designing the garden areas. It's better to use activity descriptions to start with, and label each place as a "porch" or "deck" after that. I can imagine, in planning this home, that the designer couple made something akin to the following list:

Place to sit outside in the evenings and look out over the street—possibly with the ability to talk with passersby. (This function served by the front porch; A.)

Place that's private, shaded, and free of bugs, where we can go to eat or have a drink—needs to be close to kitchen, and should have a secluded view to the garden. (This function served by the screened porch; B.)

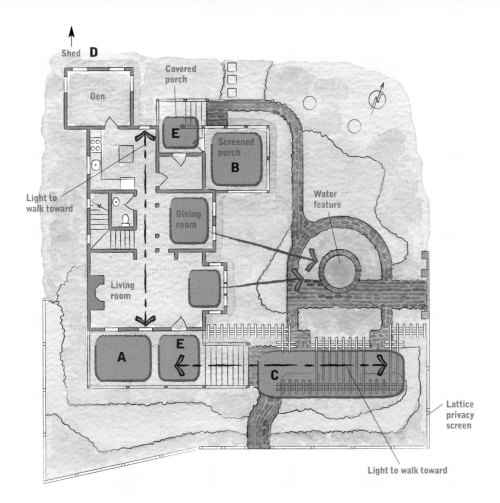

### Light to Walk Toward

**IT'S IMPORTANT** to compose the views connecting activity places so that they will draw you through from one room to the next, engage you. It's clear that at either end of this hallway is a window. Notice how the brightness of the glass area beckons you into the living room, its light reflecting off the hardwood floor, providing a cheerful glow to the room. Remove the window, however, and you have nothing to draw you toward the room.                —*Sarah*

Shaded pathway for strolling in the garden. (This function served by the entry arbor and brick walkways; C.)

Place for storing garden equipment and tools that doesn't shriek "garden shed" when you look at it. (This function served by the shed; D.)

Welcoming entries that are covered from above so those entering have protection from rain. (This function served by the front and rear entry porches; E.)

This list can then be turned into a sequence of outdoor places that are natural extensions of their indoor counterparts.                —*Sarah*

This spacious terrace is the perfect extension of the home. With ample places to relax, vivid plantings that add beauty and privacy, and the gentle bubbling of the garden pool, this area is transformed into a small paradise.

# Good Fences

"Good fences make good neighbors"—at this home near Washington, D.C., the old adage certainly holds true. Every inch of the back and side yards has been thoughtfully enclosed, either with walls, fencing, or hedging, to create a series of private outdoor rooms for the family who lives there. These rooms literally bring the inside out into the fresh air and under the stars, offering the family a completely different living experience. Outside, they can grill, dine, entertain, read the paper, and even sunbathe with abandon, since they are secluded by perimeter hedges and fences. In fact, it's a little like a having a summer home attached to your primary residence.

Located on the corner of a busy pedestrian route to the nearby subway station, the house at first glance looks much like other homes built on quarter-acre lots in this leafy Maryland suburb.

## NOT SO BIG INSIDE OUT

The home you see here presents the same kinds of challenges that face most homeowners in the inner-ring suburbs: A site that isn't very big, neighbors close at hand, and streets flanking two sides, making privacy both important and difficult to attain. What struck both of us about this property is its simple and effective approach to "room making" beyond the boundaries of the house to create places for everyday living. *—Sarah*

∧ Adding a touch of whimsy in a planter by the front door can soften the hardness of the handsome stone wall and steps.

∧ A massive shade tree stands tall over a row of evergreens adding a high privacy screen above the board fence and shielding the entertainment terrace from the street. For people who live on corner lots or busy streets, this level of privacy is essential.

∨ A narrow stepping-stone path suggests an alternative route from the front door to the entertainment terrace, one that winds between trees and through shade-loving ground covers to open, sunny lawn.

Trees shade the street, a handsome magnolia protects the front door, and lawn sweeps up to plantings of shrubs and evergreen ground covers that hide the foundation of the house. But the difference is in the details. Just off the front walk, a stepping-stone path meanders through carefully edged beds of Lenten rose, foamflower, and pachysandra, weaving past stands of birches like a stream that winds through natural woodland, luring visitors in.

Along the way, the path changes from natural fieldstone to square-cut bluestone, heralding the paving material of the terrace that forms the first of a series of outdoor rooms encircling the sides and back of the house. The path continues through an open gateway at the center of a 4-ft.-high wooden fence, offering passersby a glimpse of the realm within. Terminating three steps up, it widens into a large outdoor space for family entertainment.

## The World Behind the Wall

When seen from the street, the entertainment terrace is almost completely hidden from view. The fanlike form of a mature tree casts high and wide to bring upper-story privacy. Below it, a tall hedge of evergreens adds

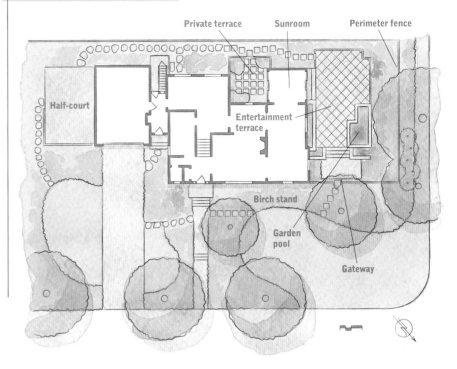

another level of screening between the tree's branching structure and a 6-ft. board fence that encloses the back and side yards of the property. Inside is a space large enough to hold a small party tent. Set apart physically and psychically, this world behind the wall becomes a kind of safe zone for the family. The sense of seclusion is further bolstered by a lovely garden pool, built at the corner of the terrace that houses a bubbler, fish, and water lilies.

Designed by landscape architect Sandra Clinton, the terrace is a study in the elegant details that make an enclosed space feel larger than it really is. Every square inch holds value; every corner is revealed. The middle becomes a place for dining and socializing, and the background stays respectfully behind the fence.

## Rooms Inside and Out  The rooms inside the house are just as carefully designed to relate to the living spaces outside as the outside rooms relate to the interior. Architect Winn Faulkner worked with the family to create an

∧ The path crosses through a sea of perennial foamflower in bloom, moves through a wooden gateway, and ascends to the terrace. Here, shade gives way to sun; low becomes high; narrow becomes broad.

< A triangular clerestory window above the doors brings the outside into this congenial sunroom. If it were closed in as a wall, the room would feel far smaller, darker, and less open to its environs.

V This picture window becomes a central focal point of the living room with its divided panes of glass breaking up the attractive view beyond into smaller fragments, each more interesting than the next.

∧ The narrow passageway between house and lot line beckons visitors to follow, thanks to a slight bend along the way. A deviation like this curve can make all the difference between the unexpected and the predictable.

addition on the side of the house that fronts onto the entertainment terrace. Two small *tempietti*—little templelike rooms with high gabled windows—form matching bookends to a living-room addition in the middle. Each façade offers views onto the terrace. On one end of the quarry-tiled garden room are French doors that open onto the entertainment terrace; the other end steps out onto a private terrace sized just for one person. This enclosed court is the perfect away room, nestled just outside the dining room, offering a quiet zone for reading or reflection.

In the new living-room addition, a large picture window has been subdivided into 16 panes to frame the view to the garden pool, an echo of the 16 squares that form the floor of the outdoor away room. Such attention to detail, as well as the contemporary artwork, floral displays, and furnishings in rooms that open onto one another, make this house comfortable both inside and out.

## Private and Public Realms

The term realm describes the environment over which you have influence: the house and land you call your own. People often present a different public and private face to the world and, unconsciously, do the same with their realms. This home presents a public face that is very different than its private side. The expanse of lawn that extends from house to street acts as a visual buffer zone, further screened by the birch trees and ground-cover beds that surround the front façade. The effect is to preserve a certain anonymity for its owners while presenting an attractive face to the street. You can't tell much about who lives here, beyond the fact that they enjoy their privacy and have a handsome front yard.

In this home, you will find out more about who the owners are when you pass through the gate into the realm behind the fence (see p. 304). The ample terrace with multiple seating areas suggests a vibrant place for entertainment and family dining. Multiple containers of plantings and a reflecting pool with lily pads and water plants indicates a private realm that is well tended, loved, and fully enjoyed and appreciated.

*—Julie*

# outside
## parallels

## Diagonals

**DIAGONALS ENERGIZE,** elongate, and expand an area. Like an arrow pointing back into space, a diagonal points to the broadest expanse, making a garden seem bigger than it is. The designers here used bluestone pavers set on the diagonal to give a sense of greater spaciousness and depth to the entertainment terrace (below).

A diagonal can feel, paradoxically, both dangerous and desirable. Our minds are inexorably drawn to follow something at an angle that focuses and expands our sense of depth. Because it's such a dynamic element, a diagonal needs a resolution point at the end, such as a T-intersection to stop its relentless move forward (see the drawing at right).　*—Julie*

## The Weaving of Inside and Out

As you move through this house, there's a gradual progression from public to private spaces, and the outdoor terraces are an important part of this sequence. Although the home is ostensibly a set of defined rooms, because the framed openings between the rooms are wide, the interior becomes a sequence of places along a diagonal view as described in the sidebars.

When interior and exterior spaces are designed in conjunction with one another, the views from place to place are composed in such a way that you are as aware of the outdoor "rooms" as the inside ones. Take, for example, the dining room. Seated here, you can see out to the garden in three directions. The window looking into the outdoor away room is centered on the room, so the view here is to a contained space with an intimate feel. Positioned at 90 degrees to this is a view through the sitting room to the terrace and pond

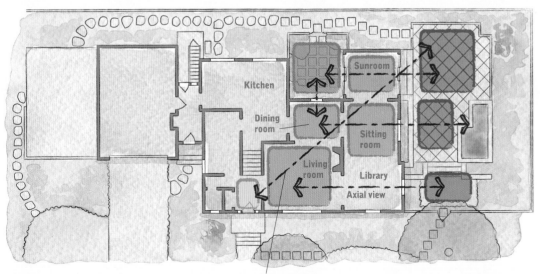

Long diagonal view

## Diagonal Views

**DIAGONAL VIEWS** work the same way in the interior of the house as they do outside. By connecting rooms with wide, framed openings along the diagonal as they are here, the house appears significantly larger than it is. You are able to experience with your eyes the longest enclosed view through the house, in this case from one end of the original living room to the opposite corner of the new sunroom. The view, in this case, is extended further yet—out into the terrace beyond.           *—Sarah*

beyond, a more focused view. The third, more oblique view leads the eye along the diagonal through the sunroom windows to the terrace. Each space along the diagonal keeps enticing you toward this outdoor area.

The sunroom itself becomes an interior bridge between two outdoor sitting places—one the most public and expansive, the other much more private and contained. It's a flow-through space with sliding doors that can open wide to the entertainment terrace on one side and the outdoor away room on the other. The inside destination is set up by the diagonal view, so that on a rainy day, you'd feel quite satisfied to sit here and enjoy gazing out in both directions. But on a beautiful day, it's the place that welcomes you into the garden. Its wide windows and sturdy French sliding doors make the transition to the outside areas a gracious and satisfactory experience.

*—Sarah*

This home shows the importance of containing space so that different functions can happen in discrete spaces. Starting with the most obvious kind of container—a reflecting pool in which water is held in by low stone walls—you can find a host of different sizes and shapes around the house.

| 1 | 2 | 3 |
|---|---|---|
| 4 | 5 | 6 |
| 7 | 8 | 9 |

**4** **5** **Containers of billowing** annuals and perennials grace the garden pool, extending the blooming season and providing focal accents. Behind the pool, bamboo, golden ray (*Ligulana x* "The Rocket") and hakonegrass (*Hakonechloa macra* "Aureola") provide a lush border.

**7** **To the left** of the garage is an outdoor room (a room-size container) for basketball with a concrete half wall and white-painted pipe railings that look like a fenced terrace. The hoop peeks over the Kousa dogwood and ornamental grasses planted in front.

**8** **A garden room** can be a container, too. Here, a slider opens from the sunroom onto this three-sided, fenced terrace, designed as a space for contemplation. The enclosures set this outside room apart from its surrounds while allowing it to feel linked to the life of the family when the sliders are open.

Rooms inside and out organize this 4-acre site into manageable parts. Here, a rectangular panel of grass sits just outside the house. Its walls are formed by the soft billows of plants, which also help define the edges of the flowing lawn.

# Rooms Inside and Out

Most of us seek to create a home that feels welcoming to family and friends. So many qualities come into play to make this happen. With a house like this suburban Boston residence, it's the projections that open out to engage the landscape. The little dormer windows peek out from the shingled roofline of the gambrel-style house, and the many "ells" push off into the landscape, occupying space and creating inhabitable corners—an outside version of the Not So Big principle "shelter around activity." The landscape responds to these architectural moves by pushing out and pulling back to hide and reveal a series of outdoor garden rooms.

The indoor and outdoor rooms and passageways define the essence of this home. Giant spruce trees line the driveway as an evergreen allée, allowing a sense of formal passage while creating

## NOT SO BIG INSIDE OUT

**Not So Big** doesn't necessarily mean small. It's more about the sensibility toward space both inside and out. This beautiful home includes intimate and expansive outdoor places, all of them woven together with the house to create a veritable wonderland, and all perfectly proportioned to accompany the scale of the house. There's a simple elegance to the composition of the various elements of this garden that greatly enhances the experience of everyday living.    *—Sarah*

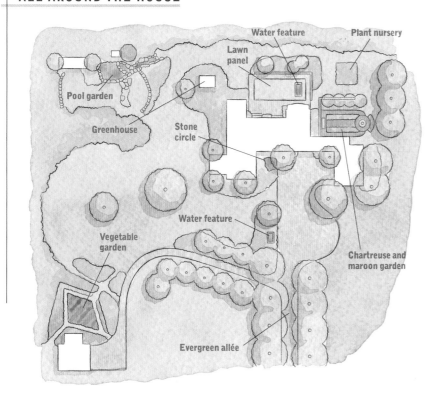

Water feature

Plant nursery

Lawn panel

Pool garden

Greenhouse

Stone circle

Water feature

Vegetable garden

Chartreuse and maroon garden

Evergreen allée

∨ Creating color echoes in your garden helps bring rhythm and harmony to its composition. This wonderful chartreuse and lime agave responds to the low-growing bamboo leaves, set off by the deep green of the clematis vine growing up a wooden trellis on the side of the house.

∧ A granite trough anchors one end of this oblong lawn. Owner and designer combined their horticultural talents to create a lushly-planted garden.

a visual and psychological barrier between house and public road. Similarly, a brick path acts as a corridor between outdoor rooms. Its planted "walls" provide linkage and screening at the same time.

## A Garden Full of Rooms

Landscape designer and horticulturist Gary Koller, working closely with his client, began by developing rooms around the house. He started with a beautiful herb garden, a plant nursery, and a lawn parterre that parallels the living room to the rear; all use planted and built enclosures to wall themselves from the rooms around them. If you think of the lawn as sitting on a horizontal plane, and of the plants as occupying a vertical plane, you can see how Gary designed this space. The bluestone path defines the edge of the lawn plane, and the stunning Japanese maple, sourwood tree, and ornamental onion below fill in the palette of the vertical plane.

Bulbs soften the low, oblong stone water basin, placed on axis with the kitchen ell. So simple, it is a place that is equally effective for contemplation as for entertainment. By the driveway, a similarly shaped stone water basin—this time supported between two vertical stones—stops the eye. It is a small event along the way. A grander event—a greenhouse—draws you inside to view seedlings and tender plants that need protection through the winter months. It hides in a flurry of plantings at the end of the lawn panel. Other events include spectacular trees and unusual shrubs that provide visiting gardeners many hours of horticultural delight.

A guest cottage sits in another corner of this 4-acre parcel. The owner decided to use it as a foil for her vegetable garden. Vegetables grown in raised garden beds often do better than their counterparts on the ground. Edges unify the design, contain the soil, and make maintenance—tilling the soil, weeding, watering—easier. The surrounding gravel pathways also make gardening

∧ Both clients and designer treated every last corner of this yard as a garden. Even along the driveway—normally considered a purely functional area—they placed a water feature, an echo of the rectangular pool in the terrace garden.

∧ Every serious gardener has a plant nursery. This former vegetable garden became too shady and was turned into a place for the owner to nurture seedlings, hold plants until they are ready to be planted, or nurse them back to health.

∧ This low-growing variety of bamboo has lime-green leaves with a velvety underside.

∨ A neat brick walkway edged in cobblestones takes a visitor under a mature Japanese maple to a turn in the path. The trunks of the tree obscure the view, adding to the sense of anticipation about what lies ahead.

easier by choking out weeds while radiating the sun's warmth into the adjoining beds. As you can see on the plan, the vegetable garden sits many yards away from the house—a kind of "away garden" that allows the owner a room of her own for growing.

## An Outside Away Room

In *The Not So Big House*, Sarah defined an "away room" as a space in the home that allows the activities that require peace and quiet to be separated from those that generate noise. The same can be said for outside a Not So Big House. A swimming pool can be a source of noisy activity, so locating it away from quieter pursuits around the home can be helpful. Here, Gary placed the swimming pool in an upper corner of the garden. This pool garden is reached by a secret stairway of stone that follows the hillside in a series of steps and platforms. Near the top of the slope, the stepping-stones begin to meld together to create a

< Some entry points are obvious; others, like this one, are more subtle. This path up to the pool garden, constructed of large, flat fieldstones, winds through plantings and alongside a falling stream.

terrace with one long stone breaking free to cross a small pool of water lilies, iris, and red and green cut-leaf Japanese maples (*Acerpalmatum dissectum* cultivars) along its shores. At the swimming pool, the stones become steps in the water and curl around the pool as a terrace, nestled back into a ledge-strewn hillside and surrounded by trailing shrubs and perennials. A charming pool house, swathed in Japanese hydrangea vine (*Schizophragma*

> Flat fieldstones are tightly jointed to form a sitting terrace. Looser joints allow small-leafed plants like thyme (*Thymus spp.*) to spread over the stones, while the cantilevered coping becomes a set of steps into the pool itself.

> The pool garden is a special outdoor destination announced by a handsome ornamental iron gate. The irregular shape of the pool, along with the pockets of plantings that soften its edge, makes it feel like a natural pond.

> **A fieldstone bridge fords the artificial stream on the way to the pool garden, just one of the many pleasures on this delightful journey.**

## Points of Entry

Here, a driveway is a garden, too, and it deserves the special consideration given to all parts of the landscape. Designer Gary Koller created a series of gestures that make this one an entry court. You enter under an allée of high spruce trees that screen the house from view. At the first of two parking areas, Gary created a special event: a stone water basin with a veil of water trickling over its edge, humidifying the air as it dampens the crunch of tires on gravel. You park and look for the front entrance, located at the corner created by two ells of the house. Here, the front door opens onto a circle of bluestone and cobbles surrounded by plantings that defines the point of entry into the house.

Another point of entry invites you directly into the garden. An extension of shingled wall links garage to house and acts as a gateway to the garden rooms beyond. Because there is no glass in the windows, the structure looks like the wall of the house but acts like a garden fence. A stone ramp allows a wheelbarrow access to the garden rooms beyond.　　　　*—Julie*

*hydrangeiodes*), offers a small shelter. Passing out of the garden through a decorative iron gate, the stones loosen up once more to become stepping-stones set in grass. The entire pool space feels like a dream landscape, hidden away yet self-sufficient.

This home shows us that you can organize a whole property as a series of garden rooms—some close to the house, others farther away. Like the rooms in your house, each outdoor room divides a large space into a series of manageable parts that can be of different sizes, uses, and styles.

# outside
### parallels

## Alignment

**SYMMETRY CAN BE** a satisfying organizational device for an outside landscape. Here, brick paths define the edges of this garden room, with rows of plantings linking foreground to background, like stripes on the earth. Flanked by birdhouses, a curved teak bench offers a secure viewing position that aligns with the house and the focal stone lantern that occupies the center of the garden space.

A sunroom window (at far right on the facing page) offers a direct line of sight onto this garden when open. Choosing plants that grow to a height just below a window jamb underlines the view. In this case, a low-growing bamboo gives color and texture to this lime-green and emerald garden. *—Julie*

## Outdoor Focus

Many traditional houses, like this one, have relatively small windows that make it difficult to really invite the outside in. These houses were designed during an era when glass was expensive, when the cold that they allowed in made the house a challenge to heat, and when direct sunlight caused fading of fabrics and rugs. There are two common solutions for today's owners of such houses who want more connection with their gardens. You can increase the size and number of windows, or you can add a room like this one (below right), devoted to appreciation of the surrounding landscape.

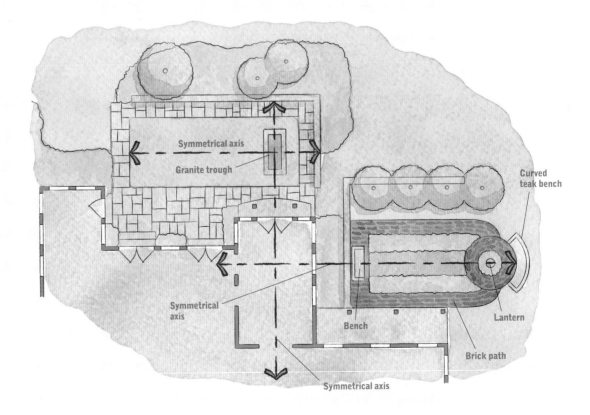

In 1987, the homeowners added this sunroom to provide a comfortable place to sit that gave them the sense of being outside. In the winter, when the doors and windows are closed, the volume of the space, with its high clerestory windows, provides a light and airy embrace, or sanctuary, from the snow-covered tree limbs. In the summer, the high windows transform into a green frieze that filters direct light.

A room that has such an outdoor focus can give you the feeling that you are sitting inside a prism or crystal, looking out through the many facets into the beauty of nature. The experience is enhanced by the use of multipaned windows. The divisions in the glass create a simple pattern overlay that breaks the view into bite-size pieces. They give you a set of mini frames to see through, which, in turn, draw your attention to particular features in the landscape.

*—Sarah*

## Alignment

**WHEN A WINDOW** or doorway is aligned with an important feature in the surrounding landscape, there's a powerful sense of order and balance. We can literally feel the interconnection between inner and outer worlds. Julie has described the symmetrical composition of this linear garden, but it's not until you view it from inside the sunroom that you really appreciate the full extent of the alignment. The center set of large casement windows, over 6 ft. tall, invite in the view to the garden beyond. The flanking casements align with the brick path. The effect from the sunroom is to experience the room and garden as components of a single place, part of it inside and part of it outside.

*—Sarah*

# A Garden of Earthly Delights

L andscape designer Rosalind Reed and her husband, Howard Walker, don't mind creating a stir in their neighborhood. When you drive down their street in the leafy suburb of Oak Park, Illinois, you can't miss their home: The three towering spires of arborvitae act like a verdant billboard advertising the delights of her garden's design. In the shadow of the 25-ft. trees lies a landscape of diverse plant species with multiple textures, colors, and sizes, all weaving together around the boxy gray house. With its hipped roof pulled down low over the upper windows and its portico of bright yellow columns announcing the front door, the house looks surprised and delighted at what its owners have wrought. Their immediate neighbors are particularly pleased, since Roz, as she's known, has begun helping them landscape their front yards as well.

## NOT SO BIG INSIDE OUT

In planning this book, we wanted good examples of houses on Not So Big lots that still use the space to create a sequence of outdoor spaces. Here, the challenge is even greater due to the fact that there are neighbors on three sides of the property. This garden eloquently illustrates how good design can bring into being a magical and secluded universe that's completely unexpected and quite transporting in its beauty.                                                                 —Sarah

The clean lines of the front façade of the Reed-Walker house contrast with the large brick courtyard, whose abundant plantings blanket the front yard. Offset from the front porch is a broad brick path that seems to flow under the concrete sidewalk that parallels the street. By not aligning front walk to front door, Roz ensures that everyone who walks onto her property will stroll through the garden court, enjoying the plantings, benches, and small but effective focal points along the way. She uses planting beds to carve out space, creating a circular path of reddish gravel around an island full of a mix of annuals, perennials, and shrubs, all artfully combined to create a voluptuous whole.

The delights continue as you are beckoned around the house by a series of large stepping-stones that winds along a dry streambed. In this narrow side yard, Roz intensifies the sensory experience by closing down space. Moving underneath a limb of a magnolia tree that acts as a gateway into the tunnel-like shade, you soon realize that you've left the open, sunny experience of the front court far behind. The soothing sounds of water beckon, traveling from basin to basin. Further along lies a recirculating pond, which appears out of the dry streambed. Roz has cleverly designed a watery journey, with sounds and cooling atmospheric effects that lure you to the back garden.

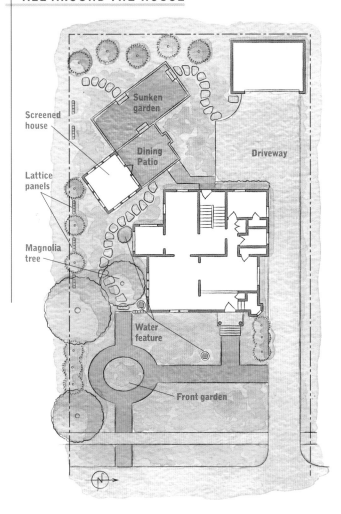

Screened house

Sunken garden

Dining Patio

Driveway

Lattice panels

Magnolia tree

Water feature

Front garden

N

∨ The public sidewalk crosses a brick path that turns into a circle in the front garden. This island planting breaks up the path and brings a point of interest to the space.

> Three vertical evergreen spires baffle the front porch and bring the house into scale, a treatment that is unlike any other on the block.

326

∧ A turquoise blue pot bobs in a sea of verdant textures. By featuring different shades of green in this garden, the home-owner has an endless array of plants to choose from. A different colored pot here might ruin the harmonious effect.

## Away Rooms in the Garden

Although planted down to the last square inch, the back garden is made up of a number of rooms—some big and some small; some for entertaining and some for getting away. The focal point of the backyard is a detached screened house placed on the diagonal from the main house. While built as an outdoor room for eating and entertaining, it also allows Roz and Howard a spot to quietly enjoy a glass of wine or read the paper, just a few steps from the back door of the house. When lit at night, this outdoor away room glows warmly on a summer's evening, providing shelter from inclement weather and unwelcome insects.

∧ This "dry landscape" was influenced by Japanese design, then filled with flowers. Here, the "stream" of gravel tumbles past false dragonhead and under an old magnolia tree.

∧ Who wouldn't be drawn to sit in this purple Adirondack chair? This contemplative place is carved out of beds of large-leafed hostas— an indestructible shade-tolerant plant with an astonishing number of varieties.

∨ The homeowners' backyard feels like a completely different experience from the front yard. Common and inexpensive landscape materials— concrete block, concrete brick, and red gravel—were used with flair.

While the screened room acts as fulcrum for the whole design (see p. 330), two terrace areas occupy most of the backyard. A sunken garden offers space for large numbers of people. A simple oblong filled with the same red gravel used in the front yard, it demonstrates an inexpensive way to carve out backyard space. Concrete block walls that retain the earth around the perimeter provide both seating and an edging that holds in the gravel. The upper dining patio houses a Mexican clay oven, a grill, and a table and chairs; its location just a few steps down from the kitchen makes it an easy destination. Peeking out among the lush plantings, you can also find several spots that lure you to sit and look back on this realm of sensory delights.

## Vertical Screening

Roz uses tall vertical elements to provide screening, yet allow the neighbors views into her garden wherever she deems it appropriate. In the front yard, a weeping pine tree blocks direct views into the garden while creating a clear sightline to the front door. In the backyard, she employs a wonderful technique to ensure that her next-door neighbors can enjoy her garden. Three lattice panels, measuring 4 ft. wide by 6 ft. high, are spaced 5 ft. apart. In the space between panels, Roz has planted an evergreen tree that will grow high and wide enough to block direct views, yet be a living, growing divider, a welcome break from the relentless separation of a wooden fence.

∧ **Roz didn't want to block her neighbors from looking into her garden, so she used latticework panels and left openings for conifer trees, which will eventually grow to fill the space.**

### The Beautiful Line

What is it about a curving path that so excites the mind? Think of the beauty of an oxbow of a river or the inward curving eddies in a rushing brook. Such beautiful lines form the backbone of landscape design, deriving from the geometric forms of architecture and the curvaceous lines of nature.

Such curves often stand in stark contrast to the buildings that define their edges. Within leftover rectilinear spaces, curves feel especially right to the eye. These voluptuous curves are the yin of nature that completes the yang of the architecture.

When I explain the beauty of curves to a client, I'll use orange biodegradable spray paint. I love to draw out the unfurling of a fern frond, or the inward spiraling of a path up to the top of a mount, or the location of a pinched "waist" in a walkway, like an hourglass shape on the land. As I sketch, I feel as though I am caressing the ground I walk upon, honoring it by giving it form, by offering up the most beautiful silhouette I can create. No matter what kind of garden I'm designing, finding the beautiful line is my perpetual quest.      —*Julie*

# outside
## parallels

### Outdoor Room

**THE COMPONENTS** of an outdoor room are the same as for one that's indoors: some walls, a floor, and a ceiling. In a landscape, walls can be high or low, of hard materials or soft. In homeowner Rosalind Reed's sunken garden, masonry walls are only 15 in. high, with plants providing upper-story screening from view.

Outdoor flooring can be made of wood, stone, tile, or even grass; Rosalind chose a gravel ground cover as the floor of the sunken garden. The out-of-doors equivalent to a ceiling could be a trellis, a pergola, a garden house, an arbor, a tree canopy, or in this case, the sky itself.　　*—Julie*

## Implied Walls

Unlike a solid wall, which can seem like an affront to neighbors, an implied wall of plant material (see p. 329) is almost always welcomed, especially when it's an enhancement for everyone. Even when there's nothing particularly exciting to look at in a surrounding garden, the tree foliage itself provides a deeply satisfying and ever-changing tableau from the interior of the house—especially when windows are large enough to invite the outside in, as here. The delightfully shaped beech tree, which stands to the southeast of the living room, is close enough to the house that it feels like the outer wall of the room. As the sun moves across the sky during the day, the leaves, which are lit from above and behind, change in both color and light intensity, and the shadows cast by adjacent foliage modulate the color of the room itself.

A tree that's lit from behind, like this one, can be an awe-inspiring sight. Every vein of every leaf can be seen highlighted against the luminous green

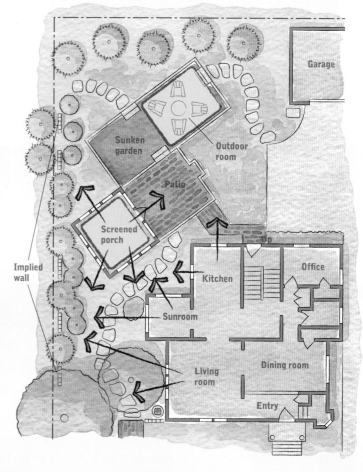

of its surroundings. This may seem minor, and even trite, but to experience this up close can be the high point of each day.

On the second floor, too, the tree canopy provides the backdrop for an

otherwise unremarkable view. The neighbor's house predominates from this angle, but when Rosalind sits at her drafting table, her gaze is directed to the tree. So even if you can't move windows—or trees—how you locate your furnishing with respect to the available views can make a big difference to the quality of your experience. —*Sarah*

### Outdoor Room

**MOST PEOPLE** conceive of an outdoor room as a porch, screened or not, attached to the house. If only one side is open to the elements, it hardly feels outdoors at all. Three open sides, and we really start to feel the connection with the surroundings. We are projected out into the landscape, but there's still a strong connection to the house.

The outdoor room shown here, however, is even more of an exterior space, with all four sides exposed. It's more akin to a gazebo than to an attached porch, yet it's close enough to the house to be remembered and so used daily. Just as with interior rooms, if you can't see a space, or if it's out of the way, it won't be used very often. But make it easily seen, and usage increases. —*Sarah*

**R**osalind Reed's backyard is designed for dining and entertainment—a set of terraces that seem as if they sit in a secluded clearing in the forest, yet are surrounded on three sides by neighbors. Details are simple, inexpensive, and completely successful.

| 1 | 2 | 3 |
|---|---|---|
| 4 | 5 | 6 |
| 7 | 8 | 9 |

**3** **When this hybrid rose mallow bud** opens in the sun, it will have 8-in. to 10-in. flowers. Placed in a protected location, it thrives in colder climates like Chicago.

**1** **It's hard to find** well-designed outdoor lighting for a garden, but this little copper-roofed fixture is just the right size for the small-leafed creeping Jenny (*Lysimachia nummularia* "Aurea") at its feet.

**6** **The Mexican clay oven** has its own place on the concrete-block retaining wall.

**9** **Brick and limestone** make a handsome couple, especially when paired with purple coneflower (*Echinacea purpurea*) blossoms.

**8** **One shrub that looks great** weeping over walls is called cotoneaster. Its dense, arching branches form layers where they overlap with creeping Jenny.

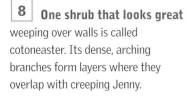

One of the three cabins peers out from behind a forest of Douglas firs and madrone trees, looking as if it has always been there. This one is the couple's primary living space.

# Three Cabins in a Forest

**M**any of us long to live a simple life in a cabin in a forest, far away from the stresses and strains of the world. This couple does just that, living on a cliff above the Straits of Juan de Fuca in Port Townsend, Washington, in a self-contained village of three shingled huts set among towering Douglas fir and madrone trees. Although equal in size, each structure houses a different set of activities: One contains the living space, another accommodates a guesthouse and office, and the last structure holds an artist studio over a garage. The first two sit at right angles to one another, enclosing a woodland garden, while the third angles outward to allow space for a lap pool and terrace. Merging the enchantment of forest, high bluff, and distant views, the site is further enhanced by gardens, water features, and six bald eagles that nest in nearby trees.

## NOT SO BIG INSIDE OUT

**Some properties** are large and ranging, while the houses upon them are small and personable. These sites present a challenge for their homeowners, who have to decide how much of the territory they are going to manicure and develop, and how much to leave in its natural state. This home finds a wonderful balance between the two, and the three structures that collectively form the house define exterior places and pathways at the heart of the site. —*Sarah*

∧ The entry porch floats above the forest floor, its supporting posts nearly indistinguishable from the tree trunks beyond. Forming the link between the residence and the guesthouse, this roofed aerial platform offers a place to choose your destination.

∨ From the guest parking lot, a reverse-curve path offers the first indication of how to move through the forest to reach the house.

< Metalwork is used as a subtle thematic idea throughout the property. The fence railings relate to the metal hinges, joinery, downspouts, fountain, fire bowl, and metal roofs, all of which bear a similar color and patina.

When approaching the property, visitors turn up a path, which, like a bend in a road, piques their curiosity about what's up ahead. The lane winds through the trees, leading them to a small parking lot where a stone path beckons. Framed by redbud trees, the path funnels guests up a hill toward the house, catching a glimpse of its roof ahead in the trees. Path lights are twinkling guideposts at night.

The long wood and metal bridge allows visitors to fully experience being in the forest. The diagonal lines of the madrone trees—an orange-barked native of California—interrupt the vertical trunks of the Douglas fir, the signature tree of America's scenic Northwest. The varied topography of the land naturally creates a variety of outdoor spaces, with more than half of the site's seven acres remaining in its natural state. Visitors walk a distance of 200 ft. with a grade change of more than 40 ft. from guest parking to entrance level.

At the end of a long wooden staircase, an entry porch seems to float above the forest floor, its supporting posts nearly indistinguishable from the tree trunks beyond. Forming the link between the residence on the left and the guesthouse on the right, this roofed aerial platform offers a place to choose one's destination.

∧ A long bridge leads visitors to a steep stairway that reaches the roofed entry porch joining two of the cabins. Orange-barked madrone trees lean across the end of the bridge, reaching up to find sunlight above the tree trunks.

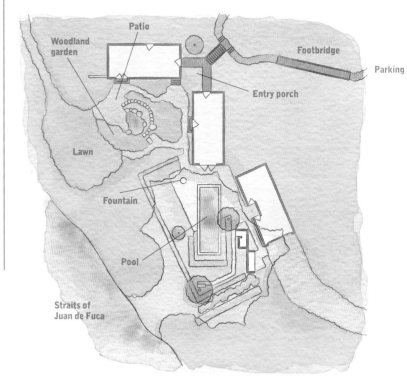

∨ At the edge of the property, erosion has torn trees from their roots to create a dramatic view of the straits.

> Beneath the bay window, a beam seems to pass through the post, connecting inside to outside. We are drawn to places where such boundaries are blurred, for they help us visually link our houses to their surroundings.

∧ On a large site like this, it looks best to shape planting-bed edges in sweeping curves with attention to the quality of the line between grass and plantings.

Wandering through the garden, you arrive at the very edge of the world: a sheer drop to the Straits of Juan de Fuca hundreds of feet below. High vantages with steep drops alternately repel us out of fear and draw us outward to the view. Here, overcoming our trepidation is worthwhile: Sailboats, barges, and steamers glide past islands across the straits.

## The Woodland Garden
This landscape is a place of soft layers that filter sunlight onto the forest floor below. The residence

∧ Two species of shrubs intertwine wonderfully to form soft hillocks in the landscape (*Hebe* "Red edge" and *Alchemilla ellenbeckii*) are pruned together with shears to create these billowing shapes, so effective at the base of tall trees.

∨ A small stone pool is fed by a central bronze water feature, sculpted by a local artist. Echoing the forms of adjacent tree trunks, it also offers a moist atmosphere and gentle sounds to this sylvan place.

## Softening Hardness

One of the things I love most about working in the land-scape is that there are so many ways to soften something that is hard. What is hard in a garden? Buildings, terraces, decks, arbors, walls, fences, and paths are elements whose solidity, rigidity, linearity, or stiff nature tends to look better with something softening their edges. Usually, plants can do the trick. Climbers can soften vertical elements, cascading forms can weep over containers that sit on decks and terraces, and ground covers can grow over the edges of driveways and fences. Plantings that grow up from the ground or down from the planting bed can soften the hardness of a wall. Rather than demolishing these curved cobble retaining walls, the landscape architect chose to leave some, build steps and terraces next to others, and bury some with soil and plantings. Using the many forms of plants to soften hardness helps inter-weave the elements that make up the landscape of home.

*—Julie*

> The owners thought carefully about matching the color of landscape elements to the building's trim color. Here, a soft mauve paint on the window mullions is echoed in the large clay vessel that stands as a focal point on the bluestone terrace.

and guesthouse form a sheltering corner for a garden that flourishes beneath the forest canopy. The horizontal branching structure of the Japanese maple trees adds a middle story between the high fir trees overhead and the billowing shrubs at their feet. Different colors and textures weave together into soft mounds that contrast with the fissured trunks of the Douglas firs. By planting species with similar growth habits in odd-numbered groupings, a sense of continuity is created.

On most properties, contractors clear away all the trees around a house, but not here. Instead, trees grow right up to the walls, and clearings are few and far between. Light descends in long shafts through the tall trunks to highlight details such as the central fountain with its trunklike metal water rod or the pools of light that dapple across the long lines of lawn.

< Sharply angled beds of hair grass (*Nasella tenuissima*) and native evergreen huckleberries (*Vaccinium ovatum*) stand out against the more natural forest floor beyond. The delicate texture of the grasses also contrasts effectively with the bluestone that edges the pool.

< This huge, faceted vessel is made of Lunastone, a fired clay that can stand up to freezing and thawing in colder climates. Behind, palmetto trees screen a small building and stand in stark contrast to the Douglas firs beyond.

∧ The atmospheric delights of a heated swimming pool combined with scented plants, the sounds of birds, and the thermal delight of this fire bowl offer an enticement to enjoy the twilight out of doors and late into the evening.

< Plants like this Lenten rose (*Hellebore sp.*), with chartreuse leaves and mauve flowers, were selected to echo the color theme around the pool.

## Reflecting the Sky

**A FORESTED SPACE** can feel dark if there is no sense of sky. To heighten the sky's presence, find a way to recline in the landscape, with a chaise lounge or deck chairs like these that allow you to look up through the trees. Another way is to bring the sky down into your plane by reflecting it on a continuous smooth surface. Here, the unmullioned windows bring the changing colors of sky, clouds, and treetops directly into the garden. Similarly, a reflecting surface on the ground, such as a pool, pond, or polished dark stone, can mirror the sky, bringing it down to your level. Finally, find or develop an edge condition, where you can get out from under the tree canopy and look out onto a wide expanse, directly into the sky. *—Julie*

## Shelter Around Activity

We are physiologically programmed to seek out places that offer a modicum of protection, particularly for our backs, so that we feel less vulnerable and more comfortable. It's why we tend to seek out a corner seat in a public place or restaurant, and the principle is just as applicable for outside spaces as inside. Readers familiar with my work know that I refer to this as "shelter around activity."

In this beautiful but rambling property, the architect and landscape architect have collaborated to create outdoor spaces that give the homeowners a sense of shelter. By breaking the house into three separate structures and locating them at angles to one another, corners have been made. Although these corners are outside spaces, they still have the characteristics that make all corners so appealing. In each case, two surrounding walls provide protection, but there's also a wide-open view to the surrounding landscape on the other two sides. In the corner made by the house and office structures, the landscape architect, Linda Attaway, has crafted a comfortable sitting area adjacent to a small pond, which in turn is circumscribed by a semicircular stone wall.

Another corner, this one created by the short end of the office and the wide side of the garage/studio, shelters the pool in much the same way. Low hedges on both sides offer a little more protection without obstructing views to the cliff edge and ocean beyond.

When you are planning the layout of a larger piece of land like this from scratch, you can use the forms of buildings to help shape and give shelter to outdoor spaces. Even if the house is a single structure, by including a wing or even a bump-out you can help create this sense of shelter around activity, which will make the outdoor sitting places more comfortable to sit in and more frequently used.

*—Sarah*

## Reflecting the Outside

**ONE OF THE** most effective ways to blur the distinction between inside and outside is to continue the materials used on the interior of the house through to the exterior, while simultaneously minimizing the frames around windows and the points at which they meet these continuous

surfaces. In the main living area, you can see just how effective this strategy can be. You could easily believe that this is a screened porch rather than an air-conditioned room. The illusion is created by the extension of beams and ceiling materials beyond the boundary created by the windows below. Instead of using standard opening windows, the architect used fixed double-pane, nonoperable glass panels, so there's no need for screens or window sashes. *—Sarah*

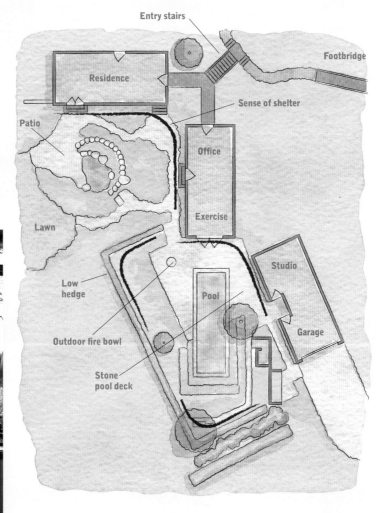

Entry stairs

Footbridge

Residence

Sense of shelter

Patio

Office

Low
hedge

Lawn

Exercise

Studio

Pool

Garage

Outdoor fire bowl

Stone
pool deck

Outdoor spaces like this patio, with a chunky stone fireplace and rustic posts, make use of local materials and signal the western style of this mountain ranch.

# At Home on the Range

Don't we all long to own a remote hut nestled into a hill-side that looks across a vast expanse to distant mountain-tops, far away from the madding crowd? The Old Snowmass Ranch in Aspen, Colorado, satisfies the need for vantage and vista while providing the comfort of snuggling into a hillside on the site of an old ranch. A *feng shui* practitioner would find this setting perfect: The house faces south, backed up by higher ground that protects it, with surface water that drains into the wide valley below. Across the way, you can see all the way to the Snowmass Wilderness Area in a wide panoramic view.

The house, designed by architect Larry Yaw for an active couple whose children were grown, was consciously located at the junction between pastureland and the hillside above. Building on this theme, landscape architect Richard Shaw chose to control the views

## NOT SO BIG INSIDE OUT

A number of houses in this book borrow from their neighbor's landscapes, but this house, located in an expansive meadow in the Colorado Rocky Mountains, gives borrowing the landscape new meaning. Designed to look and feel like a small cluster of cottages, the ranch, with its layers of garden, trees, and wildflowered meadows, provides a foreground for the dramatic surrounding mountain views. *—Sarah*

**∨ A path of local flat fieldstone wends its way from front door to garage. Hydrangeas, perennial geranium, and sweet woodruff drift in layers at the feet of native aspen trees.**

by hiding and revealing the magnificent vistas at different parts of the site. On the east, he planted cottonwood trees in rows that replicate traditional agricultural windscreens and protect the house and site from the strong winds that sweep across the valley. These trees allow him to edit the views to either side of the house, framing the panorama to the south.

Arriving from the circular driveway, visitors enter the house by traveling along a winding stone path through a lush perennial garden, located in a courtyard between the garage and the main wing of the house. On a side path to the garage, aspen trees, from the same family as the cottonwoods, provide shade and screening. In this intimate garden setting, Richard offers no hint of the vistas to come, hiding the climax of the experience from view. Only after

**> To get to the front door, visitors meander through a delicious tangle of flowers and foliage, planted with low perennials near the path and vertical ones near the buildings. It feels like walking through a river valley.**

walking through the house and coming out onto the south-facing terrace is the mountain scene revealed.

## Transitional Spaces

The terrace sits in a sun pocket protected from the western winds by the bedroom wing of the house. Here, a bent gambel-oak post supports a sunscreen structure that acts like a porch off the house, complete with glider and rockers. With corrugated fiberglass panels creating the roof, this wooden structure provides shade through the heat of the day and protection from inclement weather. Such a transitional area—the space

∧ Lines that bisect the view into foreground, middle ground, and background landscapes help flatten or carve out space. Here, the foreground is the belt of aspen trees; the middle ground is the more distant hedgerow; and the background is the mountain ridgeline.

∧ The gambel-oak post dances at the edge of the porch, where it holds up a corrugated fiberglass-covered trellis structure that lends shade to this space between house and landscape.

∧ The homeowners wanted their house to reflect their informal lifestyle. Different places to be outside offer a range of experiences: a picnic table for group dining, a pair of rocking chairs and a glider for quiet conversation, and a hot tub for soaking under the stars.

∧ Imagine removing the aspen trees at the edge of this terrace and you'd create a completely different spatial experience. Besides bringing needed shade to this outdoor living room, the trees define and enclose it.

between the house and the land—invites a different kind of use than is possible when you sit inside or out. The slight vantage of one foot above the stone terrace enables you to gaze out over the land. Having the wall of the house at your back and the structure overhead, you feel protected. Located adjacent to the living room, this is a natural outdoor extension of the room.

∧ Red, white, and pink Sweet William seed themselves with abandon in the wildflower meadow.

Two steps down bring you to a stone terrace, where a simple wooden picnic table invites alfresco dining and informal entertaining. At night, the homeowners enjoy access to an outdoor fireplace and a stone-sided hot tub for warmth in the cool summer evenings. The whole is contained by a stone sitting wall that acts like a balcony or parapet, meant to protect you from a steep or dangerous drop. Beyond the wall is a lovely swath of lawn that leads to a wildflower meadow where pasture used to be. When you add in the magnificent views, this outdoor living space creates a protected and comfortable vantage for contemplating the larger landscape.

Another outdoor space is connected to the main terrace by a stepping-stone path and sits directly outside of the country kitchen and the dining room with its built-in window seat. Here, a small breakfast terrace is screened from the road by conifer trees and a pruned hedge, under the shade of a white canvas umbrella that matches the color of the clouds. Just off the master bedroom, you can enjoy yet another vantage point: a deck to take in the view under the protection of the wooden roof. From inside the house, the majestic views continue.

> With such a broad panorama as this out the back door, it's important to establish a sense of definition and rootedness for those taking in the view. Here at the breakfast terrace, low hedges surround the teak table and chairs, bringing intimacy to an otherwise immense space.

## A Village on the Land

The Old Snowmass Ranch was designed to look like a little village or a compound of separate buildings that happen to share the same walls. By using different materials to clad the house, the architect creates the illusion of a house broken down into different but related parts. The main house, with its clerestory windows, board-and-batten siding, and stone foundation connected to massive stone fireplaces, contrasts wonderfully with the barnlike bedroom wing that juts out into the landscape toward the south. A red tin roof defines the main structure, while hardy asphalt shingles roof the wings. Using traditional materials to break down spaces into smaller but integral pieces, Old Snowmass Ranch carries off a deft balancing act of scale, wedding it beautifully to the mountains that surround it.

< When you look at the number of different rooflines that make up this Colorado ranch, you get the sense that it has been added onto as needed over time. The layout feels random and the materials eclectic, yet together they balance the composition.

Λ The perfect vantage: a comfortable armchair that sits on a private roofed porch set just above the treetops. From here, visitors look out to a distant view—alone.

# A Space for Gardening

Nothing beats the pleasure of harvesting your own vegetables and growing flowers for your own table. This garden is given a prime southerly location, which is the best orientation for growing full-sun plants like vegetables. Layers of compost—kitchen waste, grass clippings, and leaf cuttings—have been combined to make a soil that is rich in nutrients.

Surrounded by beds of daylilies, poppies, and other perennials, it's the fence that most pleases the eye here. Made of

gambel-oak boughs, it captures the look of an old homestead in the mountains. Keeping out errant wildlife, it brings the architecture of the house out into the garden.

—*Julie*

# outside
## parallels

### Natural Materials

**ONE OF THE REASONS** that the Old Snowmass Ranch appealed to us is because it uses local materials throughout to unite house to landscape. The outdoor fireplace with its massive chimney is rendered of local stone, as is the stone terrace underfoot.

The gambel oak of the posts and beams and the garden gateway are made from trees that were cleared

from the site in building the house. There's a pride attached to using natural materials straight off the property, for they add to the rustic charm of the place and further connect house and landscape to the mountains. —*Julie*

## Designing for the Way We Really Live

As we age, our objectives for our home life change as well. Instead of lives oriented around children, those with grown children, like the owners of this home, often want a feeling of peace and tranquility. The serenity of the majestic mountain views, along with the deep connection with the land that comes from cultivating both food and flowers, transforms the experience of life and provides a well-grounded foundation for these owners. They have no interest in formal rooms, preferring a house where every space is used every day.

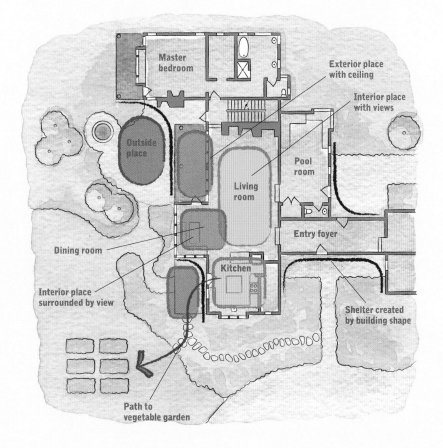

Master bedroom

Exterior place with ceiling

Interior place with views

Outside place

Pool room

Living room

Dining room

Entry foyer

Kitchen

Interior place surrounded by view

Shelter created by building shape

Path to vegetable garden

Recognizing that they were designing this house primarily for themselves, the homeowners asked their architects to make the kitchen into the social hub, with the dining and living areas suitable for everyday use as well as entertaining. The architect and landscape designer worked to create strong interconnections between inside and out. From the kitchen, you can step outside and stroll to the vegetable garden to gather the makings for lunch. From the screen door just off the living room, you can walk out onto the covered deck that runs between dining room and bedroom wing. You can sit here and enjoy the near and distant views, or you can continue out onto the stone terrace, sheltered by the L-shaped crook created by the master bedroom wing and covered deck (see the photo on p. 344). In combination, inside and outside activity areas weave seamlessly together to give the homeowners a rich variety of places to sit and enjoy their incredible surroundings.

*—Sarah*

## Natural Materials

**WHEN USED INSIDE** the house, natural materials can give an organic, timeless, and permanent feel to a space. Here, the side wall of the massive living-room fireplace juts out a little into the master-bedroom hallway, its stones splayed at the base to accentuate the sense of solidity. Because we are so familiar with images of ancient structures and castles that have lasted through the centuries, stone in particular connotes agelessness.

The architects have enhanced this sense with the use of double doors made of heavy, rustic wood. Natural materials tie us to our ancestral and historical roots and give us a sense both of security and connection with the natural world around us.

*—Sarah*

# Terraces of Grass

Symmetry can be downright boring if not detailed with care. When you compose a symmetrical landscape, the resulting design is usually restful to the eye. But it can also be too obvious, too easy for the eye to take in at a glance. Owners Scott and Norma Shannon found ways to make perfect balance seem dynamic through crafted details in the artful gardens around their 2,000-sq.-ft. house in Cazenovia, New York.

The barnlike proportions and rigid symmetry of their Dutch colonial home forced the couple to choose simple geometric forms as organizing landscape elements. In the front yard, rather than resorting to foundation plantings like the rhododendron and juniper bushes found in many suburbs around the country, they chose to create a horizontal platform retained by a low stone wall that acts as a base for the house. Centered on the front façade of

## NOT SO BIG INSIDE OUT

The Dutch colonial home shown here is familiar to many inner-ring suburbs. We selected this example because of the elegant but approachable formality of the garden's design on a lot that's pretty typical of neighborhoods established at the turn of the last century. Provisions for the automobile have been integrated in an innovative way, and there's a wonderful collaboration with the neighbors to give an expanded sense of the property's boundaries.          —Sarah

the house is an oval of grass edged by bluestone pavers, which they call "the ellipse." This lawn panel gives form to the front yard, creating an outdoor room that acts as play space and garden. Lush plantings that spill onto the sidewalk offer a certain degree of privacy yet invite passersby to look in.

This symmetrical front yard feels dynamic because the main entry to the house is on the east side. A porch is located at the center of this façade, accessed by the narrow driveway that runs along the house. When seen from the street, the symmetrical house actually sits asymmetrically on the property, energizing the otherwise perfect balance of the grass oval and making the whole feel dynamic. Scott, a landscape architect, and Norma, an experienced gardener, used the wall to provide a clear transition from the public realm of the street to the semipublic front garden.

∧ This side garden path meanders through a delightful thicket of native shade-loving perennials. Owned by the neighbors but gardened by Scott and Norma, this path links backyards and highlights the friendly relationship between the two families.

## ALL AROUND THE HOUSE

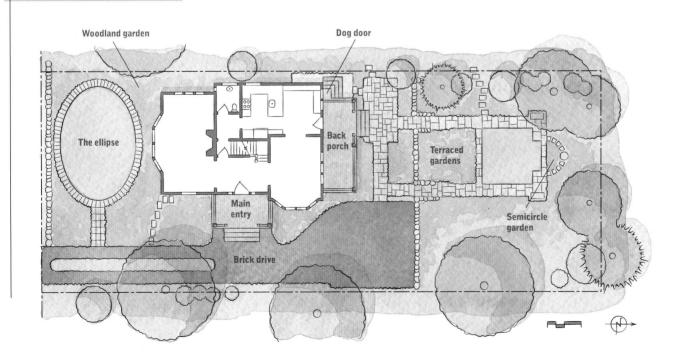

Woodland garden

Dog door

The ellipse

Back porch

Terraced gardens

Main entry

Semicircle garden

Brick drive

N

∧ The couple's lawn oval echoes the grass turf of the public park across the street. Shade-loving perennials, such as lady's mantle and different varieties of hostas and ferns, interweave to form a verdant tapestry.

< The tire tracks end at the side porch, which is the main entry point into the house. Notice how the brick drive cuts back to become a foundation for the wooden steps. This careful attention to detail is what makes the property so special.

∧ Windows over the porch and the three columns under it are set so that they are centered on the roof peak. Underneath the porch roof, the kitchen door and right-hand edge of the kitchen window grouping is also centered on the peak to achieve dynamic balance.

∨ Two kinds of stones—granite and flat fieldstone—interlock as elegantly as a dovetail joint. Creating such a seamless union between two materials brings a high level of refinement to the design of a garden.

## Gardening on the Side

The driveway itself is as carefully crafted as the ellipse. Surfaced in red brick pavers, it doubles as a path to the front porch. A grass strip—detailed with brick edging to form an elongated oval—runs down the center of the driveway. At the end of the drive, a bricked parking court is large enough to accommodate two cars at the back of the lot. With the attention Scott has given to proportion and detail, this driveway becomes a garden.

< This terrace garden of grasses and blooms is retained by a handsome stone wall. Another oblong terrace of bluestone links the porch, garden, and dog-run steps. Such panels act like a simple pool of space, a restful backdrop to the vibrant planting beds.

The garden on the west side of the house is overflowing with plants. Sandwiched between two houses and only 10 ft. wide, this naturalized woodland garden has a moist and shady microclimate. What surprises is that the neighbors, who own most of it, happily give the couple carte blanche to design and install a shared garden that benefits both properties.

### A Line of Axis
Scott and Norma decided that they wanted a stronger interior-exterior connection at the back of the house. As part of their renovation, they designed a hallway that links the pantry and kitchen areas to the breakfast nook, creating a line of axis—a path or direction of movement along a straight line—that includes the new back porch and steps and turns into a garden path. This bluestone walkway is one of two that edge the set of terraces climbing a gentle slope in the back garden. The lowest terrace is filled with flowers; one step up brings you to a terrace of grass with benches to either side. Crowned with a semicircular planting bed that has a birdbath at its center, this handsome design feels symmetrical, balanced, and perfectly proportioned for the house. Yet, because the line of axis is off center, the whole becomes dynamic.

## Events Along the Way

While the layout and design of this landscape work so well to organize space, it would not be as good a garden without the many small "events." These landmarks give pause to the flow of movement along a garden path and evoke contemplation.

Some events are tiny footnotes, like the birdbath the couple used to call attention to a step along the brick walkway. Other events stand as stronger focal points, like the standing birdbath that occupies the apex of the garden. Events should pique your interest as you make your way through the garden.

—Julie

# outside
## p a r a l l e l s

### Lining Things Up

**WHY DOES IT FEEL** so satisfying to
line up elements outside your house?
Perhaps it is because without a means
of orientation, a landscape can feel
overwhelmingly open and/or exposed.
Making a linear relationship between
house and garden serves to anchor
what's outside to that which is within.

A second reason is that an axial
path centered on an interior space like

a hallway brings the inside out and the
outside in. Here, lining up the kitchen
axis with one of the two paths that
edge the borders of the symmetrical
garden gives a sense of balance to the
two, despite the fact that the whole
is not actually centered on the house.

*—Julie*

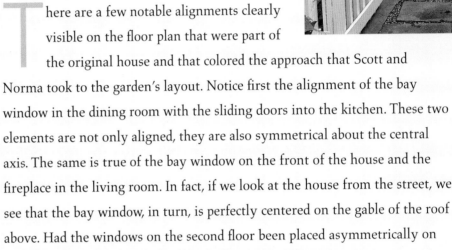

## Symmetry

There are a few notable alignments clearly
visible on the floor plan that were part of
the original house and that colored the approach that Scott and
Norma took to the garden's layout. Notice first the alignment of the bay
window in the dining room with the sliding doors into the kitchen. These two
elements are not only aligned, they are also symmetrical about the central
axis. The same is true of the bay window on the front of the house and the
fireplace in the living room. In fact, if we look at the house from the street, we
see that the bay window, in turn, is perfectly centered on the gable of the roof
above. Had the windows on the second floor been placed asymmetrically on
the front façade, the house would have a very off-kilter look.

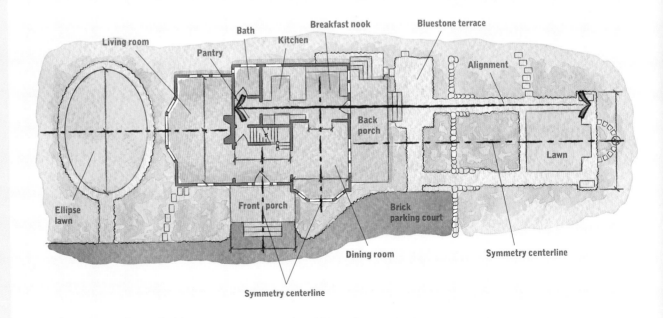

## inside
### parallels

### Lining Things Up

**OUR EYES** appreciate alignment. When things are lined up, we sense that there is harmony and balance. It's as though subliminally we know that someone thought about the arrangement of spaces, objects, or views, and that we are being well taken care of.

Just the glimpse through the open kitchen door to the garden path beyond, perfectly aligned with the direction of our movement from inside to out, gives you a feeling of order as well as an invitation to explore the world beyond the walls of the house. Looking at the floor plan, you'll see that the view from the far end of the pantry also aligns with the door and path.     *—Sarah*

So when it came to designing a garden to surround the house, the possibility existed to include some symmetrical aspects within a necessarily asymmetrical design, just like the house itself. Julie has described the delightful elliptical lawn, which has been used in lieu of the typical green carpet. But it's not just an arbitrarily located ellipse. It, like the fireplace inside and the living-room bay, is exactly aligned with the ridge of the gabled roof above.

When considering the design of your own landscape, take note of the characteristics that give the house its personality and allow this to inform what you do with its surroundings. Borrowing an attitude, as here with the use of occasional symmetry, the entire composition will be more recognizably one thing, one place, one home.

*—Sarah*

The backyard terrace is a study in how to craft landscape details. Using symmetry as an organizing device, homeowner Scott Shannon laid out two levels, with a perennial garden in the foreground and a lawn panel behind set two steps up. At the back of the garden, he created a semicircular path with a birdbath as the central focus.

| 1 | 2 | 3 |
|---|---|---|
| 4 | 5 | 6 |
| 7 | 8 | 9 |

**2** **Developing the corner** of a symmetrical garden helps stop the eye while creating a contemplative destination. Here, teak benches flank the semicircle at the end of the grass panel.

**3** **6** **Paths and place intersect** at a rectangle of bluestone that serves as a threshold for a teak bench and an indentation in the grass panel. Small "events," in this case two pots and a birdbath, allow the eye to pause, while a neighbor's garage peeks out behind a vine-clad fence.

**9** **Yellow sundrops** (*Oenothera tetragona*) and magenta meadowsweet (*Filipendula palmata*) bring zest to the perennial bed in June. You can play with plant combinations by trying them out. The beauty of most perennials is that if you don't like the effect, you can always move them around next year.

The vibrant cottage garden makes this delightfully crafted property sing. Light blue spires of delphinium rise out of drifts of lady's mantle, catmint, and iris foliage.

# A Cottage in the City

In 1988, David and Sukie Amory—he an architect, she a gardener—returned to Boston with their two young children to open a design practice. They bought a small, boxy house in the suburb of Brookline. Like many old homes, this one had its pluses and minuses. The virtues were clear: close proximity to the city, public transportation, a 10-acre park nearby, and a wonderful silver birch tree shading the backyard. The deficits were equally obvious: squat proportions, small dark rooms, pink and green concrete pavers. The Amorys assumed they would be comfortable in the house for only a few short years. Seventeen years and several renovation projects later, the couple, with children now in college, still lives here. In a row of carefully tended lawns surrounded by chain-link fences, the Amory residence stands out as a potpourri of flowers surrounding a charming cottage.

## NOT SO BIG INSIDE OUT

**Frequently,** with small homes in inner-ring suburbs, neither the interior nor the garden is much to look at. But this tidy little home is a testament to the fact that this doesn't have to be the case. A little attention to craft and detail can transform an average piece of property into a very beautiful and inspiring place to live. Both of us love the simplicity and attainability of this unassuming yet delightful home. —*Sarah*

## Cottage Gardens

Visitors open the wooden slatted gate, painted to match the trim on the house, and are immersed in a garden of plants of all types and colors and textures. Planted in the manner of a traditional English cottage garden, it consists of a seemingly casual mixture of flowering perennials, annuals, and shrubs that border the path to the front door, adorned with clematis and honeysuckle vines. And like a cottage garden, the whole is enclosed by a low picket fence, within which a changing tapestry of bulbs, herbs, grasses, ferns, and flowers weave together to wondrous effect.

Each season, Sukie's cottage garden enjoys a slightly different palette of blooms. The peak moment for color comes in midsummer, when soft blues, purples, and shell pinks are enlivened by touches of chartreuse, pale yellow, and vibrant red. In midsummer, green foliage sets off hues of blue and yellow. In fall, the subtle foliage is accented by garnet tones of sedum and the deep blue of monkshood.

∧ Modest houses nestle close in this quiet neighborhood near Boston. Every square inch of this property is planted with flowers and foliage—but no lawn—to cut for the table all year round.

## Using Every Square Inch

Sukie has gardened every square inch in her 4,000-sq.-ft. space around the house. Along the side of the house, facing southeast, she planted a garden devoted to "old" and David Austin roses that climb within a low hedging of lavender plantings. Sukie's husband David designed a wooden pergola above the garage doors that echoes the form of the rafter tails that ornament windows facing the driveway and provides a structure for a climbing clematis vine.

∧ This spectacular Persian onion is a bulb that produces 8-in. to 10-in. blossoms with half-inch silver-coated starlike florets and dried seed heads.

> The shade garden offers a cool, contemplative spot. Two sets of chairs enjoy different views: The twig chairs sit against the back of the house, borrowing the view of the neighbor's backyard; the bucket chairs, supported by the birch tree and garage, occupy the center of the garden space.

∨ Rafter tails act as supports for the homeowners' many varieties of climbing vines that adorn the house. Here, old-fashioned scented roses bordered by a row of lavender grow between house and driveway.

< Maintaining clean-edged beds where the occasional plant spills over creates a pleasing informality. Here, yellow yarrow, purple-blue catmint, and lime-green lady's mantle blur the garden path.

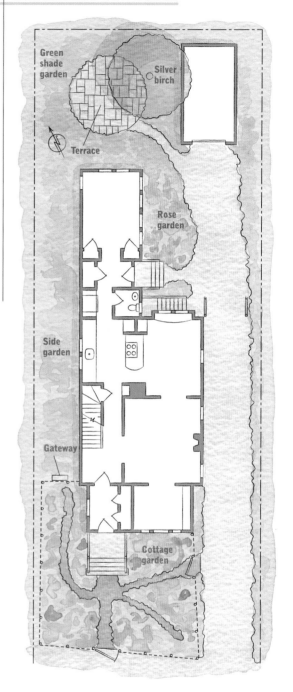

Green shade garden

Silver birch

Terrace

Rose garden

Side garden

Gateway

Cottage garden

∧ Astilbe flowers of various hues brighten the narrow side yard. In the background, honeysuckle tangles over a wooden trellis while creamy lacecap hydrangea blossoms grow tall against the picket fence.

< In the Amory's shade garden, different hues and textures of green foliage combine to bring a sense of remove on a summer's day. Fern, hydrangea, ivy, and sweet woodruff foliage stand out against the darker hues of boxwood and holly.

< The large four-sepaled blossoms of clematis vines partner well with shrubs and small trees.

## Dynamic Balance

Unless it's a highly ordered or perfectly symmetrical garden layout, I like to set objects in my landscape designs so that they feel balanced and dynamic. Owner Sukie Amory achieved this by scribing a circle of bluestone pavers in her shade garden, then setting a pair of bucket chairs on one side of the circle opposite a group of four pots of plants. Notice that three of the four are planted with the same boxwood shrub; the fourth, housing a topiary planting of variegated ivy leaves, forms a triangle in space with the two chairs. The whole composition feels ordered yet dynamic. In the planting bed behind the terrace, Sukie placed a birdbath on axis with the house and added Japanese painted fern in seemingly random order to add a dynamic element to the whole.

## The Relief of Shade

Inspiration for a garden's design can come from many sources. In her garden, Sukie referenced British poet Andrew Marvell's lines, "Annihilating all that's made/To a green thought in a green shade," by selecting evergreens and ground cover to set off the magnificent silver birch that shades the back of the property. Boxwood, holly, ferns, and English ivy—all shade-loving favorites—provide a verdant setting for daffodils and Spanish bluebells in the spring. Akebia, clematis, and Virginia creeper vines twine their way up the back corner of the house. (The old saying "clematis place their heads in the sun and their feet in the cool shade" is a good rule of thumb, since most species resent hot weather.)

To give form to her plantings, Sukie created two circular bluestone terraces: one nestled against the house and a larger one that occupies the middle of the small backyard space, both crowned with comfortable places to sit for an intimate couple. In order to make the small backyard feel bigger than it really is, Sukie chose to capture views through to the neighbor's extensive garden of yews, mountain laurel, and rhododendron by keeping plantings low along the back property line. Along the side, she also layered plantings of trees, shrubs, and perennials to create a sense of depth.

Inside the house, she used this dynamic balance with lamps, pots of plants, paintings, and furniture placed in interesting relationship to each other. Here, three windows provide a background framework that is balanced for a dynamic placement of vertical objects: two topiary standards and four white pendant floor lamps. This interior design, like its outside counterpart, will never seem predictable nor static.    —Julie

> Homeowner Sukie Amory trained rose and clematis vines to grow up against the front corner of her house to further connect the structure to the garden.

## Framed Openings

**AT THE CORNER** of the house by the side yard stands a metal archway covered in honeysuckle. This gateway illustrates what I call the "mouse hole" effect. Moving along the side garden, visitors notice the framed opening ahead, which narrows down and focuses their experience of the space beyond to one small, defined view.

From this dark mouse hole, you enter into the brightness of the garden filled with blossoms. Framing an opening in the landscape allows you to narrow down or decrease the scope of the space before you explode forth into a new garden realm.  —*Julie*

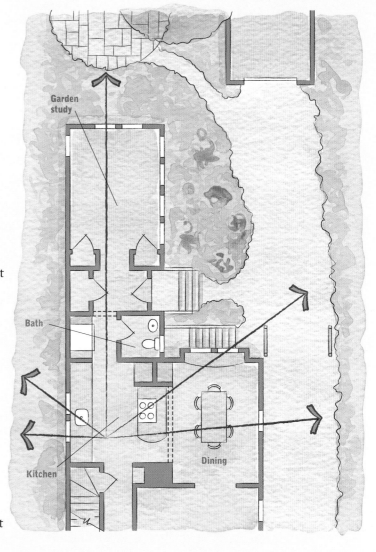

Garden study

Bath

Kitchen

Dining

# Transforming Small and Outdated into Not So Big

Many older homes present a challenge for modern homeowners in that the front part of the house, where 100 years ago most of the living occurred, is completely separated from the back part, where the kitchen and utility areas reside. This work area was often the territory of the hired help, but today it's where we tend to do most of our living. Many of these older homes are left with their original floor plans more or less intact, with most of the daily activities crowded into a tiny kitchen with one small window to the back or side yard.

In this 1920s-era home, which exhibited most of these problems, the owners implemented several simple strategies to make it more livable for today, as well as to connect the inside to the lovely surrounding gardens.

The most important was the addition of an arched opening between the original kitchen and the formal dining room. By making a wide connecting view between the two, the kitchen and dining room became defined parts of one larger space. The dining room now serves as both an informal, everyday

eating area and, when guests are over for dinner, a formal room.

Because the original dining room was designed for the visual pleasure of the primary inhabitants, there's much more connection to the outside from this space than from utility areas— a connection that can now be shared by the kitchen. *—Sarah*

## Framed Openings

**IN THE FIRST** part of the 20th century, framed openings were used frequently as spatial devices to differentiate one room from another, without blocking the view too much between them. The framed opening shown here is trimmed with the same woodwork as a doorway, yet its added width makes it feel very different.

While a doorway 30 in. to 36 in. wide tends to focus your attention on the small area you can see beyond, the wider framed opening becomes literally a frame for the entirety of the activity place beyond, sending a message of invitation. It welcomes you in, but it clearly delineates this place from the one you currently occupy. *—Sarah*

# Credits

David Linzee Amory, AIA
Amory Architects
7 Harvard Square
Brookline, MA 02445
(617) 277-4111
**www.amoryarchitects.com**
Curves and Color
Bring a Tiny House
to Life
pp. 18–25

Tina Govan
Tina Govan Architect
513 Holden Street
Raleigh, NC 27604
(919) 890-4124
**www.tinagovan.com**
Serenity
on a Budget
pp. 26–33

JDouglas Teiger
Abramson Teiger Architects
8924 Lindblade Street
Culver City, CA 90035
(310) 838-8998
**www.abramsonteiger.com**
Reinventing
the Family Home
pp. 34–41

ames Estes, FAIA
Estes/Twombly Architects, Inc.
79 Thames Street
Newport, RI 02840
(401) 846-3336
**www.estestwombly.com**
Classic Cottage
Simplicity
pp. 42–49

Jamie Wolf
Wolfworks, Inc.
195 West Main Street
Avon, CT 06001
(860) 676-9238
**www.homesthatfit.com**
A Jewel Box
of Texture and Detail
pp. 50–59

Stephen Zagorski, AIA
Stephen Zagorski Architects
P.O. Box 50196
Austin, TX 78763
(512) 789-3259
(512) 472-5156
**www.stevezagorski.com**
Texas Tuscan
pp. 60–67

Frederick Noyes, FAIA
Frederick Noyes • Architects
(formerly Modigliani/Noyes Architects)
129 Kingston Street
Boston, MA 02111
(617) 451-1962
Order in the Details
pp. 68–75

Barry D. Burgess
Insite Northwest, LLC
2339 Fairview Avenue, Suite N
Seattle, WA 98102
(206) 324-8473
A Houseboat
Full of Nautical Charm
pp. 76-83

James Strickland (design principal),
Benjamin Showalter, and Jerry Sommer
Historical Concepts, LLC
430 Prime Point, Suite 103
Peachtree City, GA 30269
(770) 487-8041
**www.historicalconcepts.com**
Laid-Back
Florida Cracker
pp. 84-91

Peter Twombly, AIA
Estes/Twombly Architects, Inc.
79 Thames Street
Newport, RI 02840
(401) 846-3336
**www.estestwombly.com**
interior consultant: Kirby Goff
Kirby Goff Interior Architecture & Design
150 Chestnut St.
Providence, RI 02903
(401) 490-5929
**Detailed
for the View**
pp. 92-99

Gail Wong and John Koppe
Gail L. Wong Architects
2609 East Garfield Street
Seattle, WA 98112
(206) 325-4025
**www.glwarc.com**
Craftsman Character
on a Narrow Lot
pp. 100-107

Gitta Robinson and Richard Grisaru
Robinson + Grisaru Architecture PC
55 Washington Street, Suite 711
Brooklyn, NY 11201
(718) 923-0040
**www.rgarch.com**
Rooms Afloat
above a Garden
pp. 108-117

Stephen Robinson Architect
2218 Lebaron Drive
Atlanta, GA 30345
(404) 636-5939
A Modest Ranch
Opens Up
pp. 118-125

CTA Design Builders, Inc.
Architects and General Contractors
Julie Campbell, AIA, and Buzz Tenenbom, AIA
2556 11th Avenue West
Seattle, WA 98119
(206) 286-1692
**www.ctabuilds.com**
The Nature
of Materials
pp. 126-133

Jim Samsel, AIA, (principal)
and Nathan Bryant (designer)
Samsel Architects, PA
60 Biltmore Avenue
Asheville, NC 28801
(828) 253-1124
**www.samselarchitects.com**
Simple Trim,
Substantial Impact
pp. 134-141

Gail A. Douglass, AIA, and Thomas R. Utley
2853 Ontario Road NW #202
Washington, DC 20009
(202) 234-1964
Grace, Elegance, and Storage—in 650 sq. ft.
pp. 142-149

Jean Rehkamp Larson, AIA,
Mark Larson, AIA, Keith Kamman,
and Susan Nackers Ludwig
Rehkamp Larson Architects, Inc.
2732 West 43rd Street
Minneapolis, MN 55410
(612) 285-7275
**www.rehkamplarson.com**
Rooms Defined
but Not Confined
pp. 150-157

Mark McInturff, FAIA
McInturff Architects
4220 Leeward Place
Bethesda, MD 20816
(301) 229-3705
**www.mcinturffarchitects.com**
The Illusion
of More Space
pp. 158-165

Tom Ellison and Leffert Tigelaar
TEA2 Architects
2724 West 43rd Street
Minneapolis, MN 55410
(612) 929-2800
**www.tea2architects.com**
Creating Coziness
in a Large Cottage
pp. 166-173

Fiona E. O'Neill, Architect
P.O. Box 108
The Sea Ranch, CA 95497
(707) 785-0040
Zen Warmth
pp. 174-181

Sarah Susanka, FAIA
www.susanka.com
Ceilings Shine
in Rooms without Walls
pp. 182-191

Playing Up the Corners
**CYNTHIA KNAUF LANDSCAPE DESIGN, INC.**
Landscape Designer: Cynthia Knauf
138 Main St.
Montpelier, VT 05602
802.223.6447
*www.cynthisknauf.com*

**SUSANKA STUDIOS**
Architect: Sarah Susanka, FAIA
(done while at Mulfinger, Susanka, Mahady
& Partners)
*www.susanka.com*

Borrowing the Landscape
**HENNING/ANDERSON**
Landscape Architects: Heather Anderson, Matthew
Henning, ASLA
4030 Everett Ave.
Oakland, CA 94602
510.531.3095
*www.henning-anderson.com*

**FOX DESIGN GROUP ARCHITECTS**
Architect: Dennis Fox
116 Washington Ave., Suite D
Point Richmond, CA 94801
510.235.3369
*www.foxdesigngroup.com*

The Attraction of Opposites
**JUDY HARMON, LANDSCAPE ARCHITECT**
Landscape Architect: Judy Harmon
706 Mountford St.
Raleigh, NC 27603
919.546.9282
*www.frankharmon.com*

**FRANK HARMON, ARCHITECT**
Architect: Frank Harmon
706 Mountford St.
Raleigh, NC 27603
919.829.9464
*www.frankharmon.com*

A Stream of One's Own
**DESIGN WORKSHOP, INC.**
Landscape Architect: Suzanne Richman
120 E. Main St.
Aspen, CO 81611
970.925.8354
*www.designworkshop.com*

**LIPKIN WARNER DESIGN AND PLANNING**
Architect: Michael Thompson, David Warner, AIA
23400 Two Rivers Rd., Suite 44
Basalt, CO 81621
970.927.8473
*www.lipkinwarner.com*

Shelter and Embrace
**DESIGN WITH NATURE, LLC**
Landscape Designer: Donna Bone
PO Box 7300
Tesuque, NM 87574
505.983.5633
*www.designwithnatureltd.com*

**ROBIN GRAY ARCHITECTS LLC**
Architect: Robin Gray
511 Agua Fria
Santa Fe, NM 87501
505.995.8411
*www.robingray.net*

Variations on a Theme
**CHARLES M. MCCULLOCH, ARCHITECT**
Landscape Architect: Charles McCulloch, ASLA
2927 Newbury St.
Berkley, CA 94703
510.548.3888
*www.cmmcculloch.com*

**FOX DESIGN GROUP ARCHITECTS**
Architect: Dennis Fox
116 Washington Ave., Suite D
Point Richmond, CA 94801
510.235.3369
*www.foxdesigngroup.com*

Japanese Journey
**JULIE MOIR MESSERVY & ASSOCIATES, INC.**
Landscape Designer: Julie Moir Messervy
Saxwin Building
18 Main St.
Saxtons River, VT 05154-0629
802.869.1470
*www.juliemoirmesservy.com*

**HAMLIN & CO., INC.**
Architect: Linda Hamlin
Contractor: David Hamlin
6 Wellington Terrace
Brookline, MA 02445
617.566.2161

Parallel Paths
**ALCHEMIE**
Landscape Architect: Bruce Hinckley
75 S. Main St. #313
Seattle, WA 98104
206.521.0358
*www.alchemiesites.com*

**SUYAMA PETERSON DEGUCHI**
Architect: George Suyama, FAIA
2324 Second Ave.
Seattle, WA 98121
206.256.0809
*www.suyamapetersondeguchi.com*

The Territory of Home
**HORIUCHI SOLIEN INC.**
Landscape Architect: Kris Horiuchi, ASLA
200 Main St.
Falmouth, MA 02540
508.540.5320
*www.horiuchisolien.com*

**MARK HUTKER & ASSOCIATES ARCHITECTS INC.**
Architect: Mark Hutker
79 Beach Rd.
Vineyard Haven, MA 02568
508.693.3344
217 Clinton Ave.
Falmouth, MA 02540
508.540.0048
*www.hutkerarchitects.com*

The World behind the Walls
**JULIE MOIR MESSERVY & ASSOCIATES, INC.**
Landscape Designer: Julie Moir Messervy
Saxwin Building
18 Main St.
Saxtons River, VT 05154-0629
802.869.1470
*www.juliemoirmesservy.com*

**CAMPBELL-KING ASSOCIATES**
Architect: Abigail Campbell-King, AIA
11 Friendship St.
Jamestown, RI 02835
401.423.3321

Living Lightly on the Land
**KINGS CREEK MANAGEMENT, INC.**
Landscape Designer: Jon Ahreus
3901-A Spicewood Springs Rd., Suite 201
Austin, TX 78759
512.615.2775
*www.kingscreeklandscaping.net*

**MAIER + ZELTER ARCHITECTS**
Architects: John Maier, AIA, Ulrike Zelter
5808 Balcones Dr., Suite 204
Austin, TX 78731
512.450.0121
*www.maierzelter.com*

Easy Living
**SITEWORKS DESIGN GROUP, LLC**
Landscape Architect: Cally Heppner, ASLA
24 Market
Beaufort, SC 29906
843.846.2259

**YESTERMORROW, LLC**
Architect: Ken Troupe
24 Market
Beaufort, SC 29906
843.846.0100
*www.yestermorrow.net*

A Landscape of Stone
**LAURA GIBSON, ASLA**
Landscape Designer: Laura Gibson
Manchester, MA 01944
978.526.8790
*www.lgld.com*

**ROBINSON + GRISARU ARCHITECTURE PC**
Architect: Richard Grisaru, Gitta Robinson
55 Washington St., Suite 711
Brooklyn, NY 11201
718.923.0040
*www.rgarch.com*

Good Fences
**CLINTON & ASSOCIATES,
LANDSCAPE ARCHITECTS**
Landscape Architect:
Sandra Youssef Clinton, ASLA
5200 Baltimore Ave., Suite 201
Hyattsville, MD 20781
301.699.5600
*www.clinton-la.com*

Rooms Inside and Out
**KOLLER AND ASSOCIATES**
Landscape Designer: Gary L. Koller
993 Park St.
Stoughton, MA 02072
617.448.7247

Garden of Earthly Delights
**ROSALIND REED ASSOCIATES**
Landscape Designer: Rosalind Reed, APLD
529 North Grove
Oak Park, IL 60302
708.524.3323
*www.rosalindreed.com*

**PAUL BERGER & ASSOCIATES**
Architect: Paul Berger
20 E. Cedar, Suite 16C
Chicago, IL 60611
312.664.0640
*www.pbadesign.com*

Three Cabins in a Forest
**LINDA ATTAWAY LANDSCAPE ARCHITECTURE**
Landscape Architect: Linda Attaway
1402 Third Ave., Suite 800
Seattle, WA 98101
206.838.4110

**CUTLER ANDERSON ARCHITECTS**
Architect: Jim Cutler
135 Parfitt Way SW
Bainbridge Island, WA 98110
206.842.4710
*www.cutler-anderson.com*

**LAWRENCE ARCHITECTURE**
320 Terry Avenue N
Seattle, WA 98109
206.332.1832
*www.lawrencearchitecture.com*

At Home on the Range
**DESIGN WORKSHOP, INC.**
Landscape Architect: Richard Shaw, FASLA
120 E. Main St.
Aspen, CO 81611
970.925.8354
*www.designworkshop.com*

**CCY ARCHITECTS**
Architect: Larry Yaw, FAIA
PO Box 529
Basalt, CO 81621
970.927.4925
*www.ccyarchitects.com*

Terraces of Grass
**SCOTT SHANNON, LANDSCAPE ARCHITECT**
Landscape Architect: Scott Shannon, ASLA
Architect: Scott Shannon
5 Emory Ave.
Cazenovia, NY 13035
315.470.6537

A Cottage in the City
**AMORY ARCHITECTS**
Garden Designer: Sukie Amory
Architect: David Linzee Amory, AIA
58 Winter Street
6th Floor
Boston, MA 02108
617.695.0300
*www.amoryarchitects.com*